Bon Travail ! 1

Junior Certificate French

Geraldine McQuillan, Marie Stafford, Carmel Timmins

Special Advisor: Breege McNally

The Educational Company of Ireland

First published 2007

The Educational Company of Ireland
Ballymount Road
Walkinstown
Dublin 12

A member of the Smurfit Kappa Group

The paper used in this book comes from Managed Forests in Northern Europe For every tree felled, at least one new tree is planted

EIQA
QUALITY CERTIFIED

Design and Layout: DTP Workshop, Design Image
Proofreaders: Claude Ducloud, Isabelle Lemée
Cover Design: Design Image
Illustrations: Brian Fitzgerald
Cover Photo: Corbis
Photos: Alamy, Corbis, Geraldine McQuillan, Céline Clavel

Teacher's CDs and script available from The Educational Company of Ireland

Speakers: Céline Clavel, Marine Debroise, Ludovic Degraeve, Clément Fabre, Haute-Claire Louis, Diane Mechani, Florian Tessandier
Recorded at Trend Studios, Dublin

The authors would like to thank their families and friends for all their encouragement and support while writing this book. Thanks to those friends who provided us with photos. A special mention to our editor, Céline Clavel, for her advice and patience and to all at Edco for their assistance in the production and marketing of Bon Travail ! 1.

Printed in the Republic of Ireland by ColourBooks
0 1 2 3 4 5 6 7 8 9

Bonjour !

Bon Travail 1 ! is the first book of a two-part series which covers the Department of Education and Science's curriculum for the Junior Certificate.

The main objectives of **Bon Travail** are:

- to help you to understand the **French language**;
- to discover how French people live their **daily lives**;
- to make your study of French **enjoyable**;
- to ensure you are **well prepared** for the Junior Certificate examination.

There are 11 **Unités** in the book. Each **Unité** covers a different aspect of the everyday life of a French teenager. In each **Unité**, you will

- **learn vocabulary** about the topic in the **Unité**;
- **hear** how words are **pronounced**;
- **write exercises** to practise what you have learned;
- **practise speaking** with your teacher and class-mates;
- **learn** the necessary **grammar rules**;
- **learn** how to write to a **French penfriend** on the topic.

Also included in each **Unité** are some **fun exercises** – crosswords, wordsearches or quizzes. There are **tips on pronunciation** and a **Lexique** of words you have met in the **Unité**. For those who like to use the internet, there are **websites** listed which will provide further information about the French way of life.

Finally, there is a short **Épreuve** at the end of each **Unité**, where you can test what you have learned in the section.

So, we wish you '**Bonne Chance**' and

Bon Travail !

Contents

La Mer du Nord
Calais
La Manche
Boulogne
Lille
Cherbourg
Le Havre
Rouen
Caen
Paris
Euro Disney
Alsace
Strasbourg
Normandie
Rennes
Bretagne
Bourgogne
Nantes
Tours
Dijon
Loire
L'Océan Atlantique
Futuroscope
Lyon
Clermont-Ferrand
Auvergne
Bordeaux
Grenoble
Les Alpes
Provence
Avignon
Biarritz
Toulouse
Marseille
Monaco
Nice
Cannes
La Côte d'Azur
Les Pyrénées
La Mer Méditerranée
La Corse

Logos

Listening activity

Reading activity

Writing activity

Speaking activity

Cultural aspects of France

Dictionary

Grammar

Classroom instructions

Les personnages dans le livre

Luc

Luc Legrane lives with his family in Toulouse, in the South-West of France. He likes reading and has a large collection of comic books. He enjoys sport and supports Toulouse's rugby team. He plays the guitar with a group of his friends.

Océane

Océane Hubert lives in Paris, the capital of France. She spends a lot of her free time surfing the internet. She is a cinema fan and she likes to read about the stars in magazines such as Starclub. She plays volleyball.

Christophe

Christophe Quéré lives in Rennes, in Brittany in North-West France. At school, he loves P.E. and he reads a lot of sports magazines. He plays the drums, which drives his family crazy! He collects stamps.

Sophie

Sophie Prioul lives in Lyon, France's third largest city. She loves to dance, especially jazz ballet. But she also loves to play football and often goes to watch the 'Olympique Lyonnais' play. She likes horses and she reads about them.

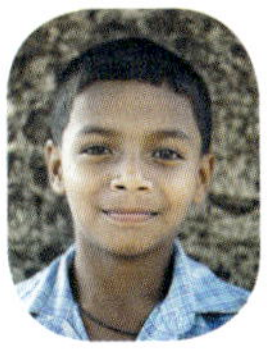

Khalid

Khalid Mansour comes from Marseille in the South of France. He is a supporter of the 'Olympique de Marseille', but because he is quite tall, his favourite sport is basketball. He is learning English at school and it is one of his favourite subjects.

Léa

Léa Rocher comes from Strasbourg in the East of France. She has a pet cat, Charley. She is not very interested in sport, but loves to paint. At school, she likes computer class. She loves reading, especially Harry Potter books.

Introduction

A beautiful destination

Three top tourist sites

- France is a beautiful country that attracts over 75 million tourists each year. Irish visitors are among these tourists – in fact, they come in the top five nations to visit France each year.
- France has lots to offer the visitor: great food, lovely villages and towns, and beautiful scenery. Paris, the capital, is one of the most beautiful cities in the world. Colourful countryside, attractive beaches, many theme parks and interesting historic sites make France the ideal tourist venue.

Some places you may know

- In the North, is **Normandy**, birthplace of Joan of Arc and location of the beaches of the D-Day landings during the Second World War. In the North-West, is **Brittany**, whose coastline resembles the west of Ireland. The **Loire Valley** is a fascinating area, with its beautiful '**châteaux**', built by French kings for holidays away from Paris. There are lots of popular holidays resorts, such as La Rochelle on the Atlantic coast. The '**Pyrénées**' mountains act as a natural border between France and Spain and the mountain slopes are used for winter sports in areas such as Andorra.

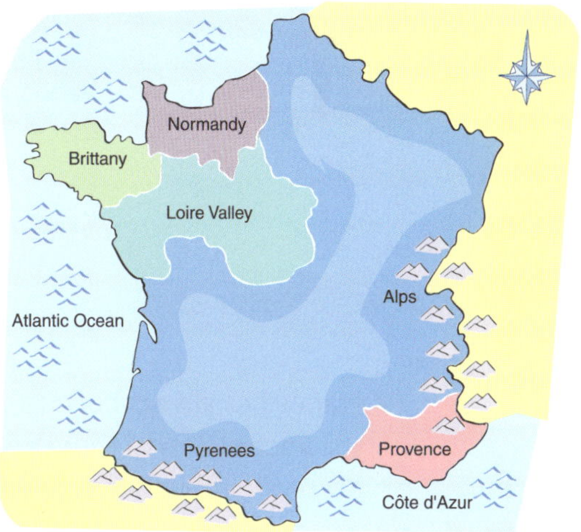

- Along the Mediterranean coast, you find the '**Côte d'Azur**', a very popular tourist destination. **Cannes** hosts the **International Film Festival** each year. The film *The Wind that shakes the Barley* won the main prize, the '**Palme d'Or**', at the festival in 2006.
- **Provence** provides acres of flower fields, in particular lavender, used in the perfume industry. You also find olive groves, fields of sunflowers and citrus fruits. The **Alps** form the frontier between France, Italy and Switzerland. '**Mont Blanc**' is the highest mountain in Europe. This area is famous for its winter sports holidays.

The French language

- The French language is spoken in many parts of the world and is one of the main languages of the European Union.
- In the past, French was the language of diplomacy and every well-educated person had to be able to speak French! French is spoken in **Canada** (in the province of **Quebec**), in **French Polynesia**, in North Africa (**Algeria**, **Morocco** and **Tunisia**) and in many countries of Africa. These countries used to be French colonies. Nowadays, they are independent.
- The **French language** has influenced our own language. We use many French words for cooking and catering, like omelette, quiche, croissant, mousse, menu, café, restaurant, hotel, chef. The Normans, who came from Normandy, were mainly responsible for this influence when they came to England and Ireland.

- Many Irish towns have **twinned** with French towns. This involves visits between local schools, sporting groups, language learners and groups that share a common interest. Twinning came about after the Second World War in an effort to re-build relations between France and its neighbours in Germany.

France and sport

- France has always been to the forefront of sport. The **Olympic Games** (**Jeux Olympiques**), the **Soccer World Cup** and the '**Tour de France**', all have French sportspeople at their origin. You will probably have your own favourite French sporting heroes or heroines.
- Almost 10 million French people are enrolled in sports groups, with football and tennis drawing the largest numbers. If you want to know more about sport in France, you can find information on: www.jeunesse-sport.gouv.fr

Activity 1

Pick some of these French sports people and find as much as you can about them.

le football

le tennis

le golf

le rugby

la natation

le judo

French culture

- Some of you may know about **French artists** such as **Monet**, **Renoir** or **Degas**. The National Gallery of Ireland and Dublin City Gallery have a number of paintings by these artists, who belonged to a group of painters known as the **Impressionists**.
- '**Le Louvre**' museum in Paris contains thousands of paintings, the most famous of which is probably the Mona Lisa, or '**la Joconde**' as she is called in France.
- The works of many **French authors** have been translated into English. Jules Vernes is well known for his adventure novels, such as *Around the World in Eighty Days*. Have you read *The Three Musketeers*? The author, Alexandre Dumas, was French. He also wrote *The Man in the Iron Mask*. Victor Hugo is famous for *The Hunchback of Notre Dame* and for the story which is now the stage musical *Les Misérables*.

French fashion

- For many years, **Paris** has been seen as the **fashion** (**la mode**) capital of the world. Designers like **Yves Saint Laurent**, **Coco Chanel** and **Jean-Paul Gaultier** have been world leaders in fashion trends. Each year, hundreds flock to see the fashion shows from the main designer houses. Perfumes and beauty products are also part of this industry.

French food and wine

- There are **63 million** people in France; that is a lot of people to be fed every day! Besides producing food for the local inhabitants, France **exports** a large amount of food products. Just look around your local supermarket and you will be surprised at the number of products originating from France!
- Well-known brand names of French products are '**Danone**' dairy products, '**Carte Noire**' coffee, '**Bonne Maman**' jams, '**Perrier**', '**Évian**' and '**Volvic**' mineral waters, and many fruits such as nectarines, figs and grapes. Look out for the labels and see how many you can find!
- France produces between 350-400 different cheeses. The ones you may know are '**brie**' and '**camembert**'.
- **French wines** are world-renowned and France is a leading exporter of wine in the world. When people want to celebrate, they often open a bottle of **champagne**. This wine is made from grapes grown in the **Champagne region** of France and produced in a special way, which gives it its sparkle and bubbles.

Activity 2

Read the clues and write the answers in your copy.

1. You will find the Mona Lisa here.
2. This is where you will find the highest mountain in Europe.
3. Important beaches used during the Second World War.
4. Area which is the centre of the perfume industry.
5. An important film festival takes place there.
6. A skiing area between France and Spain.

- France is a truly beautiful country and you are beginning to learn a beautiful language. When you visit France, you will be able to talk to the people and get to know their country.

Bon courage et bon travail !

Unité 1

Salut ! Je me présente !

Civilisation : Bonjour !

faire la bise

Kissing and shaking hands

- French people either kiss each other or shake hands with one another when they meet. For example, when they meet their friends in school each morning, they shake hands with them or kiss them!
- Boys shake hands with one another, girls kiss other girls, and boys and girls exchange kisses also. The kiss is on the cheek – sometimes it is two kisses, sometimes three or even four (this varies from region to region in France).
- Grandparents kiss grandchildren, nieces and nephews kiss their aunts and uncles and so on. The kiss is called '**la bise**' and '**faire la bise**' means '*to give a kiss*'. '**Serrer la main**' is '*to shake hands*' and '**tendre la main**' is '*to offer your hand for a handshake*'.

Saying 'Hello'

- When you want to say 'hello' in French, there are two words you can use: '**Bonjour**' or '**Salut**'. '**Bonjour**' is slightly more formal than '**Salut**', which is more like '*Hi!*'. '**Salut**' is used more often by young people. It can be followed by '**Ça va ?**' which means '*how are you ?*' '*how is it going?*'. If it is evening time, '**Bonsoir**' is used.
- Titles, '**Monsieur**' for a man and '**Madame**' for a woman, are used much more often in French than in English.

serrer la main

1.1 Écoutons maintenant !

Listen to these French people saying hello to one another.

1
– *Salut Arnaud !*
– *Salut Lucie !*

2
– *Salut maman !*
– *Salut Nicolas, ça va ?*
– *Oui, ça va bien, merci.*

3
– *Bonjour Madame !*
– *Bonjour Amandine !*

4
– *Bonsoir Monsieur !*
– *Bonsoir Madame !*

Exercice 1

Fill in the gaps in the following three conversations.

1 **Océane :** ________________ Jean-Luc !
Jean-Luc : ________________ Océane !
Océane : Ça ________ ?
Jean-Luc : Oui, ________ va bien, merci.

2 **Monsieur Legros :** Ah ! ________________ Madame Gilbert !
Madame Gilbert : Bonjour ________________ Legros !

3 **Madame Hervé :** ________________ Amandine ! Ça va ?
Amandine : ________ Hervé. Oui, ça ______ merci.

1.2 Écoutons maintenant !

Listen to eight French people introducing themselves and telling you where they live. See if you can find their towns on the map and join their names to the town in which they live. Listen to them using the phrases '**je m'appelle**' (*I am called*) and '**j'habite**' (*I live in*).

Luc

Christophe

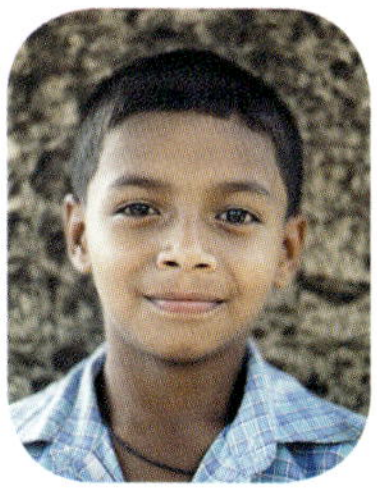
Khalid

Monsieur Réaubourg

Madame Rocher

Océane

Sophie

Léa

Écrivons maintenant !

Write a sentence using the information you have heard in the previous exercise.

Exemple : Je m'appelle Luc. J'habite à Toulouse.

1 Je m'appelle Léa. J'habite à ____________________.
2 Je m'appelle Océane. J'habite à ____________________.
3 Je __________ Christophe. J'habite à ____________________.
4 Je __________ Khalid. __________ à ____________________.
5 _____ __________ Sophie. ______________ _______ ______________.

Parlons maintenant !

Using the above sentences as an example, students in the class can practise introducing themselves individually.

Exemple : Je m'appelle Killian Keane. J'habite à Gorey.

Écrivons maintenant !

Write a sentence for each of the following people, using the phrases you have just learned.

1 Shona Dunne, who lives in Drogheda.
2 Hugh O'Brien, who lives in Kilkenny.
3 Darragh Murphy, who lives in Rathfarnham.
4 Hannah Ryan, who lives in Sligo.
5 Gary Maguire, who lives in Waterford.
6 Aisling White, who lives in Naas.

Civilisation : Carte d'identité

- All French people, even young people, have a '**carte d'identité**'. This is like a passport and each card must have the owner's photograph. It gives details of their surname (**le nom de famille**), first name (**le prénom**), where they live, their date of birth and their height.

Exercice 1

Fill in the '**cartes d'identité**' for the following people.

1 Léa Rocher, Strasbourg, 12.05.1995, 1m58
2 Khalid Mansour, Marseille, 01.10.1994, 1m52

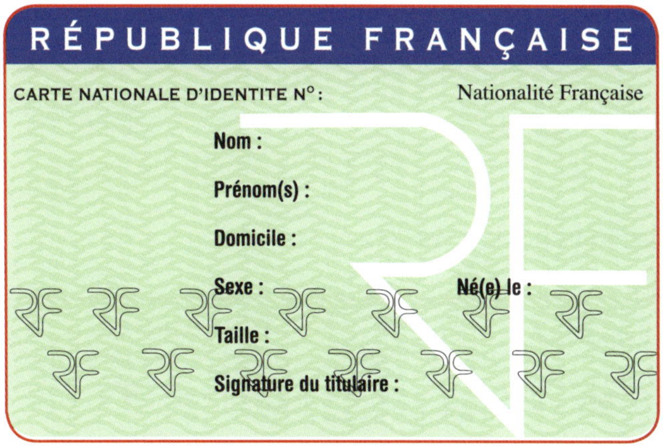

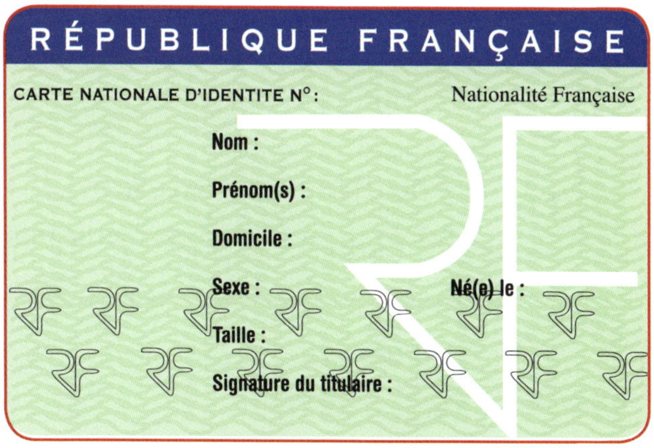

Les nombres

- Here are the French numbers from **0** to **20**.

1.3

Écoutons maintenant !

Listen to the numbers **0** to **20**.

zéro	0	**sept**	7	**quatorze**	14
un	1	**huit**	8	**quinze**	15
deux	2	**neuf**	9	**seize**	16
trois	3	**dix**	10	**dix-sept**	17
quatre	4	**onze**	11	**dix-huit**	18
cinq	5	**douze**	12	**dix-neuf**	19
six	6	**treize**	13	**vingt**	20

1.4

Écoutons maintenant !

Write the figures in your copy as you hear the French numbers on the CD. There are 16 of them.

1.5

Écoutons maintenant !

Sometimes it is hard to distinguish some of the French numbers from each other. Listen to the following numbers and mark with a tick which one you have heard.

un		**deux**		**trois**		**quatre**		**cinq**		**six**	
une		**douze**		**treize**		**quatorze**		**quinze**		**seize**	

1.6

Écoutons maintenant !

(a) Write the final scores for the football matches last weekend.

1	Monaco		**2**	Bordeaux		**3**	Olympique Lyonnais		**4**	Lens		**5**	Auxerre	
	▼			▼			▼			▼			▼	
	Paris St Germain			Marseille			Lille			Stade Rennais			St Étienne	

(b) Write the scores from the rugby results.

1	Biarritz ▼ Leinster	
2	Toulouse ▼ Ulster	
3	Perpignan ▼ Édimbourg	
4	Castres ▼ Munster	
5	Stade Français ▼ Northampton	

Exercice 1

(a) Unscramble the words and write the correct spelling of the numbers between one and ten.

1 qinC ________
2 epSt ________
3 Nefu ________
4 Huti ________
5 Dxeu ________
6 atrQue ________

(b) Match the words with the correct number.

quatorze quinze dix-sept douze treize dix-huit

13 14 18 15 12 17

(c) Count the amount of each object and write the number in French beside each picture.

1 ____________

2 ____________

3 ____________

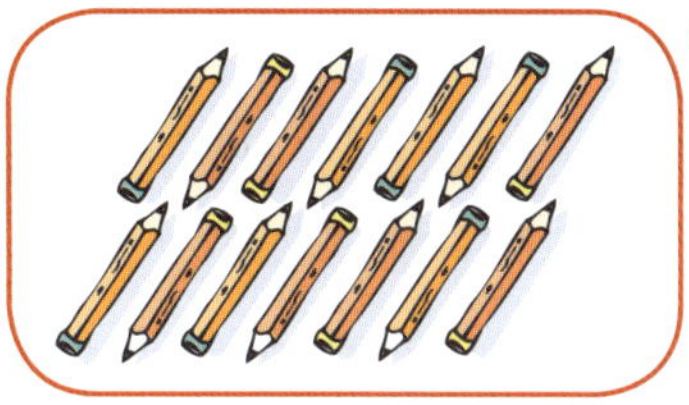

4 ____________

5 ____________

6 ____________

Exercice 2

Mots croisés ! Fill in the numbers in this crossword below.

ACROSS

- **4** 15
- **5** 8
- **6** 9
- **7** 4
- **9** 10
- **10** 13
- **11** 12
- **12** 7

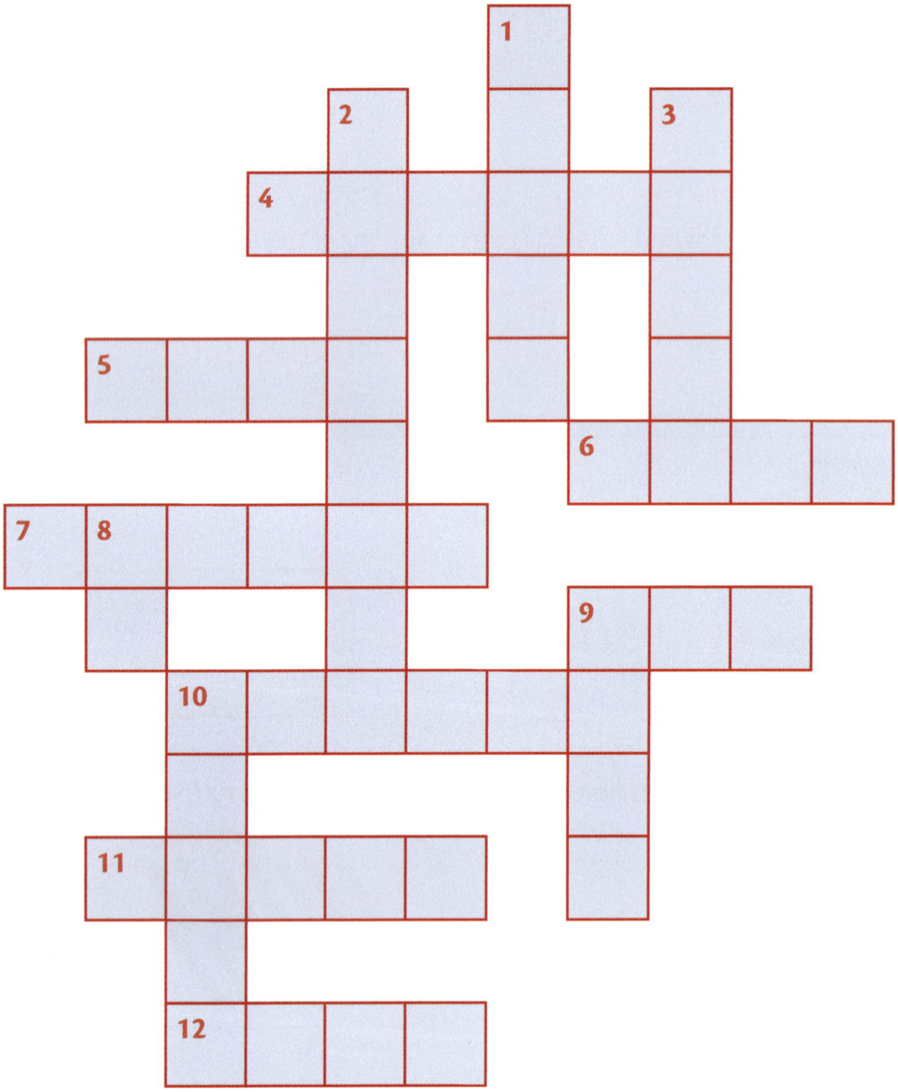

DOWN

- **1** 20
- **2** 14
- **3** 16
- **8** 1
- **9** 2
- **10** 3

1.7

Écoutons maintenant !

Draw a bingo card (three squares across and three squares down). Fill in nine numbers of your choice from 1 to 20. Then listen and tick the numbers as you hear them called out. When you have completed your card you can call '**Loto**' !

Je me présente

- Now that you know the numbers from 1 to 20, you can add in your age, as well as saying your name and where you live. The phrase you need to know is: J'ai ________ ans.

1.8 Écoutons maintenant !

Listen to the following people and fill in their ages.

1 **Suzanne :** ________	2 **Philippe :** ________
3 **Jean-François :** ________	4 **Fabien :** ________
5 **Noémie :** ________	6 **Claire :** ________

- When you meet someone who speaks French and you want to find out details about their name, age and where they live, you will need the following questions:

– Comment tu t'appelles ? (*What are you called?*)	– Je m'appelle ________.
– Tu as quel âge ? (*What age are you?*)	– J'ai ________ ans
– Tu habites où ? (*Where do you live?*)	– J'habite à ________.

Parlons maintenant !

(a) Working in pairs, ask your partner the questions above and note down their answers. Then change roles. You can make up your own personal details.

(b) Pretend you are being interviewed for a French radio programme. Give the following details about yourself. You and your partner can take turns to be the interviewer and the interviewee.

1 **Eoin O'Connor:** 14 years old, Tralee	2 **Luke Burke:** 12 years old, Tuam
3 **Nessa Kelly:** 15 years old, Monaghan	4 **Hannah McGrath:** 16 years old, Waterford
5 **Ruth Stafford:** 13 years old, Swords	6 **Richard Mulins:** 16 years old, Mullingar

L'alphabet français

1.9

Écoutons maintenant !

(a) Écoutez et répétez les lettres de l'alphabet en français.

a b c d e f g h i j k l m n o p q r s t u v w x y z.

(b) Now listen to the vowel sounds.

a e i o u y.

(c) Listen to the consonants and circle with a pencil those which sound like their English counterparts.

b c d f g h j k l m n p q r s t v w x z.

Les accents

- There are **three** accents which can be written on vowels. They affect the way words are pronounced:

  accent aigu : é **accent grave :** à; è; ù **accent circonflexe :** â; ê; î; ô; û

- **La cédille:** The cedilla is sometimes written under the letter 'c' (**ç**). It looks like a small apostrophe. The '**cédille**' softens the letter '**c**' to make it sound like the 'c' in the English word '*face*', e.g. '**Ça va ?**'.

1.10

Écoutons maintenant !

Listen to these three people spelling their names.

1	Je m'appelle	LAURENCE	GEFFROY.
2	Je m'appelle	CLAIRE	DELABROSSE.
3	Je m'appelle	PHILIPPE	HAVÉ.

1.11

Écoutons maintenant !

Now listen to the following names and see if you can fill in letters. There are five first names (**prénoms**) and five surnames (**noms de famille**).

1 J ___ L ___ E	**6** D ___ P ___ N ___
2 N ___ C ___ L ___ S	**7** M ___ R ___ I ___
3 N ___ T ___ AL ___ E	**8** T ___ T ___ ___
4 S ___ ___ D ___ A	**9** B ___ ___ A ___ D
5 A ___ M ___ ___	**10** L ___ ___ L ___ ___ C

Parlons maintenant !

Spell your own name in French and some of your friends' names.

Coin grammaire : Nouns ('les noms') and articles ('les articles')

Nouns ('les noms')

- As you probably know a **noun** is the name we give to a person (Marie, Conal, boy, niece), place (Cork, Norway, house, school) or thing (cup, tree, bus, phone).
- Nouns have a **gender**. In French there are **two** genders, **masculine** or **feminine** (there is no neuter, as in English).
- Nouns can be **singular** (one person or thing) or **plural** (more than one person or thing).
- When you are learning a new noun in French, always learn whether it is masculine or feminine. You will usually find this information in a dictionary or vocabulary list.

Articles ('les articles')

- There are **two types** of articles. The **definite** article '**the**', which points out a particular person or thing. The **indefinite** article '**a/an**' is a little more vague. For example, you might say: 'She is **the** girl who lives in Paris'. You are being very definite about that girl. On the other hand, if you say 'She is **a** girl who lives in Paris', she might be one of many.

The definite article ('l'article défini')

- In French there are **three** ways of saying '**the**':
  1. '**le**' is used for masculine singular nouns;
  2. '**la**' is used for feminine singular nouns;
  3. '**les**' is used for all plural nouns.

- '**Le**' and '**la**' are **shortened** to '**l'** ' before a **singular noun** starting with a **vowel** or a **silent** '**h**'.

1.12 Écoutons maintenant !

(a) Listen and repeat the words.

a. le café

b. la serviette

c. les restaurants

d. l'hôtel

e. l'omelette

f. le garçon

g. la fille

h. les enfants

(b) Listen and put the missing article in front of each of the following words.

a. _____ chat

b. ____ maison

c. _____ tables

d. _____ porte

e. _____ homme

f. ______ livres

g. ____ cahier

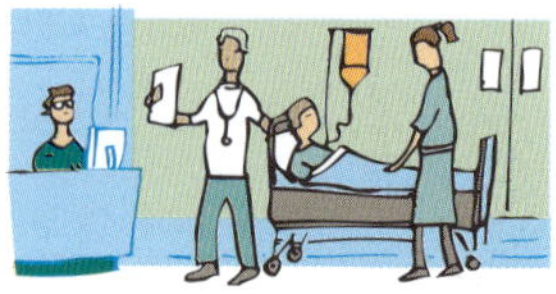

h. ____ hôpital

Coin Prononciation : The letter '**h**' at the beginning of a French word is generally not pronounced, e.g. '**habiter**', '**huit**', '**Henry**', '**hôpital**', '**hôtel**'.

The indefinite article ('l'article indéfini')

- In English we have **two** indefinite articles, '**a**' or '**an**'. In French, there are **three** forms:
  1. '**Un**' for masculine singular nouns;
  2. '**Une**' for feminine singular nouns;
  3. '**Des**' for all plural nouns. This translates as '*some*'.

1.13 Écoutons maintenant !

(a) Listen and repeat the following words.

a. une chaise

b. un chien

c. des stylos

d. un vélo

e. un portable

f. des filles

g. une table

h. des cahiers

(b) Écoutez et remplissez les blancs ci-dessous avec l'article indéfini '**un**', '**une**' ou '**des**'. Listen and pick the correct indefinite article for each of the following words.

Coin Prononciation : '**Les**' and '**des**' are pronounced 'lay' and 'day'.

a. 

________ café

e. 

________ cahiers

b. 

________ fille

f. 

________ garçon

c. 

________ tables

g. 

________ vélos

d. 

________ serviette

h. 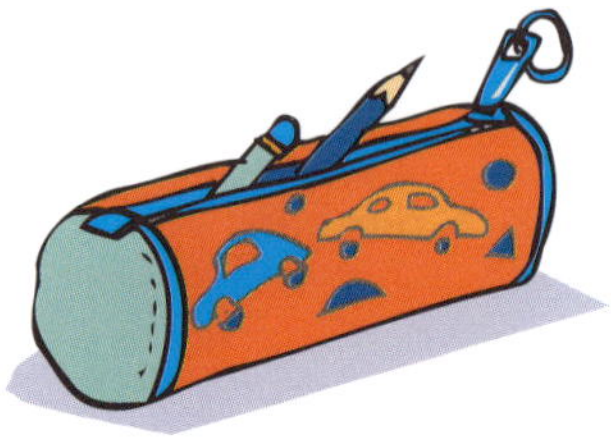

________ trousse

Coin dictionnaire : Signs and abbreviations

- Some dictionaries will provide a guide to pronunciation in brackets, followed by '**nf**', '**nm**', '**a**' or '**v**'. This indicates whether the word is a **noun feminine**, **noun masculine**, an **adjective** or a **verb**.
- There is usually a list of signs and abbreviations to be found at the beginning of your dictionary along with tips for pronunciation or phonetics.

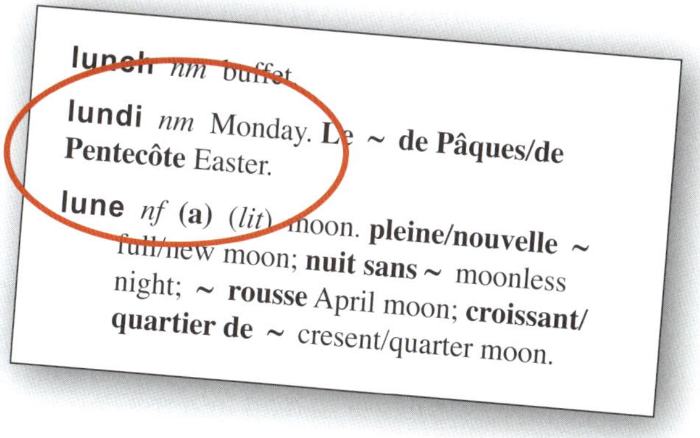
lunch *nm* buffet
lundi *nm* Monday. **Le ~ de Pâques/de Pentecôte** Easter.
lune *nf* **(a)** *(lit)* moon. **pleine/nouvelle ~** full/new moon; **nuit sans ~** moonless night; **~ rousse** April moon; **croissant/ quartier de ~** cresent/quarter moon.

Exercice 1

(a) Look up the following words in your dictionary and write them out in French in your copy with the correct definite article ('**le**', '**la**', '**l'** ' or '**les**'). By adding an '**s**', you can make the word plural.

1 pencil	**2** office	**3** window	**4** schoolbag	**5** maps
6 mother	**7** father	**8** pupils	**9** ice cream	**10** brothers

(b) Using the same nouns, put '**un**', '**une**' or '**des**' in front of each one.

Did you notice? When you used '**le**' in front of the noun in **(a)**, you used '**un**' in **(b)**. When you used '**la**' in **(a)**, you used '**une**' in **(b)**. And, if you used '**les**' in **(a)**, you used '**des**' in **(b)**. It is important to remember this!

Civilisation: Les célébrités françaises

- Many famous French people have had a great influence in areas of life such as sport, politics, fashion, science, medicine, cinema, literature and music. The French like to commemorate their famous daughters and sons by naming streets, schools and other public places after them.

Voulez-vous surfer ce soir ?

- To find lots of information about France and the French, visit: http://french.about.com/
- Use the site to help find the answers to the clues below.

Exercice 1

Answer the following clues about famous French people.

1. This **P** is a former French President. A famous art centre in Paris is named after him.
2. This **B** invented a system of reading for the visually impaired.
3. This **M** is a French artist who loved to paint water-lilies.
4. This **C** is a famous fashion designer and creator of well-known perfumes.
5. This **T** is a French actress who we know as the star of *Amélie*.
6. This **Z** is an important French novelist of the 19th century.
7. This **P** discovered how to pasteurise milk.
8. This **L** had a hit single with 'Complicated'.
9. This **J** led the French army against the English and was burnt at the stake.
10. This **M** is a well-loved master of the art of mime.

Coin grammaire : Verbs ('les verbes')

Why do we use a verb?

- Verbs are an essential part of every sentence. If you said '*The boy... to training...*' or '*Sinéad... sport*', no-one would understand you. The verb is missing from each sentence. The verb is the action or doing word. If you say '*The boy **goes** training*' or '*Sinéad **plays** sport*', everything is clear.

Subject pronouns ('les pronoms personnels sujets')

- The person or thing doing the action is called the subject of the sentence. It can be a **noun** (**un nom**) 'the boy', Sinéad', 'my teachers' or a **pronoun** (**un pronom**) 'we', 'she', 'they'.
- The **subject pronouns** are:

singular pronouns		plural pronouns	
je	*I*	**nous**	*we*
tu	*you (one person)*	**vous**	*you (more than one person or showing respect)*
il	*he/it (masculine)*	**ils**	*they (masculine)*
elle	*she/it (feminine)*	**elles**	*they (feminine)*

- The French also sometimes use the **pronoun** '**on**', when they want to say '*someone/ somebody*', or '*people in general*'. You will learn about that later on.

The infinitive ('l'infinitif')

- When you look up a verb in the dictionary, the form you find is called **the infinitive** (**l'infinitif**). The **tense** is the time at which an action is done, e.g. present tense (what **is** happening), future tense (what **will** happen), etc.

Verb groups ('les groupes')

- French verbs in the infinitive end in one of the following endings:

group 1	group 2	group 3
–**er** ending	–**ir** ending	–**re** ending

- Each group follows a particular set of **rules** to make its various tenses. When you learn the rule for **one** verb from each group, you know the rule for other regular verbs in that group.
- There is a fourth group of verbs, which may end in '–**er**', '–**ir**', or '–**re**', but which follow no particular rule. These verbs are called **irregular verbs** and have to be learned individually.

Exercice 1

Put the following verbs into three columns according to their endings.

écouter

parler

saisir

finir

vendre

jouer

regarder

choisir

attendre

- When you remove the endings '**–er**', '**–ir**', '**–re**' from the verb, the part you are left with is called the **stem** (or **root**).

Stage 1

You take the verb and remove its ending.

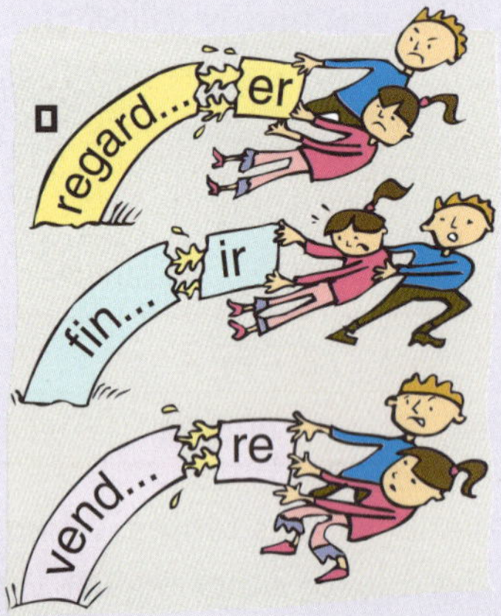

Stage 2

You are now left with the stems:

regard–

fin–

vend–

Stage 3

Then you add on the tense endings you need, which you will learn in future units.

Exercice 2

Take the ten verbs from the previous exercise and write the stem for each one.

Civilisation: 'Tu' et 'vous'

- You will have noticed that, in the subject pronouns list on page 21, there were **two** words for 'you' in French:

tu and **vous**

Singular: 'Tu'

- **Someone you know well:** a member of your family; a friend; a person your own age.

tu →

Plural and respect: 'Vous'

- **Someone you do not know well:** older people who are not members of your family; people in authority; a group of people.

vous →

Exercice 1

Would you use '**tu**' or '**vous**' when speaking to the following people?

1 Your best friend	2 Your teacher	3 Your cousin	4 A waiter
5 Your brother	6 Your doctor	7 A shop assistant	8 An elderly neighbour

Exercice 2

Look at the pictures below. Match each picture with the correct speech bubble.

1

2

3

4

5

6

a. Vous écoutez la radio, Monsieur ?

b. Tu joues au foot avec moi ?

c. Vous vendez de l'aspirine ?

d. Tu parles anglais, maman ?

e. Mes enfants, où est-ce que vous habitez ?

f. Tu regardes les Simpson ?

Tips

- '**Comment vas-tu ?**' and '**Comment allez-vous ?**' (*How are you?*) are used to greet people in French.
- '**Ça va ?**' is used in a casual way, when talking to friends. It is like '*Hiya!*'

Exercice 3

Remember the rule for '**tu**' and '**vous**' and complete the exercise.
Put in either '**Comment vas-tu ?**' or '**Comment allez-vous ?**'.

1 Bonjour, Madame, ______________________________ ?
2 Salut, Nicolas, ______________________________ ?
3 Bonjour, Monsieur l'agent, ______________________________ ?
4 Oui, et toi, ______________________________ ?
5 Oncle Henri, ______________________________ ?

1.14

Écoutons et écrivons maintenant !

Here is a letter from Sylvie to her new Irish pen-pal who is called Clodagh. Unfortunately, her little brother spilt some orange juice on the page and some of the words have become unclear! Listen to Sylvie and fill in the missing words. You will find them in jumbled order in the box.

Tip: A pen-pal is called a '**correspondant(e)**' in French.

âge – ans – correspondante – France – habites – m'appelle – professeur – 4

Guichen, le ___ mai 2007

Chère Clodagh,

Je suis ta nouvelle ______________ Mon ______________ m'a donné ton adresse.

Je me présente. Je ______________ Sylvie Jautier. J'ai douze ______________. J'habite á Guichen, en ______________.

Et toi ? Tu as quel ______________ ? Tu ______________ où en Irlande ?

Amitiés,

Sylvie

Écrivons maintenant !

Using Sylvie's letter as an example, write to your new French-speaking penpal, called Julien/Julie. Tell him/her your name, your age and where you live. Ask him/her some questions.

Tip: When you are writing to a boy, use the word '**cher**' for '*dear*'. When writing to a girl, use '**chère**'.

Communication en classe !

Lexique

âge	*age*
aimer	*to like*
ambulance (f.)	*ambulance*
amitiés	*best wishes*
anglais	*English*
ans (m. pl.)	*years*
s'appeler	*to be called*
attendre	*to wait for*
au revoir	*goodbye*
banque (f.)	*bank*
bise (f.)	*kiss*
bonjour	*hello*
bonsoir	*good evening*
ça va ?	*how is it going?*
café (m.)	*coffee/café*
cahier (m.)	*copybook*
carte d'identité (f.)	*identity card*
chaise (f.)	*chair*
chat (m.)	*cat*
cher/chère	*dear*
chien (m.)	*dog*
choisir	*to choose/to pick*
comment on dit… ?	*how do you say…?*
correspondant(e)	*penfriend*
crayon (m.)	*pencil*
domicile (m.)	*residence*
donner	*to give*
écouter	*to listen to*
élève (m./f.)	*pupil*
enfant (m.)	*child*
faire la bise	*to kiss*
fille (f.)	*girl*
finir	*to finish*
français	*French*
garçon (m.)	*boy*
habiter	*to live*
homme (m.)	*man*
hôpital (m.)	*hospital*
hôtel (m.)	*hotel*
jouer	*to play*
livre (m.)	*book*
magazine (m.)	*magazine*
maison (f.)	*house*
merci	*thank you*
mordre	*to bite*
nom de famille (m.)	*surname*
monument (m.)	*monument*
nombre (m.)	*number*
nouveau/velle	*new*
omelette (f.)	*omelette*
ouvrir	*to open*
parler	*to speak*
perdre	*to lose*
pharmacie (f.)	*chemist's shop*
porte (f.)	*door*
portable (m.)	*mobile phone*
poste (f.)	*post office*
prénom (m.)	*first name*
se présenter	*to introduce oneself*
professeur (m./f.)	*teacher*
regarder	*to look at*
remplir	*to fill*
restaurant (m.)	*restaurant*
saisir	*to grab, snatch*
salut	*hi!*
serrer la main	*to shake hands*
serviette (f.)	*towel*
sortir	*to go out/take out*
station-service (f.)	*petrol station*
stylo (m.)	*pen/biro*
supermarché (m.)	*supermarket*
table (f.)	*table*
trousse (f.)	*pencilcase*
vélo (m.)	*bicycle*
vendre	*to sell*

Épreuve

Question 1

You will hear six people introducing themselves. Copy the headings into your copybook and then listen to their statements and fill in their personal details.

Exemple :

first name	family name	age	where they live
Luc	Hamel	13	Rennes

Question 2

Write the following numbers in French.

1, 11, 2, 12, 3, 13, 4, 14, 5, 15, 6, 16, 7, 17, 8, 18, 9, 19, 20.

For **help** with this exercise, see page 10.

Question 3

Mots cachés ! Find the French words for the above numbers (1-20) in the '**mots cachés**'.

R	A	B	V	I	T	S	D	H	A	S	Y	D	F
C	U	J	I	T	R	D	O	U	Z	E	D	I	G
S	C	I	N	Q	E	C	Z	F	G	I	H	X	E
K	I	Q	G	B	I	T	A	E	X	Z	F	N	X
W	J	V	T	L	Z	S	I	X	R	E	N	E	M
D	W	U	D	S	E	T	Q	U	P	G	Q	U	E
P	I	Y	I	U	N	T	R	H	V	W	U	F	O
V	Z	X	X	F	K	I	R	O	Q	D	A	C	B
D	E	C	S	D	I	X	H	U	I	T	T	P	Q
H	O	B	E	O	N	Z	E	S	W	S	R	T	U
S	U	X	P	J	E	R	D	K	X	P	E	O	I
E	M	I	T	L	U	Y	G	E	O	L	J	M	N
P	N	A	T	Q	F	Z	M	H	U	I	K	A	Z
T	Q	U	A	T	O	R	Z	E	N	X	L	N	E

Question 4

Listen to place names in France being spelled and write them down. There are eight of them.

Question 5

Fill in the blanks in this introductory letter from a '**correspondant(e)**'.

Nice, le 2 octobre

Cher Robert,

Je suis ton nouveau ____________. Mon ____________ m'a donné ton adresse.
Je me ____________. Je ____________ Alexis. J' ____________ douze ans. J'habite á ____________________ en France.

Et toi ? Tu ____________ quel âge ? Tu habites où en Irlande ?

Amitiés,

Alexis

Question 6

(a) Le/la/les Write the three headings below in your copy and put the following nouns in the correct column.

masculine singular	feminine singular	plural

la banque ; les maisons ; le café ; les ambulances ; le supermarché ; la pharmacie ; les monuments ; la poste ; les magazines ; la station-service.

(b) Using your '**dictionnaire**', look up the meanings of the above words and write them in your copy.

Question 7

Listen to the CD and write in the indefinite article '**un**', '**une**' or '**des**' in the gaps below.

1	________ moment	6	________ glace
2	________ minute	7	________ gâteaux
3	________ heure	8	________ tente
4	________ crayons	9	________ caravanes
5	________ cinéma	10	________ sandwich

Question 8

Find the stems of the verbs below. Then, write down their meanings.
You can use your '**dictionnaire**' or '**lexique**' (see page 27).

aimer – choisir – mordre – chercher – perdre – remplir

Question 9

Listen to what is being said in the classroom and write down the caption for each of the following illustrations.

1

____

4

____

2

____

5

____

3

____

6

____

Unité 2

En classe

Civilisation : L'école

L'école maternelle

- In France, children attend state-run pre-school from the age of three. The pre-school is called '**l'école maternelle**'. Small children spend all day at the '**maternelle**' and even have an afternoon sleep (**la sieste**) there. The classes are called '**les petits**', '**les moyens**' and '**les grands**'.

L'école primaire

- At the age of six, children begin '**l'école primaire**' (also known as '**l'école élémentaire**') for five years. Here they spend a full day, until 4.30pm. Primary-school pupils are called '**les élèves**'. At primary school level, pupils learn **three** main groups of subjects:

1 French, History, Geography and Civic Studies;

2 Maths, Science and Technology;

3 Physical Education and Sport, Arts and Crafts and Music.

- Pupils receive twenty-six hours of teaching per week. In some regions, children now have school four days per week: Monday, Tuesday, Thursday and Friday! To ensure that children do not lose out on school hours, such schools may have slightly shorter holidays.

les classes à l'école primaire	âge
cours préparatoire (CP)	6 ans
cours élémentaire 1 (CE1)	7 ans
cours élémentaire 2 (CE2)	8 ans
cours moyen 1 (CM1)	9 ans
cours moyen 2 (CM2)	10 ans

Le collège

- At the age of eleven, children attend '**le collège**' where they spend four years studying for '**le brevet**'. This exam is like our Junior Certificate. In Ireland, you begin secondary school in first year and finish in sixth year, but the French system is the opposite: the first year in '**collège**' is called '**la sixième**', followed by '**la cinquième**', '**la quatrième**' and '**la troisième**'. Having completed '**le brevet**', French students then move to another school, called '**le lycée**'. As in Ireland, school is compulsory until the age of 16. Students who want to go straight into training for a trade, office or shop job can go to '**un lycée professionnel**'.

les classes au collège	âge
sixième	11 ans
cinquième	12 ans
quatrième	13 ans
troisième	14 ans

Le lycée

- Some '**lycées**' are in fact attached to the '**collège**', but, in many cases, transfer to a '**lycée**' means moving school to a much bigger establishment. '**Le lycée**' is like an American high school or sixth-form college in Britain. There can be up to 2,000 students. There are just three classes in a '**lycée**'.

les classes au lycée	âge
seconde	15 ans
première	16 ans
terminale	17 ans

- Students spend three years studying for their final exam, called '**le baccalauréat**' (or '**le bac**'), which is similar to our Leaving Certificate. In '**le lycée**', the first year is called la '**seconde**'. This is followed by '**la première**' and, finally, '**la terminale**'.

2.1 Écoutons maintenant !

Listen to these six pupils and tick **(a)** the type of school they attend and **(b)** which class they are in.

	primaire	collège	lycée	terminale	1ère	5ème	3ème	CE1	CM1
Benoît									
Cécile									
Alexandre									
Élodie									
Paul									
Solène									

Les devoirs

- Just like you, French pupils have homework to do most evenings. Here are some of the **instructions** a teacher might give to the class.

dessinez

écrivez

répondez

apprenez

lisez

écoutez

2.2

Écoutons maintenant !

Match each instruction with a suitable ending. Listen to the CD and see if you were correct.

1	Dessinez…	(a)	… le poème !
2	Écrivez…	(b)	… à la question 5 !
3	Répondez…	(c)	… le CD !
4	Lisez…	(d)	… une carte de la France !
5	Écoutez…	(e)	… le texte !
6	Apprenez…	(f)	… une lettre !

La salle de classe

2.3 Écoutons maintenant !

Listen to these French words being called out and link them to the correct picture.

Coin grammaire : Il y a...

- '**Il y a**' is a really useful little phrase in French. It means '*there is*' or '*there are*'. It is particularly useful when you are describing the contents of a room, such as your classroom.

Exercice 1

(a) Complete the sentences below with the help of the pictures.

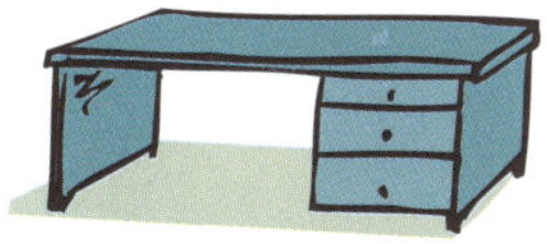

1 Dans la salle de classe, il y a un ________________.

2 Dans la salle de classe, il y ______ une ____________.

3 Dans la salle de classe, il ____ ____ des ______________.

4 Dans la salle de classe, ____ ____ ____ des ______________.

5 Dans la salle de classe, ____ _____ _____ ______ ________________.

(b) Dessinez votre salle de classe. Label each item in French.

Coin grammaire : Irregular verbs ('les verbes irréguliers')

- In **Unité 1**, we mentioned a group of verbs called **irregular verbs** ('**verbes irréguliers**', see page 21). These are verbs which follow no particular pattern and must be learned '**par cœur**' (*by heart*).
- The first of these verbs you are going to learn is the verb '**être**' (*to be*).

2.4

Écoutons maintenant !

Listen to how the verb '**être**' sounds.

être		**to be**
je	**suis**	*I am*
tu	**es**	*you are*
il	**est**	*he is*
elle	**est**	*she is*
nous	**sommes**	*we are*
vous	**êtes**	*you are*
ils	**sont**	*they are*
elles	**sont**	*they are*

Exercice 1

Fill in the missing parts of the verb '**être**' in the grid.

je	**suis**
	es
il	
	est
nous	
vous	
ils	**sont**
elles	

Exercice 2

By taking one item from the each bag, match the subject with the correct form of the verb '**être**'. One is done for you as an example. Write the answers in your copy.

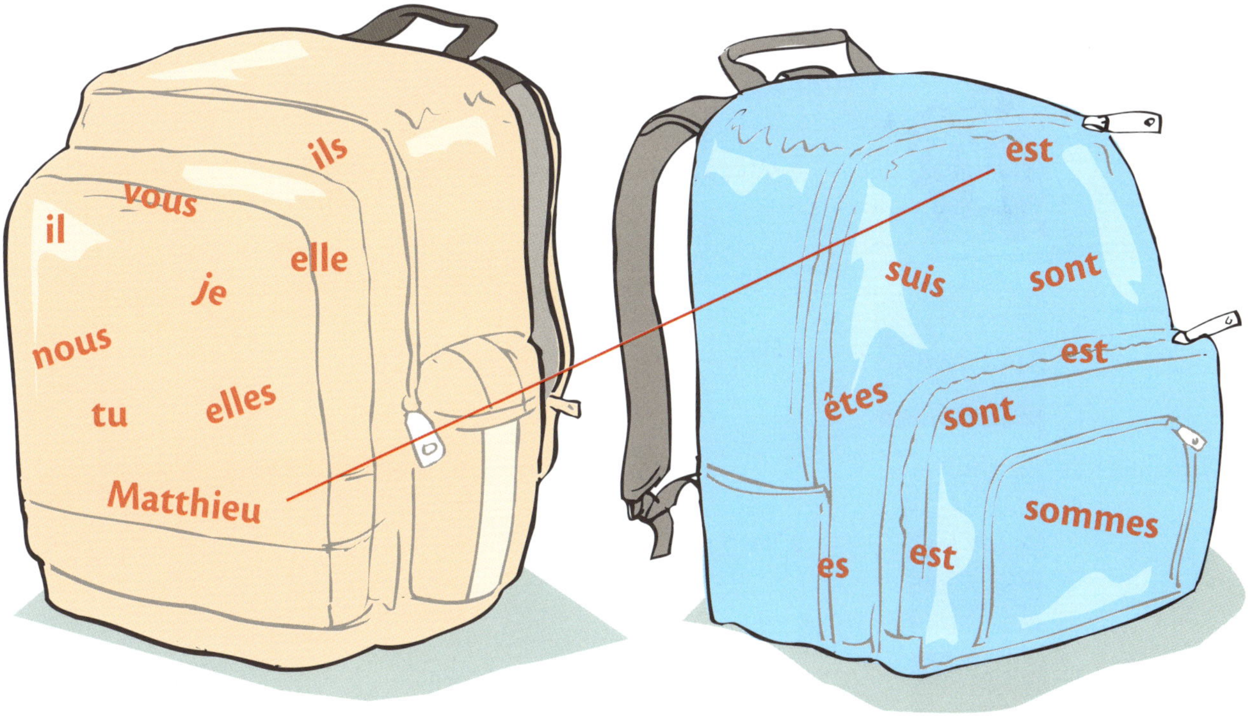

Exercice 3

Can you complete the missing parts of the verb in the following sentences?

1 Je ______________ sous la table.

2 Maman ______________ au restaurant.

3 Nous ______________ à l'école.

4 Ils ______________ dans la salle de classe.

5 Tu ______________ au téléphone ?

6 Elles ______________ à Paris.

7 Tu ______________ dans le train ?

8 Il ______________ devant le cinéma.

Coin grammaire : Negative of 'être'

2.5 Écoutons maintenant !

Listen to how the negative sounds.

This is the **negative** of the verb '**être**'. The word '**ne**' (or '**n'**') goes in front of the verb and '**pas**' goes **after** it.

je	**ne**	suis	**pas**	*I am not*
tu	**n'**	es	**pas**	*you are not*
il	**n'**	est	**pas**	*he is not*
elle	**n'**	est	**pas**	*she is not*
nous	**ne**	sommes	**pas**	*we are not*
vous	**n'**	êtes	**pas**	*you are not*
ils	**ne**	sont	**pas**	*they are not*
elles	**ne**	sont	**pas**	*they are not*

Tip: You can learn more about negatives, on page 66.

Exercice 1

Put '**ne**' and '**pas**' in the correct place in the following sentences. Write them in your copy and say what each sentence means.

1 Il ________________ est ________________ au cinéma.
2 Elle ________________ est ________________ à l'école.
3 Nous ________________ sommes ________________ dans la salle de classe.
4 Ils ________________ sont ________________ dans les Alpes.
5 Brhona ________________ est ________________ pas française.
6 Tu ________________ es ________________ à Sligo.
7 Vous ________________ êtes ________________ à l'école.
8 Je ________________ suis ________________ le professeur.

La salle de classe

Exercice 1

Can you write these words under the correct drawing? Don't forget the definite article!

e.

____

d.

____

g.

____

h.

____

f.

____

a.

____

c.

____

b.

____

la poubelle

le magnétophone

l'horloge

la carte

le poster

les étagères

l'ordinateur

la brosse

Parlons maintenant !

Take it in turns to ask each other '**Qu'est-ce que c'est**' (*What is it?*) by pointing to items in the classroom.

Exemple : – Qu'est-ce que c'est ? – C'est la poubelle.

Coin grammaire : Prepositions ('Les prépositions')

- Prepositions are useful little words which usually tell you **where something is**, e.g. the book is **on** the table, the teacher is **in front of** the board. Here are some useful prepositions for you to learn.

2.6 Écoutons maintenant !

Écoutez et regardez les dessins.

Je suis **dans** la poubelle.

Je suis **sur** le placard.

Je suis **devant** l'horloge.

Je suis **derrière** la porte.

Je suis **sous** le livre.

Je suis **entre** mon professeur et le directeur !

Écrivons maintenant !

Regardez le tableau et complétez les réponses ci-dessous.

1 **– Où est la poubelle ?** – La poubelle est…	3 **– Où est le livre ?** – Le livre est…	5 **– Où est l'élève ?** – L'élève est…
2 **– Où est l'horloge ?** – L'horloge est…	4 **– Où est la carte ?** – La carte est…	6 **– Où est le bureau ?** – Le bureau est…

Exercice 1

Un petit puzzle ! Qui est assis où ? *'Who is sitting where?'* Read the clues carefully and then fill in the names of the students under their pictures.

1	Louis est assis entre Loïc et Charles.
2	Charles est assis devant Christine.
3	Jonathan est assis derrière Louis.
4	Amandine est assise derrière Loïc.
5	Anissa est assise devant Louis.
6	Charles est assis derrière Tony.
7	Anissa est assise entre Noémie et Tony.

Tip: When the sentence refers to a girl, '**assis**' has an '**e**' at the end.

2.7

Écoutons maintenant !

Dictée ! Listen to these six sentences describing the location of items in the classroom. Write out each sentence.

Encore des nombres !

- Once you have learned your numbers from 0-20 (see page 10), the next set are not very difficult. Notice that you **join** the two words together with a **hyphen** (-).

Tip: For the number **twenty-one**, the hyphens are optional (older texts will not have them but a recent decision by the French authorities makes it possible to include the hyphens).

vingt	20
vingt et un	21
vingt-deux	22
vingt-trois	23
vingt-quatre	24
vingt-cinq	25
vingt-six	26
vingt-sept	27
vingt-huit	28
vingt-neuf	29
trente	30

2.8 Écoutons maintenant !

Listen to the numbers **20** to **30**.

Exercice 1

Un peu de maths ! Complétez les questions suivantes en français. Give the answers to these maths problems in French.

(a)	12	+	1	= ___________		(f)	7	x	3	= ___________
(b)	15	+	1	= ___________		(g)	5	x	5	= ___________
(c)	14	+	10	= ___________		(h)	3	x	9	= ___________
(d)	9	+	20	= ___________		(i)	4	x	7	= ___________
(e)	16	+	6	= ___________		(j)	3	x	10	= ___________

Parlons maintenant !

You wish to get your key from the desk in the French hotel where you are staying. What would you say to the receptionist?

Exemple : La vingt-quatre, s'il vous plaît !

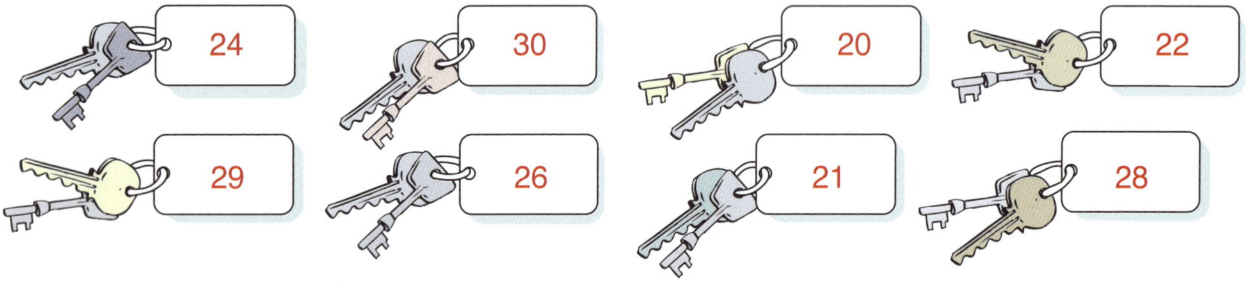

Exercice 2

Find the prices of the items below and write the price on the label.

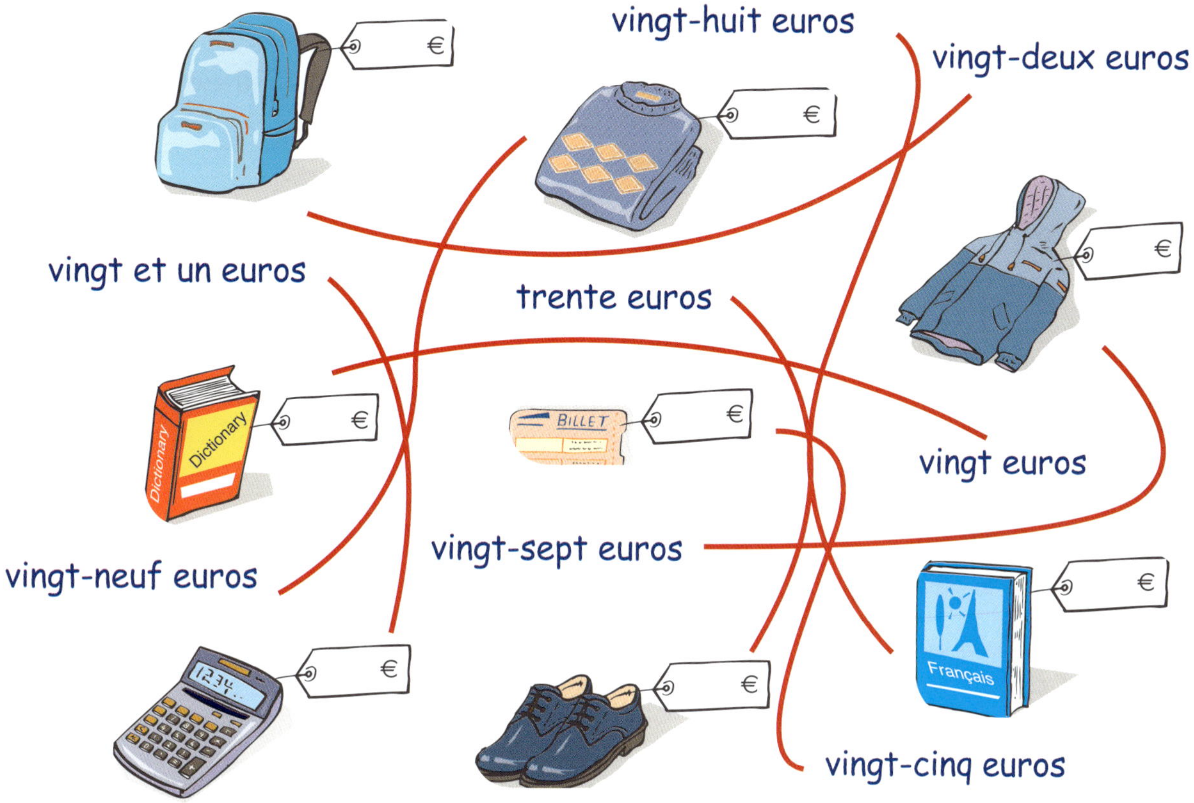

2.9

Écoutons maintenant !

Où habitent-ils/elles ? Some mischief-makers have been out and about in the town of St Pierre. They have removed the numbers from the hall doors. Listen and put the correct number back on each hall door.

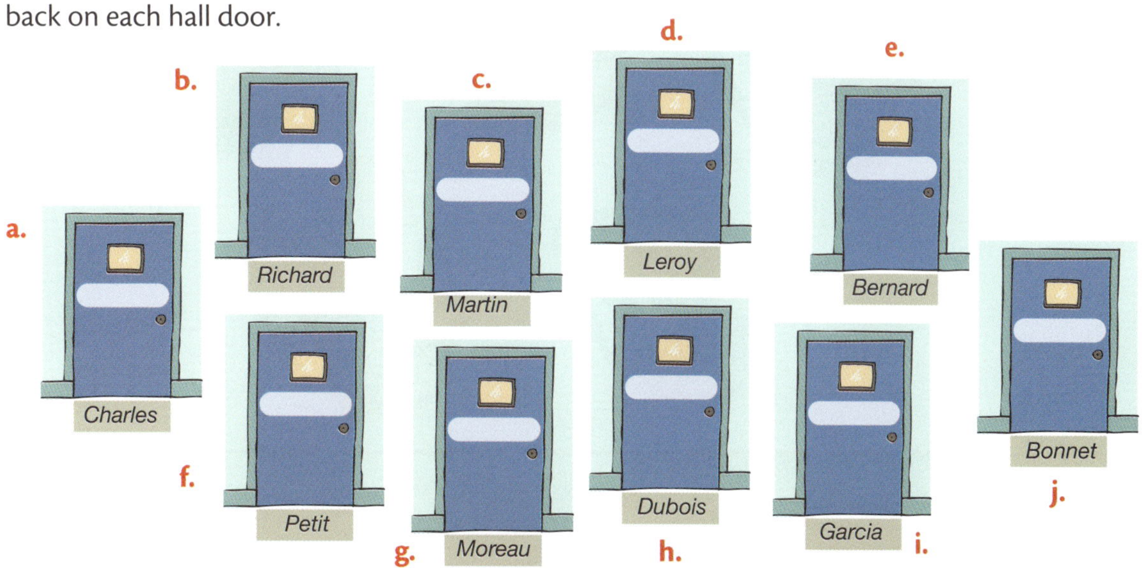

Écrivons maintenant !

Exercice 1

Using your '**dictionnaire**' or '**lexique**' (see page 52), find the meanings of these items and put them into either '**le cartable**' (*schoolbag*) or '**la trousse**' (*pencil case*).

le stylo	le livre
le carnet	l'agenda
le taille-crayon	le classeur
la règle	

le crayon	la gomme	le cahier
le feutre	la calculatrice	le compas

Écoutons maintenant !

2.10

Listen to the following people who are describing what is in their schoolbag and decide which schoolbag belongs to which person.

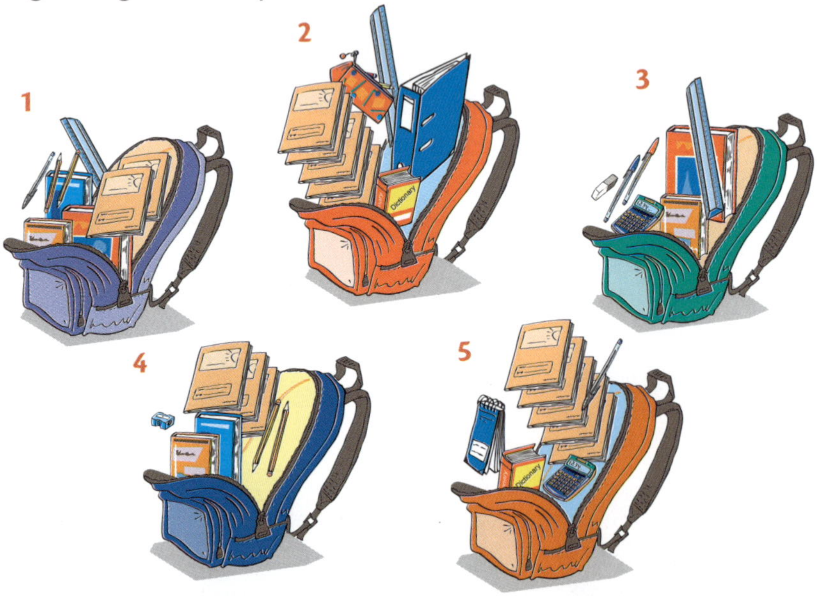

(a) Claire = (b) Olivier = (c) Alexandre = (d) Leila = (e) Suzanne =

Écrivons maintenant !

Fill in the missing French words in these ads for back to school items. The words you need are in the pencil-case.

Promo Rentrée

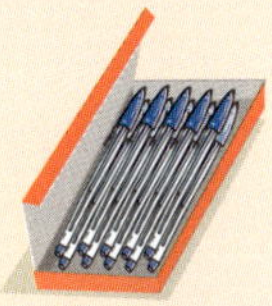

10 __________ bille, coloris assortis
2,35 €

__________ affichage 8 chiffres
1,95 €

__________ **à levier**, en carton, dos. 80 mn
1,80 €

__________ Existe en gris ou bordeaux, polyester
15,95 €

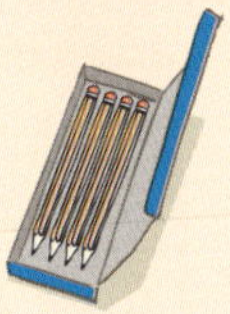

__________ **graphite**, HBCA1,
0,99 € le lot de 4

Lot de 3 __________, 96 pages
2,70 €

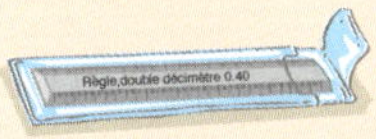

__________, double décimètre
1,40 €

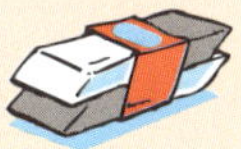

Lot de 2 __________
1,55 €

Parlons maintenant !

(a) Ask your partner to describe what he/she has in his/her pencil-case and schoolbag.

(b) Play the following memory game. Place at least six items from your schoolbag and pencil-case on the table in front of you. Give your partner 60 seconds to study them. Then, cover them up and your partner must try to recall all the items which were there. Then, reverse the situation.

Civilisation : Les vacances scolaires

Holidays and regions

- School holidays in France are standardised. The country is divided into three zones. In each zone, all schools follow the same dates for holidays. Parents must have permission to take their children out of school, other than during official holiday time.

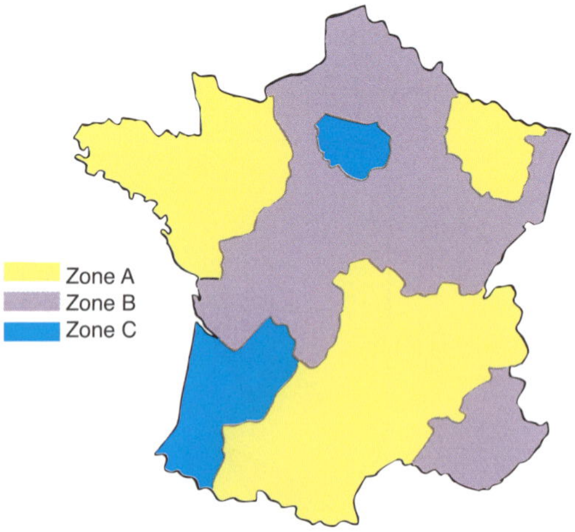

School holidays for the year 2007-2008

	Zone A	Zone B	Zone C
Back to school	3 septembre	3 septembre	3 septembre
November break	27 oct. - 8 nov.	27 oct. - 8 nov.	27 oct. - 8 nov.
Christmas	22 déc. - 7 jan.	22 déc. - 7 jan.	22 déc. - 7 jan.
February mid-term	16 fév. - 3 mars	9 fév. - 25 fév.	23 fév. - 10 mars
Easter time	12 avr. - 28 avr.	5 avr. - 21 avr.	19 avr. - 5 mai
Summer holidays	3 juillet	3 juillet	3 juillet

Tip: Voulez-vous surfer ce soir ?
To find more information on the school holiday system in France, visit: www.education.gouv.fr

La rentrée

- Going back to school in September is always a busy time for French students. It is called '**la rentrée**'. From August onwards, there is a lot of advertising for back to school necessities. For those going to '**le collège**' for the first time, it is quite exciting! They are going to a much bigger school, often having to travel there by coach (**le car scolaire**). As in primary school, French school children do not wear a school uniform in secondary schools. You will see in the next unit that the school day is longer than yours, but most French students have a half day on Wednesday. However, there is sometimes school on Saturday mornings!

Lisons maintenant !

Read the following advertisements and answer the questions which follow.

Facile la rentrée

Le lot de trois cahiers piqûre, 96 pages, grands carreaux, **2,20 €**

Classeur à levier, plastique couleur, **1,95 €**

Le lot de 3, couverture vernie, 96 pages, grands carreaux, **2,90 €**

+**100 gratuites**, Ramette de papier, 400 feuilles + 100 gratuites, 90 g, **3,60 €**

1. How many copies are there in the offer at €2.20?
2. Give **one** feature of the cover binding on the folder.
3. In which offer do you get something free?

Rentrée des classes

Agenda, couverture souple, 360 pages 1 jour/page **3,64 €**

Sac à dos, en polyester et coton **12,23 €**

Dos et bretelles matelassées

Existe aussi en sac à dos à roulettes au prix de **29,60 €**

1. How many pages per day are there in the '**agenda**'?
2. Can you name the **two** materials used in the school bag?
3. What is the difference between the bag at €12.23 and the one at €29.60?

Écrivons maintenant !

Lettre symbole ! Mark is writing to his French speaking '**correspondant**' Christophe. He describes his class and his classroom. Écrivez un mot pour chaque symbole. Rewrite the letter in your copy, replacing each symbol with the appropriate French word.

Longford, le 3 septembre

Cher Christophe,

Merci pour ta lettre avec les détails de ta classe. Moi, je suis dans une classe de **28** élèves. Nous sommes en quatrième.

La salle de classe est grande. Il y a trois  et une . Il y a des  et des  pour les élèves. Sur le mur, il y a des 

de la France ! Il y a aussi une  sur le mur. Le professeur a un . Sous les fenêtres, il y a des . Il y a deux  et un 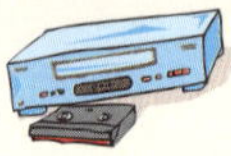. C'est bien, n'est-ce pas ?

Je dois finir maintenant. J'ai des devoirs à faire. Je dois dessiner une 

de la France et le professeur est strict !

Amitiés,

Mark

Communication en classe !

Lexique

agenda (m.)

allumer

anglais (m.)

appel (m.)

apprendre

assis(e) (m./f.)

baccalauránt (m.)

school journal

to turn on

rollcall

rollcall

seated

baccalauréat (m.)

brevet (m.)

exam like Leaving Cert.

exam like Jun. Cert.

bretelles (f. pl.) straps brosse (f.) duster

bureau (m.) teacher's desk/desk

copybook cahier (m.) calculatrice (f.) calculator notebook carnet (m.) cartable (m.) schoolbag carte (f.) map chaise (f.) chair ringbinder classeur (m.) collège (m.) secondary school compas (m.) compasses

compas (m.) compasses
cours (m.) lesson
courriel (m.) email
couverture (f.) blanket
crayon de couleur (m.) colouring pencil

crayon (m.)

dans

derrière

dessiner

devant

devoirs (m.pl.)

pencil

behind

to draw

to draw

homework

directeur/directrice (m./f.) school principal dos (m.) back école maternelle (f.) preschool école primaire (f.) primary school

écouter to listen to to write écrire écriture writing school pupil élève (m./f.) between entre Spanish espagnol (m.) shelf étagère (f.) to turn off éteindre

fatigué(e) fenêtre (f.)

feutre (m.) felt-tip pen finish/end finir gomme (f.) eraser grand(e) big/large gratuit free clock horloge (f.) Irish irlandais (m.) salle de classe (f.) classroom lecteur CD/DVD (m.) CD/DVD player

lettre (f.) letter
lire to read
livre (m.) book

lycée (m.) secondary school magnétophone (m.) tape recorder magnétoscope (m.) video recorder moyen(ne) medium/middle

wall mur (m.) numéro number ordinateur (m.) computer petit(e) (m./f.) small, little placard (m.) cupboard poème (m.) poem porte (f.) door poster (m.) poster poubelle (f.) bin prix (m.) price professeur (m./f.) teacher ruler règle (f.)

rentrée (f.) return to school répondre to reply roulette little wheel

sieste (f.) afternoon sleep/nap

sous under
stylo (m.) pen/biro
sur on
tableau (m.) board

taille-crayon (m.) pencil sharpener terminale (f.) final-year at lycée

train (m.) train
trousse (f.) pencilcase
vacances (f.pl.) holidays

Épreuve

Question 1

Look into your school-bag and write five sentences about what you find there.

Exemple : Dans le cartable, il y a dix cahiers.

1 Il y a ______________________.   **2** Il y a ______________________.

3 Il y a ______________________.   **4** Il y a ______________________.

5 Il y a ______________________.

Question 2

Listen to Nadia describing her classroom and answer the questions.

1 How many students are there in the class?

2 The teacher's desk is between the ______________ and the cupboard.

3 What is under the windows?

4 Where are the dictionaries kept?

5 Name **one** item which the teacher has on the desk.

Question 3

Write sentences in French saying where each numbered item is.

Exemple : Le professeur est devant la carte. (Number 8)

Question 4

Read these advertisements for school books and answer the questions which follow.

1.

Maternelle

Pour accompagner votre enfant tout au long de ses années de maternelle.

7,50 €

Une collection complète animée pour aider votre enfant à bien démarrer la lecture, l'écriture et les mathématiques.

4, 90 €

2.

Les cahiers scolaires

10 minutes par jour pour apprendre en s'amusant tous les jours de l'année scolaire.

10,90 €

3.

Série Réussite

Sciences, Nature, Langues, Histoire, 100 pages. Fun pour les élèves !

3,50 €

Advertisement 1: This series is produced for children in which type of school?

Apart from reading and writing, which other school subject is covered by these workbooks?

Advertisement 2: How long each day is suggested for using '**les cahiers scolaires**'?

Advertisement 3: The '**Série Réussite**' is available for which **two** languages?

Question 5

Léa has written an email (**un courriel**) to her Irish penpal describing her classroom. Read her email and say whether the statements which follow are true or false (**vrai ou faux**).

Je suis en cinquième cette année. C'est super ! Il y a vingt-neuf élèves dans ma classe : quinze garçons et quatorze filles. Notre professeur d'anglais s'appelle Monsieur Brown. Il vient de Manchester. Il est très strict !

Nous avons une grande salle de classe, numéro neuf. Il y a quatre fenêtres et la salle est très claire. Le tableau est derrière le bureau du professeur. Sur les murs, il y a des posters et une carte d'Europe. Sur le bureau, il y a un magnétophone et un rétroprojecteur. Entre le bureau et les fenêtres il y a un placard. Les cahiers et les livres sont dans le placard. Il y a aussi un magnétoscope et deux ordinateurs.

Et toi ? Comment sont les élèves de ta classe et ta salle de classe ?

Répond-moi vite !

Léa

		vrai	faux
1	This is Léa's first year in secondary school.		
2	There are more boys than girls in his class.		
3	Their English teacher comes from Scotland.		
4	The teacher's desk is in front of the board.		
5	There is a map on the wall.		
6	The cupboard is between the windows and the door.		
7	Books and copybooks are kept in the cupboard.		
8	The room has two computers.		

Question 6

Destination – Faites des paires ! Where am I going? Read the sentences and write the name of the city to which I am travelling.

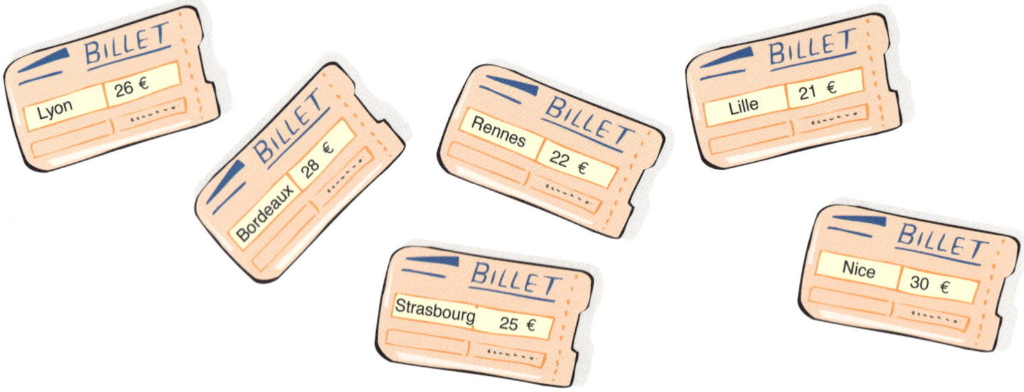

1 Je paie vingt-huit euros : ______________

2 Je paie vingt-deux euros : ______________

3 Je paie vingt-six euros : ______________

4 Je paie vingt-cinq euros : ______________

5 Je paie vingt et un euros : ______________

6 Je paie trente euros : ______________

Question 7

Listen to these advertisements in a supermarket for back to school items and write the correct price on the labels. You will hear them in the correct order.

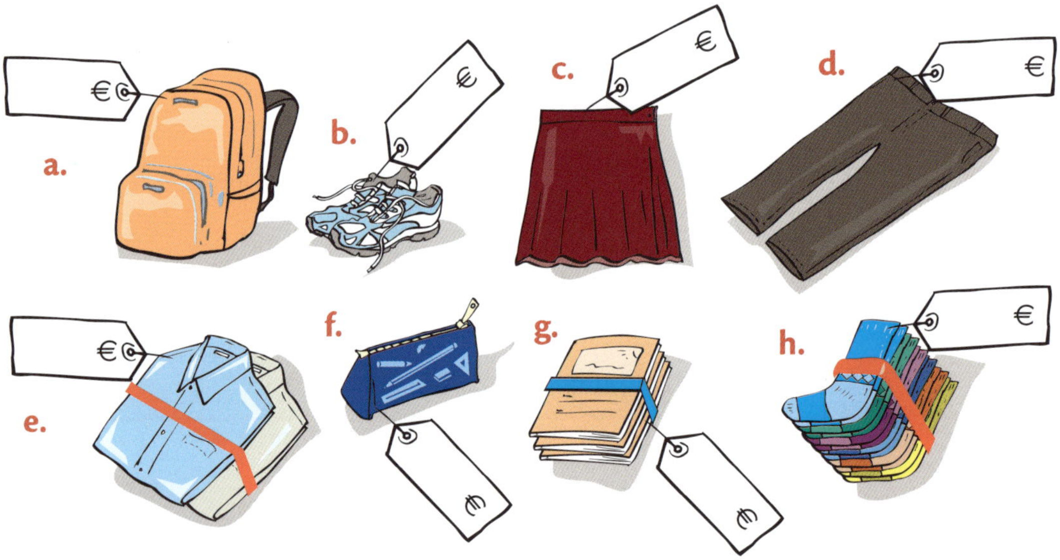

Question 8

Write out the classroom instructions in French for the following illustrations.

____________________ ! ____________________ ! ____________________ !

____________________ ! ____________________ !

Unité 3

Au collège

Civilisation : Les classes

- During the first two years at '**collège**', in '**sixième**' and '**cinquième**', pupils spend approximately twenty-six hours a week in school. They study a wide range of subjects (**les matières**) just as you do. In '**sixième**', they start to learn their second language, usually English.
- Two years later, in '**quatrième**', students take on another language such as Spanish, German or Italian.

Les matières

3.1

Écoutons maintenant !

Faites des paires ! Listen to see which student studies which subject.

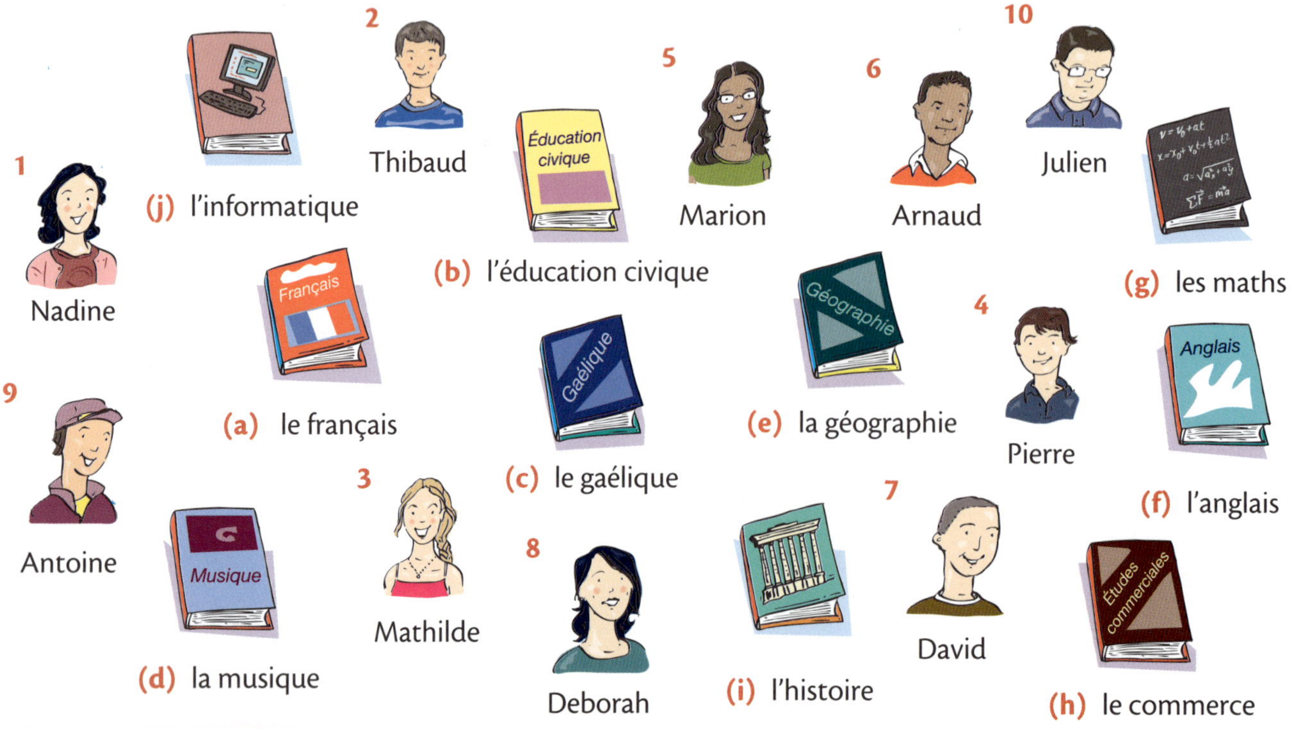

Écrivons maintenant !

(a) Can you sort out the following school subjects? The space bar has got jammed! Insert the '**le**', '**la**' or '**l'** ' in front of each one in your copy.

Tip: Generally, when talking about the subjects, '**les matières**', you use '**le**', '**la**' or '**les**' in front of the subject, exemple '**le** français', '**la** musique' and '**les** maths'.

anglaisinformatiquemusiquehistoiremathsfrançaisgaéliquegéographie

(b) Based on what you noted in the listening exercise on page 58, write out ten sentences in your copy saying what each student is studying.

Exemples : Nadine étudie la géographie.
Thibaud étudie ______________________.
Mathilde ______________ ______________________.

Encore des matières !

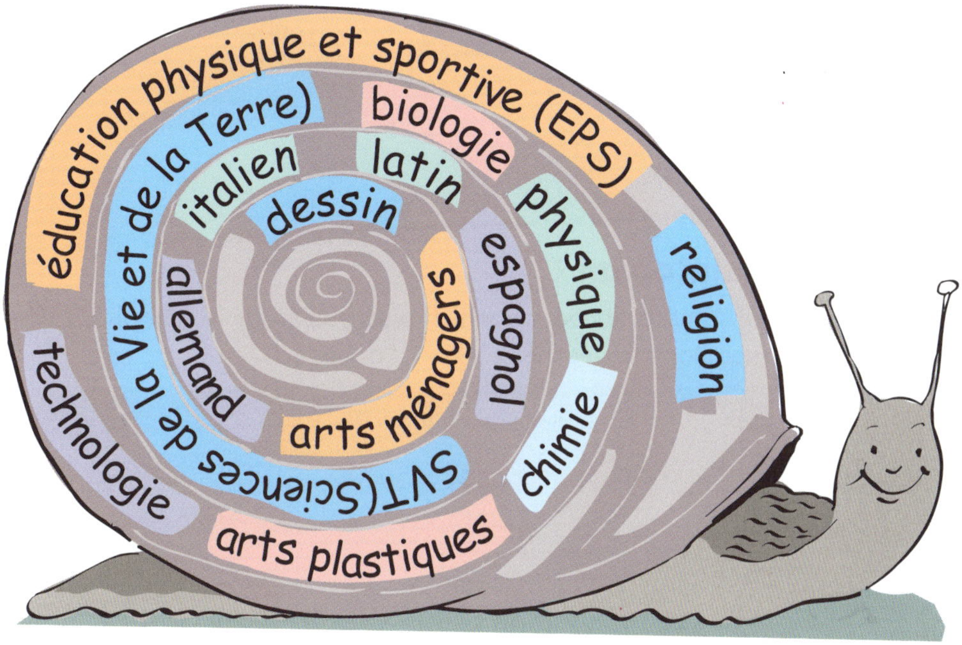

Parlons maintenant !

Draw an icon for each of the school subjects above and ask your partner to guess which French subject this is.

Exercice 1

Link the subject to the correct book.

1 les arts ménagers

(a)

(c)

6 le latin

(b)

10 l'EPS

7 les arts plastiques

2 la biologie

(j)

(d)

(g)

(e)

4 la technologie

3 l'allemand

5 la chimie

(h)

(f)

(i)

8 le dessin

9 la physique

Parlons maintenant !

From the list of subjects above, say which ones you study in school. Say which subjects your classmates study. Don't forget the '**le**', '**la**', '**l'** ' or '**les**' !

Exemples : J'étudie l'anglais, le gaélique, les maths, le ______________________________.

Niall étudie ______________________________.

3.2 Écoutons maintenant !

Listen to Khalid and Sophie talking about their school subjects and answer the questions.

1 What age is Khalid?

____

2 What class is he in?

____

3 Apart from French, what other language does he learn?

____

4 What subject does he not like?

____

5 Why is this?

____

1 How many subjects does Sophie study?

____

2 Name **three** subjects she likes.

__________ __________ __________

3 Name **one** subject she doesn't like.

____

4 Why does she hate German?

____

Giving your opinion

Find more expressions on page 62.

3.3 Écoutons maintenant !

Listen to these French pupils talking about school subjects. What subject are they talking about and what comment do they make?

	subject	comment
Luc		
Océane		
Christophe		
Sophie		
Léa		
Khalid		

Parlons maintenant !

Pick any five of your school subjects and make a comment about it.

Exemples : – Moi, j'étudie les maths. C'est cool ! – J'étudie l'allemand. C'est difficile !

Coin grammaire : Present tense ('Le présent')

Useful verbs

- To discuss your subjects in French, you need verbs like 'aimer', 'adorer', 'préférer' or 'détester'.
- To talk about what you do in school, you need verbs like 'écouter', 'regarder', 'parler' and 'travailler'.
- You use these verbs in the **present tense** (le présent).

Present tense of '-er' verbs

- These verbs belong to the first and largest group of French verbs which all end in '-er'. These are regular verbs, which means that they all form 'le présent' in exactly the same way. In French, the ending of a verb changes depending on the subject.
- When there is a mixture of masculine and feminine, you keep the masculine form and use the plural. For example, if you wish to say that a group of boys and girls like chocolate, you say:

Rappel! Remember the subject pronouns you learned in Unité 1, on page 21: 'je', 'tu', 'il', 'elle', 'nous', 'vous', 'ils', 'elles'

Ils aiment le chocolat.

- 'Le présent' of 'regarder' is formed in two steps:
 - **Step 1:** Take away the **-er** ending. What remains is the stem:

Step 2: Add the endings to the stem for each person as follows:

	THE REAL PROPERTY OF THE PERSON NAMED IN COLUMN 1	THE RESIDENCE OF THE PARTY OF T	
je	-е	nous	-ons
tu	-es	vous	-ez
il	-е	ils	-ent
elle	-е	elles	-ent

3.4 Écoutons maintenant !

Listen to how the verb '**regarder**' sounds in the present tense. You will notice that although the spellings are different, some of the words sound the same.

> **Rappel !** You never hear the final '-**ent**' in the present tense

je	regard**e**	nous	regard**ons**
tu	regard**es**	vous	regard**ez**
il	regard**e**	ils	regard**ent**
elle	regard**e**	elles	regard**ent**

You need to learn these endings by heart (**par cœur**):

- When you have the subject's name, e.g. Pierre or Julie, you use the '**il**/**elle**' form.

  Exemples : Pierre aime le chocolat. Julie adore le français.

- Use the '**ils**/**elles**' form if the subject is named in the plural.

  Exemples : Les enfants aiment les bonbons. Les filles adorent la musique.

- Where any verb begins with a vowel or a '**h**', '**je**' is shortened to '**j'** '.

  Exemple : The verb '**aimer**' (*to like*), begins with a vowel.
  So, to say '*I like*', you say '**j'aime**'.

Exercice 1

Some parts of the present tense of the verb '**parler**' are missing in the grid. Can you fill in the missing parts?

je	parl**e**	nous	parl**ons**
	parl**es**	vous	
	parl**e**		parl**ent**
elle		elles	

Exercice 2

Write out the missing parts of the verb '**aimer**' in the grid.

j'			aim**ons**
tu			aim**ez**
il	aim**e**	ils	
elle		elles	

Exercice 3

Now fill in the empty grid with the verb '**travailler**'.

je	nous
tu	vous
il	ils
elle	elles

Exercice 4

Link the descriptions with the pictures.

8 Nous aimons le français.

(g)

2 Maman prépare le dîner.

(e)

(c)

(h)

6 Elle regarde la télé.

5 Ils commencent le match de ping-pong.

(f)

1 Ils écoutent la radio.

(b)

(d)

3 Je travaille à l'école.

(a)

7 Vous commencez l'école à huit heures ?

4 Il regarde le match de foot.

Coin grammaire : Negative form ('La forme négative')

- To make a verb negative in French (to say something is **not** happening) you need to use **two** little words '**ne**' and '**pas**'.
- Put the '**ne**' in front of the verb and the '**pas**' after it.

Exemple : Je parle italien. Je

italien.

- If the verb begins with a vowel or silent '**h**', put '**n'** ' in front of the verb and the '**pas**' as normal.

Exemple : Clara aime la géo. Clara

la géo.

Exercice 1

Write the following sentences in the negative form in your copy.

Then, translate them into English.

1. Je déteste le rugby.
2. Elle regarde la télé.
3. Vous aimez la musique.
4. Ils habitent à Paris.
5. Suzanne étudie le gaélique.
6. Michel regarde les Simpson.
7. Tu habites dans le Donegal.
8. Nous aimons le volley.

Les jours de la semaine

- As in some other European languages, the days of the week in French come from **Latin**, which was the language the Romans spoke. The Latin word for day was '**dies**'. As a result, most of the days of the week end with the letters '–**di**'.

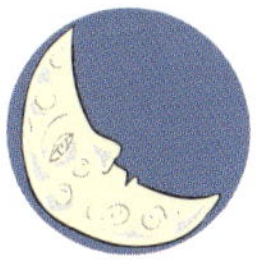	lunae dies →	**lundi** →	jour de la lune (*the day of the moon*)
	martes dies →	**mardi** →	jour de Mars (*the day of Mars*)
	mercoris dies →	**mercredi** →	jour de Mercure (*the day of Mercury*)
	jovis dies →	**jeudi** →	jour de Jupiter (Jove) (*the day of Jupiter*)
	veneris dies →	**vendredi** →	jour de Vénus (*the day of Venus*)
	sambati dies →	**samedi** →	jour du Sabbat (*the day of the Sabbath*)
	dies Dominicus →	**dimanche** →	jour du Seigneur (*the day of the Lord*)

Tip: In French, there is **no** capital letter for the days of the week.

3.5 Écoutons maintenant !

Listen to and repeat after the speaker the days of the week in French.

lundi	mardi	mercredi	jeudi	vendredi	samedi	dimanche

Comptines

- As in all countries there are rhymes which little children like to hear, but which also teach them certain information. You probably learned some when you were very young. In French, these are called '**comptines**'.

3.6 Écoutons maintenant !

Listen to this '**comptine**' which helps French children to learn the days of the week.

Bonjour lundi
Ça va mardi
Très bien mercredi
Dites à jeudi
De venir vendredi
Danser samedi
Dans la salle de dimanche

Exercice 1

Faites des paires dans votre cahier. Can you sort out each group of letters to make a day of the week?

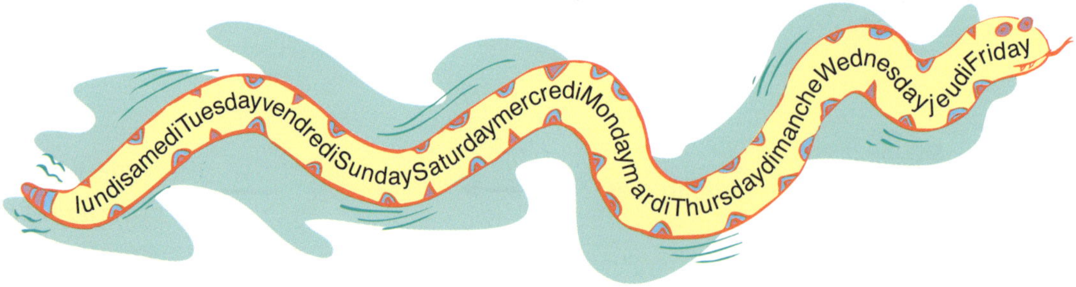

Lisons maintenant !

La semaine de Nounours ! Nounours is a busy bear. Read below what he is doing this week.

lundi :	*Maths. Je déteste ça !*	
mardi :	*Géographie. Super !*	
mercredi :	*Basketball*	
jeudi :	*Sciences. J'adore ça !*	
vendredi :	*Informatique. Compliqué !*	
samedi :	*Musique avec mon groupe…*	
dimanche :	*Je mange au restaurant.*	

Exercice 1

Quel jour ? Complete the following sentences.

1 Nounours has problems in his computer class on ______________________.
2 Nounours eats out on ______________________.
3 Nounours has a subject that he doesn't like on ______________________.
4 Nounours plays sport on ______________________.
5 Nounours is in a musical mood on ______________________.

Coin grammaire : Asking questions ('Poser des questions')

Est-ce que tu aimes le français ?

- Besides giving information about yourself, you will want to ask French people questions: *Do you like school? Do you play football? Does Julien live in Paris?*
- There is a simple way in French to turn a statement into a question, using the little group of words '**Est-ce que**…' and inserting a question mark '**?**' at the end of the sentence.

Examples :

Statement:	Tu joues au foot.	*You play football.*
Question:	**Est-ce que** tu joues au foot **?**	*Do you play football?*
Statement:	Julien habite à Paris.	*Julien lives in Paris.*
Question:	**Est-ce que** Julien habite à Paris **?**	*Does Julien live in Paris?*

- If the subject of your sentence (the person or thing doing the action) begins with a vowel or silent '**h**', simply shorten the word '**que**' to '**qu'**'.

Examples :

Statement:	Elle aime le basket.	*She likes basketball.*
Question:	**Est-ce qu'**elle aime le basket **?**	*Does she like basketball?*

Coin Prononciation : the letter '**q**' is pronounced with a '**k**' sound in French, e.g. '**que**', '**qui**', '**qu'**', '**quand**'.

Exercice 1

Turn these statements into questions in your copy. Then, translate them into English.

1. Manon regarde *Lost* à la télé.
2. Luc et Sophie habitent à Grenoble.
3. Tu aimes les maths.
4. Il déteste le volley-ball.
5. Élodie adore les chiens.
6. Elles parlent le gaélique.
7. Vous écoutez le professeur.
8. Tu joues au football.

Quelle heure est-il ?

Being able to tell the time in French is very useful. To start with, you will learn how to say the time on the hour. Note that when you write one o'clock you write '**une heure**', but when you say any other hour after that, the word '**heure**' gets an '**s**' (**cinq heures**).

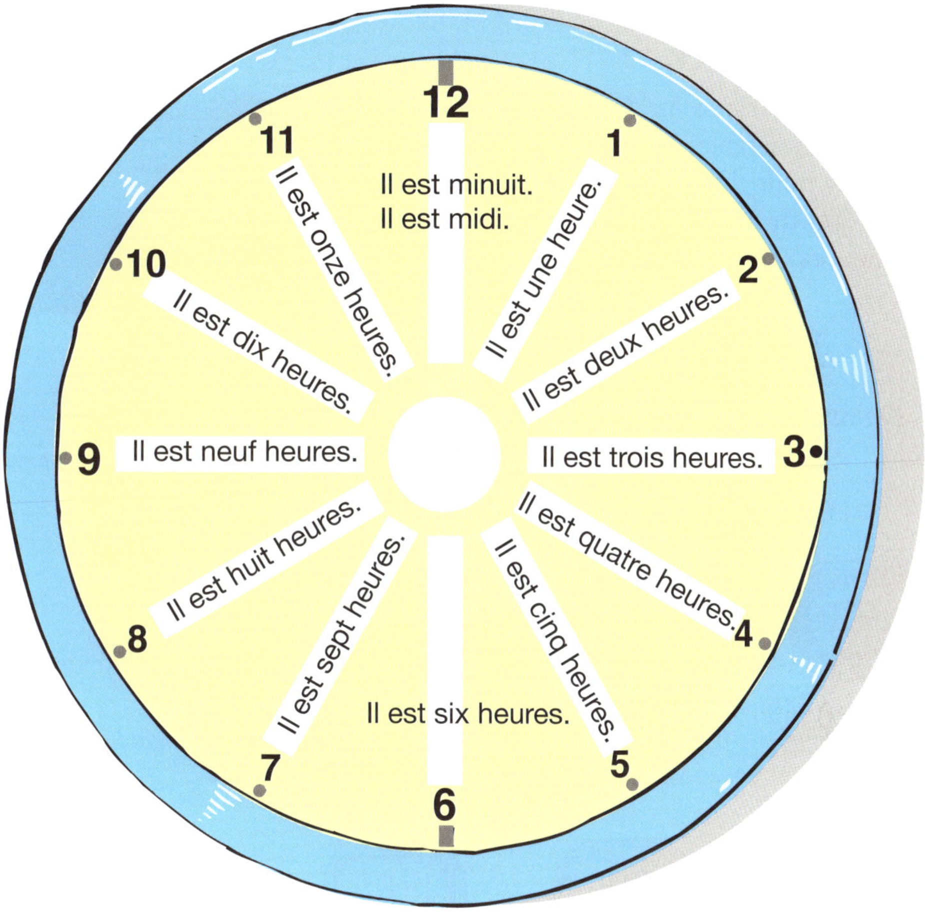

3.7

Écoutons maintenant !

Listen to the following times being called out. Indicate the order in which you hear them (1 to 8).

(a) 05.00		**(b)** 03.00		**(c)** 09.00		**(d)** 11.00	
(e) 01.00		**(f)** 07.00		**(g)** 10.00		**(h)** 06.00	

Écrivons maintenant !

Write these times in your copy in French.

3 o'clock; 5 o'clock; 9 o'clock; 2 o'clock; 1 o'clock.

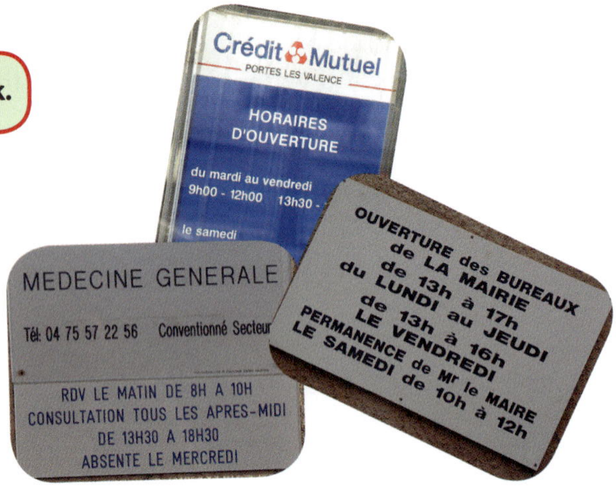

24-hour clock

- In France, times for TV and radio programmes, travel timetables and many public signs are given as 24 hour times. You do not use 'am' and 'pm' in French. 1pm becomes '**13 heures**', 2pm is '**14 heures**', etc.

Exemples : Le train arrive à seize heures. *The train arrives at 4 pm.*

Le film commence à vingt heures. *The film starts at 8 pm.*

Il est douze heures.

Il est treize heures.

Il est quatorze heures.

Il est quinze heures.

Il est seize heures.

Il est dix-sept heures.

Il est dix-huit heures.

Il est dix-neuf heures.

Il est vingt heures.

Il est vingt et une heures.

Il est vingt-deux heures.

Il est vingt-trois heures.

Il est vingt-quatre heures.

Coin grammaire: The verb 'aller' (Le verbe 'aller')

- A useful verb to learn at this stage is the verb '**aller**', which means *to go*. It is an **irregular** verb which means you must learn it '**par cœur**'.

3.8 Écoutons maintenant !

Listen to how the present tense of the verb '**aller**' sounds.

je	v**ais**	nous	all**ons**
tu	v**as**	vous	all**ez**
il	v**a**	ils	v**ont**
elle	v**a**	elles	v**ont**

Tip: You may recognise this verb from the greetings you have already learned '**ça va ?**' and '**comment vas-tu/allez-vous ?**'.

Exercice 1

Fill in the missing parts of the verb '**aller**'.

je	
tu	vas
il	va
elle	
nous	
vous	allez
ils	
elles	vont

Exercice 2

Choose a subject from column A and join it to the correct part of the verb in column B. Then, write the sentence in your copy.

	A		B
1	Je	(a)	vas au collège à 7h30 ?
2	Marine	(b)	allez en classe maintenant.
3	Nous	(c)	vais au cinéma samedi.
4	Tu	(d)	vont au parc pour le match à 15h00.
5	Vous	(e)	allons à Nice pour les vacances.
6	Romain et Nicolas	(f)	va chez ses grands-parents dimanche.

Civilisation : La journée scolaire en France

L'emploi du temps

- The school day can start at 8 in the morning and continue until 4 in the afternoon. Most class periods are of 50-60 minutes duration. Students start the school day when the teacher calls the roll, '**faire l'appel**'. There is a short break during the morning, '**la récré**', and a much longer break at lunchtime, called '**la pause déjeuner**'. Most students eat in the school canteen, '**la cantine**', which is like a self-service restaurant. They have a choice of starter, main course and dessert. Students may have classes on Saturday mornings, but instead have a half day on Wednesday. All second-level schools are mixed and there is no school uniform.

Lisons maintenant !

Luc has just received his timetable for the new school year.
Look at it and answer the questions which follow in your copy.

EMPLOI DU TEMPS 2007–2008

	lundi	mardi	mercredi	jeudi	vendredi
8.00- 8.55	hist/géo	français	maths	maths	anglais
9.00- 9.55	technologie	anglais	éd. physique & sportive	français	éd. physique & sportive
10.00-10.50	arts plastiques	maths	éd. physique & sportive	français	éd. physique & sportive
10.50-11.00	**RÉCRÉATION**				
11.00-11.55	français	hist/géo	anglais		français
12.00-13.30	**DÉJEUNER**				
13.30-14.25	maths			hist/géo	sc. de la vie & de la terre
14.30-15.25	anglais	technologie		musique	sc. de la vie & de la terre
15.30-16.30	sc. de la vie & de la terre	technologie			

1. How many periods of French does Luc have each week?
2. What does he have on Thursdays before school ends?
3. At what time does he have art and craft class?
4. In which subjects does he have double classes?
5. On what day does he **not** have an English class?

Écoutons maintenant !

3.9

It is the first day back for the class of '5ème' in the collège Gustave Flaubert. Madame Delabre is calling out the new timetable for the year. Listen to her and complete the timetable for Mondays in your copy.

Lundi
8

Exercice 1

Write out your own '**emploi du temps**' in French.

3.10

Écoutons maintenant !

Thomas has forgotten to bring home his timetable (**emploi du temps**). He telephones Océane to ask her for details of tomorrow's classes. Listen to their conversation and answer the questions.

1 What day is tomorrow?
(*a*) Tuesday; (*b*) Wednesday; (*c*) Friday.

2 Which of the following is the first class tomorrow morning?
(*a*) English; (*b*) French; (*c*) Spanish.

3 At what time do they have their lunch break?
(*a*) 11.00; (*b*) 12.00; (*c*) 1.00.

4 In the afternoon, which class will they have after Science?
(*a*) Maths; (*b*) Computers; (*c*) History.

5 What is the last class of the day?
(*a*) Music; (*b*) Art and Design; (*c*) CSPE.

Une journée typique

3.11

Écoutons maintenant !

Listen to Léa describing her school day and fill in the times on the clocks.

1  J'arrive à l'école. 

2  J'étudie la géographie. 

3  Je mange à la cantine. 

4  Je joue au basket. 

5  Je prends le bus scolaire. 

6  Je commence mes devoirs. 

7  Je téléphone à Claire. 

8  Je regarde la télévision. 

Parlons maintenant !

Ask your partner the following questions and using the indications in brackets give the answers. Then, your partner can ask you the same questions and this time use your own times for the answers. Use the 24-hour clock.

1 – Tu arrives à l'école à quelle heure ?	– J'arrive à l'école à ____________ (9) heures.
2 – Tu étudies l'histoire à quelle heure ?	– J'étudie l'histoire à ____________ (11) heures.
3 – Tu manges à quelle heure ?	– Je mange à ____________ (1) heures.
4 – Tu joues au football à quelle heure ?	– Je joue au foot à ____________ (4) heures.
5 – Tu commences les devoirs à quelle heure ?	– Je commence les devoirs à ____________ (7) heures.
6 – Tu regardes la télé à quelle heure ?	– Je regarde la télé à ____________ (9) heures.

Bulletin scolaire

BULLETIN SCOLAIRE		
Collège Jean Macé		
6 rue Gambetta, 31000 Toulouse		
Nom : Dauvergne	**Classe :** quatrième	
Prénom : Mathieu	**Trimestre :** 1	
Français	*13*	*Bons résultats*
Mathématiques	*11*	*Peut mieux faire*
Langue vivante 1 : Anglais	*15*	*Bon travail*
Sciences de la Vie et de la Terre	*13,5*	*Satisfaisant*
Éducation Physique et Sportive	*14*	*Bien*
Arts plastiques	*12*	*Moyen*
Langue vivante 2 : Espagnol	*16*	*Très bonne participation en classe*
Histoire/Géographie	*18*	*Excellent travail*
Éducation musicale	*9*	*Peu d'effort*
Technologie	*7*	*Très peu d'effort*

- As you can see from Mathieu's '**bulletin scolaire**', the French marking scheme is not the same as ours. Instead of grades or percentages, students are marked out of a maximum of twenty marks. These are the values given to the different marks, ranging from weak (**faible**) to excellent (**excellent**).

19–20	*excellent*
16–18	*très bien*
12–15	*bien*
10–11	*assez bien*
8–9	*passable*
6–7	*insuffisant*
0–5	*faible*

Exercice 1

Answer the following questions about Mathieu's '**bulletin scolaire**' in your copy.

1. Which class is Mathieu in and what is the equivalent in an Irish school?
2. In which subject did he get his best result?
3. In which subject did he get his worst result?
4. What was the comment about Science?
5. Was the comment for Spanish a good one? Give a reason for your answer.
6. What comment was made about French?

Écrivons maintenant !

Lettre-symbole ! Eoin is writing to his French '**correspondante**' Élodie, telling her about his school subjects and his daily routine. Replace each symbol by the French word. Then, rewrite the letter into your copybook.

Oughterard, le 18 septembre

Chère Élodie,

Comment vas-tu ? Ma nouvelle  est super. Elle s'appelle St Joseph's College. Elle est à Galway. Je suis en '1st year', l'équivalent de la sixième. J'étudie 10 matières. J'aime la , c'est intéressant. Ma matière favorite, c'est le . Le  est super ! Je n'aime pas  C'est une matière difficile. J'adore l'  parce que je suis sportif.

L'école commence à  heures. Nous avons une pause à . Je  avec mes amis. À une heure, je  le déjeuner. Je finis à quatre heures. Je rentre à Oughterard en  et je fais mes devoirs.

Je te laisse maintenant. Je dois écouter mon CD de français.

Amitiés,

Eoin

Le personnel de l'école

- A teacher in a second-level school is called '**un professeur**', but a teacher in a primary school is called '**un instituteur**' or '**une institutrice**'.
- '**Un/une surveillant(e)**' is someone who supervises pupils when they are not in the classroom. They are often college students. Sometimes they help students with their work.

Exercice 1

Faites des paires ! Can you join the people with the description of what they do around school?

(a) la directrice

(b) le directeur-adjoint

(c) le professeur

(h) la déléguée de classe

(d) le concierge

(f) le surveillant

(g) la conseillère d'orientation

(e) la secrétaire

Qui fait quoi ?

1. Il/Elle s'occupe de l'école.
2. Il/Elle aide le directeur/la directrice.
3. Il/Elle représente les élèves de la classe.
4. Il/Elle surveille les élèves et aide avec les devoirs.
5. Il/Elle enseigne aux élèves.
6. Il/Elle conseille les élèves en ce qui concerne les matières et les problèmes.
7. Il/Elle travaille dans le bureau de l'école.
8. Il/Elle est le chef de l'école.

Communication en classe !

- Tu étudies quelles matières ?
- Tu aimes l'anglais.../les maths.../le français… ?
- Le français, c'est cool !
- Tu parles espagnol/gaélique/allemand ?
- Les cours commencent à 9 heures ?
- Tu arrives à la maison à quelle heure ?
- Nous sommes quel jour aujourd'hui ?
- L'exercice est pour jeudi.

Lexique

aider	*to help*
aimer	*to like*
adorer	*to love*
allemand (m.)	*German*
anglais (m.)	*English*
arts ménagers (m. pl.)	*home economics*
arts plastiques (m. pl.)	*art and craft*
assez bien	*fairly good*
bien	*good/well*
biologie (f.)	*biology*
bulletin scolaire (m.)	*school report*
car scolaire (m.)	*school bus*
chimie (f.)	*chemistry*
commencer	*to start/begin*
compliqué(e)	*complicated*
concierge (m./f.)	*caretaker*
conseiller	*to advise*
conseiller/ère (m./f.)	*guidance counsellor*
cours (m.)	*lesson/class*
déjeuner m.	*lunch*
délégué(e) de classe (m./f.)	*class rep.*
dessin (m.)	*art/drawing*
détester	*to hate*
devoirs (m.pl.)	*homework*
difficile	*difficult*
directeur/trice (m./f.)	*school principal*
directeur/rice adjoint(e) (m./f.)	*deputy principal*
écouter	*to listen to*
éducation civique (f.)	*civics (CSPE)*
élève (m./f.)	*pupil*
emploi du temps (m.)	*timetable*
enseigner	*to teach*
étudier	*to study*
E.P.S. (Éducation Physique et Sportive) (f.)	*physical education*
espagnol (m.)	*Spanish*
études commerciales (f. pl.)	*business studies*
étudiant(e) (m./f.)	*student*
extra	*super!*
facile	*easy*
faible	*weak*
fantastique	*great*
favori/te (m./f.)	*favourite*
gaélique (m.)	*Irish language*
géographie (f.)	*geography*
heure (f.)	*hour*
histoire (f.)	*history*
informatique (f.)	*computer studies*
insuffisant	*not enough*
irlandais (m.)	*Irish*
journée scolaire (f.)	*school day*
latin (m.)	*Latin*
manger	*to eat*
marrant (familiar)	*fun/enjoyable*
maths/mathématiques (f. pl.)	*maths*
matière (f.)	*school subject*
midi (m.)	*midday*
monter/monter dans	*to climb up/into*
musique (f.)	*music*
minuit (m.)	*midnight*
nul(le)	*useless*
passable	*acceptable*
pause (f.)	*break*
pause-déjeuner (f.)	*lunch break*
peu	*a little*
pratique	*practical/useful*
physique (f.)	*physics*
professeur (m.)	*teacher*
résultats (m. pl.)	*results*
récréation (f.)	*break-time*
regarder	*to watch/look at*
religion (f.)	*religion*
rentrée (f.)	*return to school*
rentrer	*to go back/go home*
secrétaire (m./f.)	*secretary*
sportif/-ive (m./f.)	*sporting*
surveillant(e) (m./f.)	*supervisor*
surveiller	*to supervise*
S.V.T (Sciences de la Vie de la Terre) (f. pl.)	*Science and Environmental Studies*
terminale (f.)	*6th year*
travailler	*to work*
très	*very*
trimestre (m.)	*term*
vacances (f. pl.)	*holidays*

Épreuve

Question 1

Copy the following grid into your copybook. Then, listen to Luc, Christophe, Khalid, Léa, Sophie and Océane talking about their school subjects and fill out the information.

	Subject liked	Subject disliked	Why?
Luc			
Océane			
Léa			
Sophie			
Khalid			
Christophe			

Question 2

Find the nine '**matières**' hidden in this word search.

1 ANGLAIS	**2** GÉOGRAPHIE	**3** MUSIQUE
4 FRANÇAIS	**5** HISTOIRE	**6** SCIENCES
7 GAÉLIQUE	**8** MATHS	**9** TECHNOLOGIE

E	H	K	F	Z	C	W	C	Y	M	G	G	R	I	Z
I	I	W	U	R	L	Q	D	L	A	E	P	D	V	B
G	S	S	Z	G	A	D	S	E	S	D	O	K	X	Z
O	T	H	Y	T	K	N	L	W	E	G	A	M	Q	M
L	O	T	E	D	V	I	C	I	O	W	P	Y	X	D
O	I	A	D	U	Q	M	H	A	B	J	S	G	K	Q
N	R	M	C	U	Q	P	S	C	I	E	N	C	E	S
H	E	Y	E	I	A	I	I	D	Q	S	D	M	V	D
C	Y	K	J	R	X	Z	S	S	I	A	L	G	N	A
E	Q	G	G	Y	S	W	F	U	E	D	S	S	U	A
T	Z	O	H	F	U	V	Q	Z	M	K	R	J	A	M
U	E	W	G	A	W	D	H	S	V	J	J	F	C	K
G	W	F	Y	P	N	X	B	V	K	T	M	Z	U	G
W	H	Q	K	Q	M	V	Z	W	M	D	F	X	C	D
Y	W	J	O	O	Q	J	S	R	U	O	I	R	L	U

Question 3

Insert the correct endings on these verbs.

1 Luc travaill_____ dans un café le samedi.
2 J'ador_____ l'histoire.
3 Nous regard_____ Star Academy.
4 Est-ce que tu aim_____ l'éducation civique ?
5 Madame Lambert écout_____ la radio.
6 Vous parl_____ anglais.
7 Ils jou_____ dans le parc.
8 Manon et Louise regard_____ la télé.
9 Tu détest_____ l'école.
10 Les cours commenc_____ à 9 heures.

For **help** with this exercise, see page 63.

Question 4

Make the following sentences negative.

1 J'aime les films comiques.
2 Marie travaille dans le café.
3 Julie et Arnaud sont en discothèque.
4 Théo parle gaélique.
5 Sophie habite en Italie.
6 Nous écoutons la radio.
7 Madame Dubois enseigne les maths.
8 Tu aimes le professeur.
9 J'aide Marc.
10 L'informatique est difficile.

For **help** with this exercise, see page 66.

Question 5

You will hear six people talking about what they do on a particular day of the week. Fill in the correct day under each activity.

____

____

____

____

____

____

Question 6

Transform the following statements into questions using '**est-ce que**' and write them down in your copy. Don't forget the question mark!

1 Tu aimes les maths.
2 Philippe aide Michel.
3 Le professeur enseigne la géographie.
4 Claire travaille le vendredi.
5 Ils adorent Avril Lavigne.
6 Nous travaillons le samedi.

For **help** with this exercise, see page 70.

Question 7

Listen to this interview with Élodie as she describes her school day and fill in the correct time.

1 À quelle heure est-ce que tu prends ton petit-déjeuner ?
Je prends mon petit-déjeuner à ________________ heures.

2 À quelle heure est-ce que tu prends le car scolaire ?
Je prends le car à ________________ heures.

3 À quelle heure est-ce que les cours commencent ?
À ________________ heures.

4 À quelle heure est-ce qu'il y a la récréation ?
À ________________ heures.

5 À quelle heure est-ce que tu manges à la cantine ?
À ________________ heures.

6 À quelle heure est-ce que tu quittes l'école ?
À ________________ heures.

7 À quelle heure est-ce que tu arrives à la maison ?
À ________________ heures.

8 À quelle heure est-ce que tu fais tes devoirs ?
À ________________ heures

Question 8

Read Thibaud's '**emploi du temps**' and say if the following statements are '**vrai**' or '**faux**'.

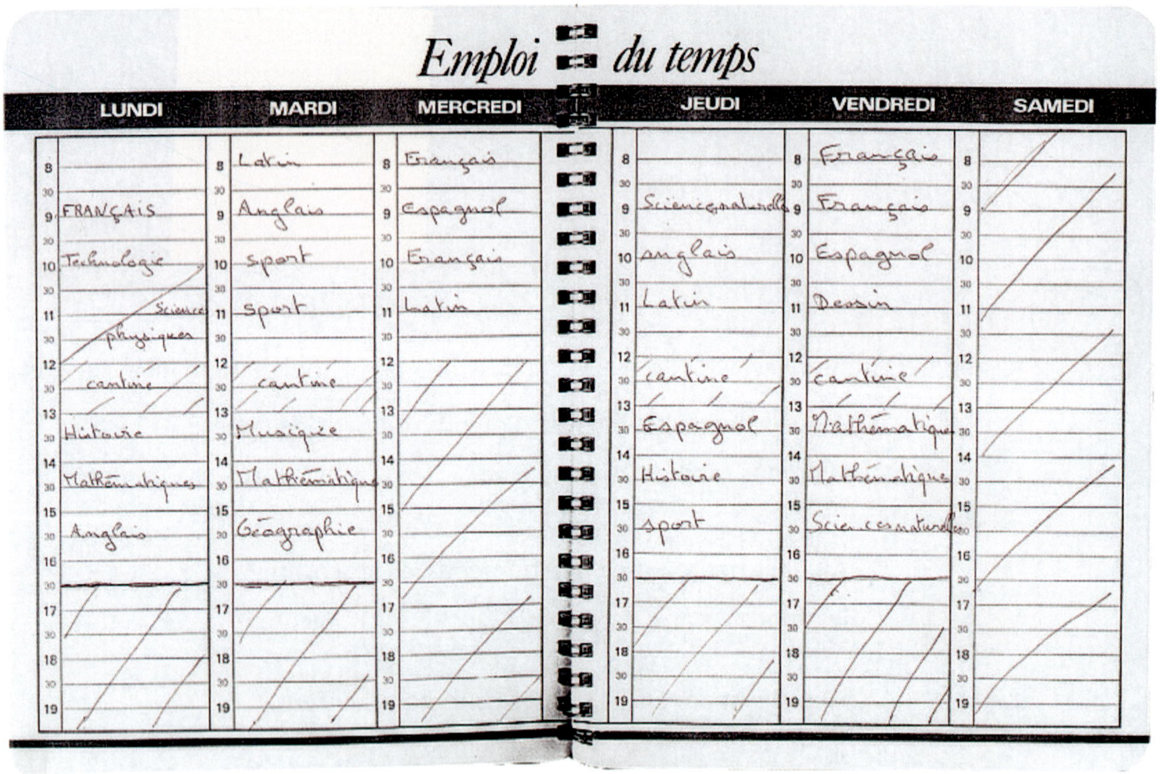

		vrai	faux
1	He has French first class on Monday.		
2	He has music on Tuesday morning.		
3	Spanish is at 10 on Wednesday mornings.		
4	He has three periods of English each week.		
5	On Thursdays, he ends the day with P.E.		
6	He has a double class of Art on Friday.		

Question 9

Read Marion's account of her school and answer the questions which follow.

Je m'appelle Marion Guillaume. J'ai quatorze ans. Mon collège s'appelle Fernand Gregh. Je crois que c'est le nom d'un poète, mais je n'en suis pas sûre. Voici les matières que j'étudie en 4ème :

- Mathématiques
- Histoire-Géographie
- Dessin
- Éducation Civique
- Français
- Musique
- Éducation Physique et Sportive (E.P.S.)
- Sciences Physiques
- Espagnol
- Sciences de la Vie et de la Terre (S.V.T.)
- Anglais

L'année prochaine (3ème), je prends une option : Latin.

1. What age is Marion?
2. What is the name of her school?
3. Apart from French, what languages does she study?
4. What option will she take next year when she is in '3ème'?
5. What are these subjects called in an Irish school: E.P.S./S.V.T.?

Question 10

Use the correct form of the verb '**aller**' to complete these sentences.

1 Florian et Camille ______________ au collège en bus.
2 Je ______________ chez mes grands-parents le week-end.
3 Mélanie ______________ au zoo samedi.
4 Nous ______________ au cinéma mercredi.
5 Tu ______________ à ton cours de maths à 10 heures ?
6 Vous ______________ bien ?

For **help** with this exercise, see page 73.

Question 11

Write a short letter to your '**correspondant(e)**' giving the following details:

- name of your school
- class you are in
- subjects you study
- **one** subject you like and why
- **one** subject you dislike and why
- when school starts and when school finishes

Unité 4

La famille

Dans ma famille, il y a…

Salut ! Je m'appelle Alexis. Voici une photo de ma famille avec mes grands-parents. Je ne suis pas sur la photo. Nous sommes cinq dans ma famille : mon père, ma mère et trois enfants. J'ai un frère et une sœur. Mon frère s'appelle Pascal et ma sœur s'appelle Caroline. Mon père s'appelle Guy et ma mère s'appelle Maryse. Mes grands-parents s'appellent Jean et Marguerite.

Exercice 1

Answer the following questions about Alexis's family.

1 What is the name of Alexis's mother?
2 Who is Jean?
3 Who is Caroline?
4 How is Marguerite related to Pascal?
5 What is the name of Guy's wife?

Exercice 2

Complétez les phrases suivantes. Still looking at the picture of Alexis's family, can you fill in the gaps in the following sentences?

Exemple : Alexis est **le frère** de Caroline.

1. Marguerite est la ________________ de Guy.
2. Caroline est la ________________ de Pascal.
3. Jean est le ________________ d'Alexis.
4. Guy est le ________________ de Caroline et de Pascal.
5. Jean et Marguerite sont les ________________ de Caroline et de Pascal.

4.1

Écoutons maintenant !

Listen to these descriptions of five families. Number the pictures according to the description.

1 Laure :
Voici une photo de ma famille. Il y a quatre personnes : mon père, ma mère, mon frère Benjamin et moi.

2 Vincent :
Dans ma famille, il y a quatre personnes. Sur la photo, c'est mon père, mon frère Éric, ma sœur Chloë et moi. Nous habitons avec mon père.

3 Camille :
Dans ma famille, il y a quatre personnes : ma mère, mon père, mon demi-frère Joël et moi. Grand-père et grand-mère sont sur la photo avec nous.

4 Nadège :
Voici une photo de ma famille. Il y a trois personnes : mon père, ma mère et moi. Je suis fille unique.

5 Thomas :
Nous sommes quatre dans ma famille : ma mère, mes deux sœurs, Rachel et Mireille, et moi. Je ne suis pas sur la photo.

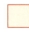

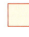

Coin grammaire : Possessive adjectives ('Les adjectifs possessifs')

My ('mon', 'ma')

- In the conversations on page 88, when speaking about members of the family, the words '**mon**', '**ma**' and '**mes**' are used to say '*my*'. These words are called possessive adjectives (**les adjectifs possessifs**).
- In English, we just have one word 'my'. In French, there are **three** different ways of saying 'my'!
- The word 'my' depends on the **gender** (masculine or feminine) of **what is owned** and whether it is **singular** or **plural**.
- It **doesn't matter who** is saying 'my'.

possessive adjectives	when to use them
mon	before a masculine noun
ma	before a feminine noun
mes	before plural nouns

mon oncle

ma tante

mes cousins

Exercice 1

Put in the correct form of 'my' in these sentences.

1 J'aime _________ parents.
2 Le français est _________ matière favorite.
3 _________ frère Paul est marrant.
4 _________ famille habite à Navan.
5 Je lis _________ livres.
6 Je ne trouve pas _________ trousse.

Your

- In French, the words used for '*your*' are '**ton**', '**ta**' or '**tes**'.
- Again, remember it is what is owned that will decide which form you use!

possessive adjectives	when to use them
ton	before a masculine noun
ta	before a feminine noun
tes	before plural nouns

Exercice 1

Faites des paires ! Using the words from the sack below, fill in the blanks in the cartoons.

His/Her

- To say '*his*' or '*her*', you use '**son**', '**sa**' or '**ses**'.
- The words '**son**', '**sa**' and '**ses**' mean '*his*', '*her*' or '*its*'. So, if you say '**sa mère**', it could mean '***his*** mother' or '***her*** mother'. The meaning will be clear from the situation.
- Remember, it is always the word which **follows** which tells you which form to use!

4.2 Écoutons maintenant !

Listen and fill in the missing form of '**son**', '**sa**' or '**ses**'.

1 Thibaud habite avec ______ famille.
2 Manon adore ______ grand-père.
3 Maman rend visite à ______ parents.
4 Il cherche ______ crayons dans ______ trousse.
5 Comment s'appelle ______ père ?
6 Thierry rend visite à ______ grand-père et ______ grand-mère.

4.3 Écoutons maintenant !

Listen to these two French students, Christophe and Léa, introducing their families and answer the questions.

Christophe

1 How many people are there in his family?
2 He has (*a*) two sisters and one brother;
(*b*) one sister and one brother;
(*c*) one sister and two brothers.
3 What does he say about Alex?
4 What is his mother's job?
5 In which city does his father work?

Léa

1 What age is Léa?
2 Including her parents, how many people are there in her family?
3 Who is Anne?
4 Where does Anne live?
5 What does she say about her mother?

Coin grammaire : The verb 'avoir'

- The verb '**avoir**' is an **irregular verb** and therefore must be learned '**par cœur**'.
- You will need to use it to talk about your family. In French, it is used to talk about your age. '**J'ai treize ans**' is like saying in English '*I have thirteen years*', in other words '*I **am** thirteen*'.

4.4 Écoutons maintenant !

Listen to how the present tense of the verb '**avoir**' sounds.

j'	**ai**	*I have*
tu	**as**	*you have*
il	**a**	*he has*
elle	**a**	*she has*
nous	**avons**	*we have*
vous	**avez**	*you have*
ils	**ont**	*they have*
elles	**ont**	*they have*

Exercice 1

Fill in the missing parts of the verb '**avoir**' in the grid.

j'	ai
tu	
il	a
elle	
nous	
vous	avez
ils	
elles	ont

Exercice 2

Can you complete the missing parts of the verb '**avoir**' in the following sentences?

J' ________ deux frères.

Ma sœur ________ vingt ans.

Luc ________ des livres et des cahiers dans son cartable.

Mes amis ________ un chien.

Tu ________ des grands-parents ?

Julie ________ trois frères.

Ma maman et mon papa ________ trente-huit et trente-neuf ans.

Vous ________ des sœurs ?

The verb 'avoir' in a negative sentence

- This is how to write the negative of the verb '**avoir**':

je	**n'**ai	**pas**
tu	**n'**as	**pas**
il	**n'**a	**pas**
elle	**n'**a	**pas**
nous	**n'**avons	**pas**
vous	**n'**avez	**pas**
ils	**n'**ont	**pas**
elles	**n'**ont	**pas**

See also page 39, the **negative** of '**être**'.

Exemples : Je **n'**ai **pas** de sœur. Il **n'**a **pas** douze ans.

Coin grammaire : Asking questions ('Poser des questions')

- In **Unité 3** (see page 70), you learned to use the little phrase '**est-ce que**' when you wanted to ask a question.
- You can also use **question words**, such as:

Combien… ?	*(how many)*	→	Il y a **combien** de personnes dans ta famille ?
Où… ?	*(where)*	→	**Où** est-ce que tu habites ?
Quel… ?	*(what)*	→	Tu as **quel** âge ?

- You will build up a store of these as you learn more French.

4.5

Écoutons maintenant !

Listen to these interviews and write in French the three questions each person is asked.

Interview 1

Bonjour, comment ________________________________ ?

• Je m'appelle Aurélie Prioul.

Où ________________________________ ?

• J'habite à Guignen, en Bretagne.

Il y a ________________________________ ?

• Il y a quatre personnes dans ma famille : mes parents, mon frère Adrien et moi.

Interview 2

________________________________ ?

• Je m'appelle Mikaël Massot.

________________________________ ?

• J'ai quinze ans.

________________________________ ?

• J'ai une sœur.

Parlons maintenant !

Working with your partner, ask each other the following questions about your family and reply to them.

Rappel ! Don't forget to use the verb '**avoir**' (*to have*). See page 93.

– Il y **a** combien de personnes dans ta famille ?	– Il y **a** ________ personnes.
– Est-ce que tu **as** des frères ?	– Oui, j'**ai** ________ frère(s).
	– Non, je n'**ai** pas de frère.
	– Non, je suis fils/fille unique. (*I am an only child*)
– Tu **as** des sœurs ?	– Oui, j'**ai** ________ sœur(s).
	– Non, je n'**ai** pas de sœur.
– Ton frère/Ta sœur **a** quel âge ?	– Il **a**/Elle **a** ________ ans.
– Tes frères/Tes sœurs **ont** quel âge ?	– Ils **ont**/Elles **ont** ________.

L'arbre généalogique (Family tree)

Exercice 1

Faites des paires ! Here are some more words for family members. Using your dictionary, can you match up the male and female pairs in this jumble of family words? You should find eight pairs, apart from the example.

Exemple : femme – mari

Exercice 2

Complétez les phrases suivantes. The word needed in each gap is a family member.

1 Le fils de mon oncle est mon ______________________.
2 Ma mère est la ______________________ de mon père.
3 La sœur de mon père est ma ______________________.
4 Mon oncle Guy est le ______________________ de ma tante Yvette.
5 La fille de tante Marie est ma ______________________.
6 Le fils de mon beau-père et de ma mère est mon ______________________.

Exercice 3

Here is Caroline's family tree. Fill in the blanks under each name using words from the list which follows.

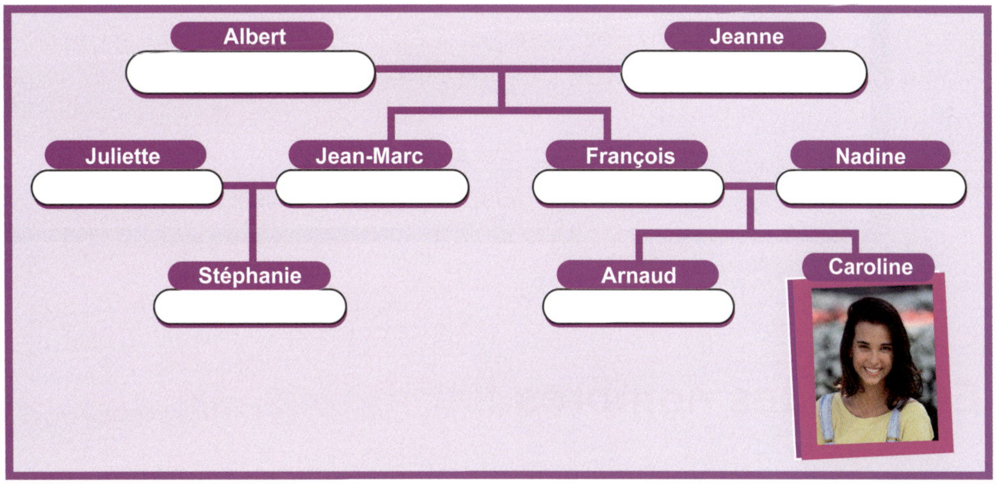

tante – père – oncle – grand-mère – cousine – grand-père – frère – mère

Écrivons maintenant !

Aurélie is writing to her new Irish '**correspondant**', Rory, to tell him about herself and her family. She has had a problem with her computer and the description of her family is difficult to read. Can you sort out what Aurélie has written to Rory and re-write her email correctly?

La Rochelle, le 10 mai

Cher Rory,

Jesuistacorrespondantefrançaisejem'appelleAuréliej'aitreizeansj'habit
eàlaRochellej'aiunesœurelles'appelleStéphanieelleadixansj'aiundemi-
frèreils'appelleJérômeilavingtansilhabiteàParismamèreestprofesseurd
'anglaisettoiest-cequetuasdesfrèresetsœurs ?

Écris-moi bientôt et parle-moi de ta famille.

Amitiés,

Aurélie

Encore des nombres !

- Now that you can count to **30**, it is not hard to count a little further.
- The pattern which you used from **21** to **29** (see page 43), is repeated for the numbers **30**, **40** and **50**.

4.6 Écoutons maintenant !

Listen to the numbers from **30** to **50**.

trente	30
trente-et-un	31
trente-deux	32
trente-trois	33
trente-quatre	34
trente-cinq	35
trente-six	36
trente-sept	37
trente-huit	38
trente-neuf	39
quarante	40
cinquante	50

Exercice 1

Now, try counting from **40** to **49** and then write these numbers in your copy.

Exercice 2

Can you write the prices under these price tags?

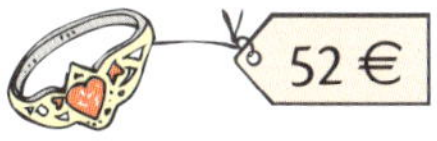

cinquante-cinq euros ____________ ____________ ____________

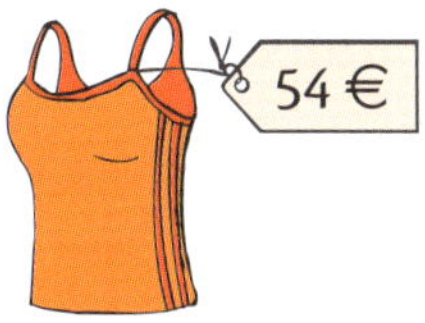

____________ ____________ ____________

Quelle heure est-il ?

- In **Unité 3** (see page 71), you learned how to **tell the time on the hour**. Now, it is time to learn some **more phrases!**
- To say '*a quarter past*', use the phrase '**et quart**'.

Il est six heures **et quart**.

- To say '*half past*', use the phrase '**et demie**'.

Il est quart heures **et demie**.

- In English, we use the phrase 'a quarter to'. French people say '*less the quarter*': '**moins le quart**'.

Il est onze heures **moins le quart**.

- To say midday or midnight, use the phrases '**il est midi**' and '**il est minuit**'.

Il est **midi**. Il est **minuit**.

Exercice 1

Faites des paires ! Match the sentences below with the correct time.

Il est dix heures moins le quart.

Il est huit heures et demie.

Il est quatre heures moins le quart.

Il est minuit.

Il est midi.

Il est quatre heures et demie.

Il est onze heures et quart.

Il est une heure et quart.

4.7 Écoutons maintenant !

À quelle heure ? Write down the times you hear called out! There are six of them.

1 Le bus arrive à ____________________.
2 Je mange à ____________________.
3 Paul rentre à ____________________.
4 J'ai un cours de français à ____________________.
5 Tu rentres à ____________________.
6 Les cours commencent à ____________________.

Coin grammaire : Reflexive verbs ('Les verbes pronominaux')

What is a reflexive verb?

- The verb '**s'**appeler' is used when people are giving their own name or the names of their family. It is a **reflexive verb**.
- Reflexive verbs (**les verbes pronominaux**) use an **extra pronoun**, called the **reflexive pronoun**. This pronoun refers back to the person or thing which is the subject of the verb (*myself, ourselves*).

Je **m'**appelle David.	*I call **myself**/I am called David.*
Ma mère **s'**appelle Laure.	*My mother calls **herself**/My mother is called Laure.*

An example of a reflexive verb

Look at the verb '**se** laver' in the present tense below. The reflexive pronouns are in **bold**.

se laver			to wash **oneself**
je	**me**	lave	*I wash **myself***
tu	**te**	laves	*you wash **yourself***
il	**se**	lave	*he washes **himself***
elle	**se**	lave	*she washes **herself***
nous	**nous**	lavons	*we wash **ourselves***
vous	**vous**	lavez	*you wash **yourself/yourselves***
ils	**se**	lavent	*they wash **themselves***
elles	**se**	lavent	*they wash **themselves***

- Using a reflexive verb is not very difficult; the verbs follow the **rules for regular verbs**.
- Most reflexive verbs are **regular '–er' verbs**.

Exercice 1

Write out the verb '**se** demander' (*to ask oneself/to wonder*) in the present tense by filling in the missing boxes in the grid.
Rewrite the full verb in your copy.

je	**me**	demande
tu	**te**	
	se	demande
elle	**se**	
	nous	demandons
vous		demandez
ils		demandent
	se	

Useful reflexive verbs

- Here are some reflexive verbs in the present tense that you can **use when writing** and **speaking French**.

s'	amuser*	*to enjoy oneself*	je	**m'**	amuse	*I enjoy myself*
s'	appeler*	*to call oneself*	je	**m'**	appelle	*I call myself/I am called*
se	brosser les dents/cheveux	*to brush one's teeth/hair*	je	**me**	brosse les dents/cheveux	*I brush my teeth/hair*
se	coucher	*to go to bed*	je	**me**	couche	*I go to bed*
se	doucher	*to have a shower*	je	**me**	douche	*I have a shower*
s'	habiller*	*to dress oneself*	je	**m'**	habille	*I get dressed*
se	laver	*to wash*	je	**me**	lave	*I wash myself*
se	lever	*to get up*	je	**me**	lève	*I get up*
se	reposer	*to rest*	je	**me**	repose	*I rest*
se	réveiller	*to wake up*	je	**me**	réveille	*I wake up*

* When the verb **begins with** '**h**' (as in '**s'h**abiller') or **a vowel** (as in '**s'a**muser'),

- the '**me**' shortens to '**m'**';
- the '**te**' shortens to '**t'**';
- the '**se**' shortens to '**s'**'.

Exercice 1

Read Pauline's description of a typical school day and fill in the missing parts of the verb in each sentence. Use reflexive verbs from the list.

1 Je me ______________ à sept heures et demie.

2 Je ________ lève à huit heures.

3 Je me ____________ dans la salle de bains.

4 Je ________ brosse les dents.

5 Je m'____________ dans ma chambre.

6 Je me _____________ à dix heures et quart.

Exercice 2

Faites de paires ! The Rocher family is on holiday in '**les Alpes**' with their cousins. They are all staying in a large family chalet. Can you see what each of them is doing? Put the number in the box to describe each picture. The first one is done for you.

1 Paul se réveille.	5 Marc s'amuse.
2 Céline se lève.	6 Maman se repose.
3 David s'habille.	7 Papa se couche.
4 Nadine se brosse les dents.	8 Mathieu se douche.

Negative form of reflexive verbs

Rappel ! Je m'appelle Nounours. Je ne m'appelle pas Paddington !

4.8 Écoutons maintenant !

Here is the negative form of the verb '**se** coucher' (*to go to bed*) in the present tense. Listen to it and repeat how it sounds.

je	**ne**	me	couche	**pas**
tu	**ne**	te	couches	**pas**
il	**ne**	se	couche	**pas**
elle	**ne**	se	couche	**pas**
nous	**ne**	nous	couchons	**pas**
vous	**ne**	vous	couchez	**pas**
ils	**ne**	se	couchent	**pas**
elles	**ne**	se	couchent	**pas**

Coin dictionnaire : Reflexive verbs ('Les verbes pronominaux')

- **Remember !** Reflexive verbs have '**se**' or '**s'** ' in front of them when you look them up in the dictionary, e.g. '**se** demander', '**s'**habiller'.

Civilisation : Bonne fête et bon anniversaire !

- French people celebrate their '**fête**' (*feast day*). The fête is the day when you receive presents, as it is the feast day of the saint you are named after.
- The girl in the picture is called Claire. Her '**fête**' is on 11 August. On that day, she has a little party and her friends and family give her presents.
- The family also celebrates birthdays (**les anniversaires**). '**La marraine**' (*godmother*) and '**le parrain**' (*godfather*) are invited and of course '**la mamie**' (*nana*) and '**le papi**' (*granddad*) also come along to celebrate. French people often celebrate with a special '**gâteau**' (*cake*) and sometimes '**champagne**'.

Les mois de l'année

4.9

Écoutons maintenant !

Listen to the months of the year in French and repeat the words after the speaker.

janvier

février

mars

avril

mai

juin

juillet

août

septembre

octobre

novembre

décembre

Rappel ! Just like the days of the week (see page 67), there is no capital letter for the months of the year in French.

Lisons maintenant !

Read the following advertisements and give the correct dates of the shows in the grid.

show	day and date
Nathalie Voisine	
Alexandre et les violons virtuoses	
Le fils Norman	
Maxime Dubois	
Laurent Carnot	
Marcel et son orchestre	

Quelle est la date de ton anniversaire ?

Exercice 1

Follow the lines and find out the dates of these people's birthdays. Then, write a sentence for each person.

Exemple : **Luc :** Son anniversaire est le 12 juin.

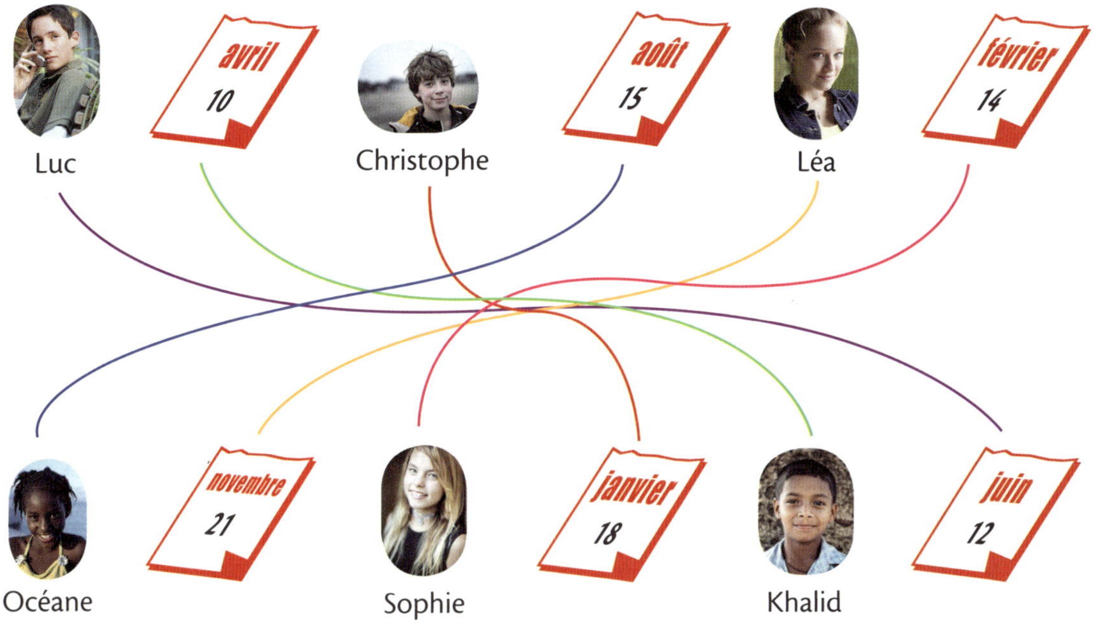

Écoutons maintenant !

4.10

Listen and mark these birthdays on the calendar. The first one is done as an example.

Exemple :

Parlons maintenant !

Note down the answers to the questions you ask. Get your partner to check if they are correct.

- Quelle est la date de ton anniversaire ? C'est le ____________.
- C'est quand l'anniversaire de ton ami(e) ? C'est le ____________.
- C'est quand l'anniversaire de ta cousine ? C'est le ____________.

Lisons maintenant !

(a) Read this interview with the actor William Moseley and answer the questions.

William Moseley

Nom : Moseley

Prénom : William Thomas

Date de naissance : 27 avril 1987

Taille : 1m80

Famille : Il a une soeur qui s'appelle Daisy. Elle est plus jeune que lui. William est l'aîné de la famille. Son frère s'appelle Ben.

1. What is William's date of birth?
2. How many children are there in his family?
3. Give the names of the members of his family and say who they are.

(b) Read this interview with the actress Natalie Portman and answer the questions.

Natalie Portman

Nom : Hershlag (Portman est un pseudonyme)

Prénom : Natalie

Date de naissance : 9 juin 1981

Taille : 1m63

Famille : Natalie n'a pas de sœur et n'a pas de frère. Son père est médecin. Sa mère est artiste peintre.

1. What is Natalie's date of birth?
2. Has she brothers and sisters?
3. What does her mother do?

4.11 Écoutons maintenant !

Listen to these people talking about recent events and match them to the cards.

a.

b.

c.

d.

e.

f.

g.

h.

1 Fatima	2 David	3 Ali	4 Estelle
5 Reda	6 Céline	7 Erika	8 Delphine

Exercice 1

Design two French greetings cards:

1. A birthday card for your French '**correspondant(e)**';
2. A Christmas card for your French teacher.

Coin grammaire : Verbs ending in '–ir'

- In **Unité 3** (see page 63), you learned how to make the present tense of '–**er**' verbs.
- You are going to learn how to use '–**ir**' verbs.
- Look at how '**le présent**' of the verb '**finir**' (*to finish*) is formed below. There are **two steps**:

Step 1: **Take** away the '–**ir**' ending. What remains is the **stem**.

Step 2: **Add** the endings for each person as follows:

je	fin**is**	nous	fin**issons**
tu	fin**is**	vous	fin**issez**
il	fin**it**	ils	fin**issent**
elle	fin**it**	elles	fin**issent**

4.12 Écoutons maintenant !

Listen to how the verb '**finir**' sounds in the present tense. You will notice that although the spellings are different, some of the words sound the same.

Tip: You never hear the final '**–ent**' of the present tense.

- You need to learn these endings '**par cœur**' (*by heart*):

Exercice 1

Some parts are missing from the present tense of the verb '**grandir**' (*to grow up/grow tall*) in the grid. Can you fill in the missing parts?

je	
tu	grandis
il	
elle	grandit
nous	
vous	grandissez
ils	
elles	grandissent

Remember : Le négatif 'ne... pas'

Je **ne** choisis **pas** un cadeau pour Marie. *I am **not** choosing a present for Marie.*

Paul **ne** finit **pas** ses devoirs ce soir. *Paul is **not** finishing his homework this evening.*

Exercice 2

(a) Write the correct form of the following '–**ir**' verbs in your copy.

1 Mon oncle (*bâtir*) ____________ un mur.
2 Maman (*nourrir*) ____________ le bébé.
3 Nous (*réussir*) ____________ aux examens.
4 Je (*rougir*) ____________ quand Paul arrive.
5 Tu (*grandir*) ____________, Luc.
6 Ils (*finir*) ____________ les cours à 17h00.
7 Vous (*choisir*) ____________ une carte.
8 Elle (*frémir*) ____________ de froid.

(b) Now, link them to the correct picture.

Communication en classe !

- Aujourd'hui, nous sommes lundi/mardi...
- Quelle est la date aujourd'hui ?
- Avez-vous vos cahiers ?
- Catherine, as-tu un stylo ?
- Les cours finissent à midi et demi.
- Voici les devoirs pour le vendredi 12.
- J'étais absente le jeudi 11.
- Finissez maintenant !

Coin Prononciation : The letters '**in**', in French, are generally pronounced like '**an**': '**in**viter', '**in**vitation', 'c**in**q', 'ju**in**', 'cous**in**'.

Lexique

aîné(e) (m./f.)	*eldest*
s'amuser	*to enjoy oneself*
anniversaire (m.)	*birthday*
s'appeler	*to be called*
aujourd'hui	*today*
bâtir	*to build*
beau-père (m.	*stepfather*
bébé (m.)	*baby*
belle-mère (f.)	*stepmother*
se brosser	*to brush*
calendrier (m.)	*calendar*
carte (f.)	*card*
cheveux (m. pl.)	*hair*
choisir	*to pick/choose*
se coucher	*to go to bed*
cousin(e) (m./f.)	*cousin*
date de naissance (f.)	*date of birth*
date (f.)	*date*
se demander	*to wonder*
demi(e)	*half*
demi-frère (m.)	*half-/step brother*
demi-sœur (f.)	*half-/step sister*
dent (f.)	*tooth*
se disputer	*to argue*
se doucher	*to take a shower*
enfant (m.)	*child*
famille (f.)	*family*
femme (f.)	*wife/woman*
fête (f.)	*feast/name day*
fille (f.)	*daughter*
fils (m.)	*son*
fille/fils unique (f./m.)	*only child*
finir	*to finish*
frémir	*to shiver*
frère (m.)	*brother*
grandir	*to grow up/tall*
grand-mère (f.)	*grandmother*
grands-parents (m.pl.)	*grandparents*
grand-père (m.)	*grandfather*
s'habiller	*to dress oneself*
homme (m.)	*man*
invitation (f.)	*invitation*
jeune	*young*
se laver	*to wash*
se lever	*to get up*
maman	*mum/mam*
mari (m.)	*husband*
mariage (m.)	*marriage/wedding*
marraine (f.)	*godmother*
mère (f.)	*mother*

midi (m.)	*midday*
minuit (m.)	*midnight*
moins	*less*
neveu (m.)	*nephew*
nièce (f.)	*niece*
Noël m.)	*Christmas*
nourrir	*to feed*
nouveau/elle (m./f.)	*new*
oncle (m.)	*uncle*
oublier	*to forget*
Pâques (f.pl.)	*Easter*
parents (m.pl.)	*parents*
parrain (m.)	*godfather*
peintre (m./f.)	*painter*
père (m.)	*father*
personne (f.)	*person*
petits-enfants (m.pl.)	*grandchildren*
petite-fille (f.)	*granddaughter*
petit-fils (m.)	*grandson*
photo (f.)	*photo*
plancher (m.)	*floor*
quart (m.)	*quarter*
se reposer	*to take a rest*
retrouver	*to meet/find again*
réussir (à)	*to succeed*
se réveiller	*to wake up*
rougir	*to blush*
sœur (f.)	*sister*
tante (f.)	*aunt*

Épreuve

Question 1

Listen and fill in the information required on the grids.

1 **Name:** Delphine
Age:
Birthday:
Number of sisters:

2 **Name:** Damien
Age:
Birthday:
Number of sisters and brothers:

Question 2

Fill in the blanks in each sentence by looking at the relationships in this family tree.

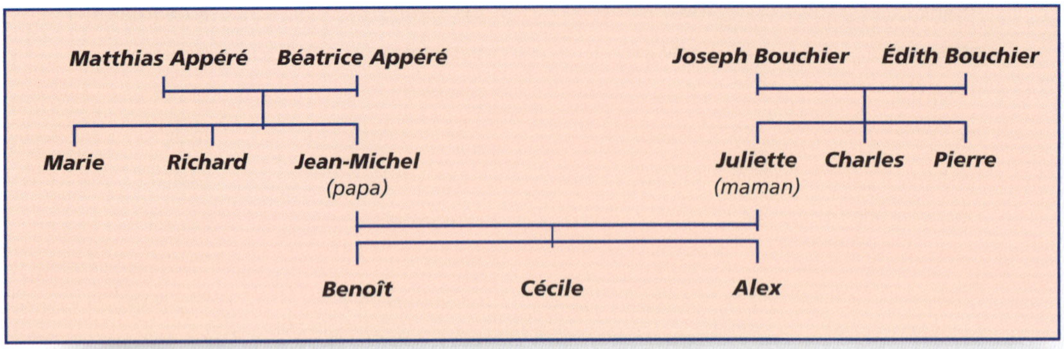

1. Cécile est la __________________ de Benoît.
2. Richard est le __________________ de papa.
3. Marie est la __________________ de Benoît, Cécile et Alex.
4. Charles est le __________________ de Joseph et Édith Bouchier.
5. Juliette est la __________________ de Benoît, Cécile et Alex.
6. Pierre est l'__________________ des enfants.
7. Cécile est la __________________ de Juliette et Jean-Michel.
8. Matthias est le __________________ de Richard.
9. Alex est le __________________ de Joseph et Édith.
10. Cécile est la __________________ de Matthias et Béatrice.

Question 3

Write the correct possessive adjectives in these sentences.

1. J'habite avec _________ parents.
2. Jean adore _________ grand-mère.
3. Sophie n'aime pas _________ cousin Louis.
4. Tu téléphones à _________ tante ?
5. Je finis _________ devoirs à 8 heures.
6. Tony travaille avec _________ oncle.
7. Tu te disputes avec _________ frère ?
8. Elle s'amuse avec _________ cousines.

For **help** with this exercise, see pages 89-91.

Question 4

Make sentences about people's ages using one item from each picture frame and put them under the correct photo.

1 

____

2 

____

3 

____

person	*verb*	*age*
Nous	ont	deux ans.
Ils	a	cinquante-six ans.
Le bébé	a	dix ans.
Ma grand-mère	avons	dix-huit ans.
Cousine Alice	a	vingt-cinq ans.

4 

____

5 

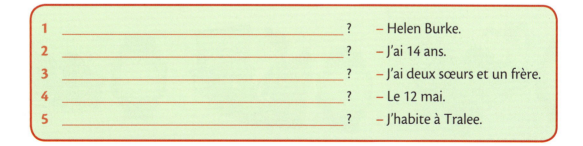

____

Question 5

Listen to these questions and write them beside the correct response.

1	____________________?	– Helen Burke.
2	____________________?	– J'ai 14 ans.
3	____________________?	– J'ai deux sœurs et un frère.
4	____________________?	– Le 12 mai.
5	____________________?	– J'habite à Tralee.

Question 6

Listen to these people, who have tickets for the local raffle (**la tombola**). What ticket number has each person?

1 Jean-Claude Havé		2 Andrée Félier		3 Christine Bernard	
4 Marcel Gachot		5 Stéphanie Dupont		6 Guy Rocher	

Question 7

Listen to Louis describing what he does each day and write the time on each clock.

1

2

3

4

5

6

7

8

9

Question 8

Write out the correct form of the verb and then match the sentences with the pictures.

a.

b.

c.

1 Les enfants (*se lèvent/se levez*) ______________.
2 Je (*me brosse/me brossent*) ______________ les dents.
3 Sabine et Paul (*se disputes/se disputent*) ______________.
4 Suzanne (*s'amuse/s'amusent*) ______________.
5 Nous (*nous habillons/nous habillent*) ______________.
6 Il (*se couche/se couches*) ______________ à 10h00.

d.

e.

f.

For **help** with this exercise, see page 101.

Question 9

Écrivez les dates suivantes en français.

1 French national holiday	le quatorze juillet
2 St Patrick's Day	______________
3 New Year's Eve	______________
4 Christmas Day	______________
5 Your birthday	______________
6 A friend's birthday	______________
7 The day you will get your next holidays	______________

Question 10

Listen to these six French students and mark on the calendar the day of their feast day.

Les fêtes

janvier

1 Jour de l'an	11 Paulin	21 Agnès
2 Basile	12 Tatiana	22 Vincent
3 Geneviève	13 Yvette	23 Barnard
4 Epiphanie	14 Nina	24 François
5 Edouard	15 Rémi	25 Conv. Paul
6 Mélaine	16 Marcel	26 Paule
7 Raymond	17 Roseline	27 Angèle
8 Lucien	18 Prisca	28 Thomas
9 Alix	19 Marius	29 Gildas
10 Guillaume	20 Sébastien	30 Martine
		31 Marcelle

février

1 Ella	11 N-DLourdes	21 P. Damien
2 Prés Seign	12 Félix	22 Isabelle
3 Blaise	13 Béatrice	23 Lazare
4 Véronique	14 Valentin	24 Modeste
5 Agathe	15 Claude	25 Roméo
6 Gaston	16 Julienne	26 Nestor
7 Eugénie	17 Alexis	27 Honorine
8 Jacqueline	18 Bernardette	28 Romain
9 Apolline	19 Gabin	
10 Arnaud	20 Aimée	

mars

1 Aubin	11 Rosine	21 Clémence
2 Charles	12 Justine	22 Léa
3 Mardi-Gras	13 Rodrigue	23 Victorien
4 Cendres	14 Mathilde	24 Catherine
5 Olivia	15 Louise	25 Annonciation
6 Colette	16 Bénédicte	26 Mi-Carême
7 Félicité	17 Patrice	27 Habib
8 Carême	18 Cyrille	28 Gontran
9 Françoise	19 Joseph	29 Gwladys
10 Vivien	20 Printemps	30 Amédée
		31 Benjamin

avril

1 Hugues	11 Stanislas	21 Anselme
2 Sandrine	12 Rameaux	22 Alexandre
3 Richard	13 Ida	23 Georges
4 Isidore	14 Maxime	24 Fidèle
5 Irène	15 Paterne	25 Marc
6 Marcellin	16 B. Joseph	26 Déportés
7 J-Baptiste	17 Vendredi-St	27 Zita
8 Constance	18 Parfait	28 Valérie
9 Gautier	19 Pâques	29 Catherine
10 Fulbert	20 Odette	30 Robert

mai

1 Fête Travail	11 Estelle	21 Constantin
2 Boris	12 Achille	22 Emile
3 P. Jacques	13 Rolande	23 Didier
4 Sylvain	14 Matthias	24 Donatien
5 Judith	15 Denise	25 Sophie
6 Prudence	16 Honoré	26 Bérenger
7 Gisèle	17 Pascal	27 Augustin
8 Victoire 45	18 Eric	28 Ascension
9 Pacôme	19 Yves	29 Aymar
10 Solange	20 Bernardin	30 Ferdinand
		31 Fête Mères

juin

1 Ronan	11 Barnabé	21 Eté
2 Blandine	12 Guy	22 Alban
3 Kévin	13 Antoine	23 Audrey
4 Clotilde	14 Trinité	24 J.-Baptiste
5 Igor	15 Germaine	25 Salomon
6 Norbert	16 J.-F. Régis	26 Anthelme
7 Pentecôte	17 Hervé	27 Fernand
8 Médard	18 Léonce	28 Irénée
9 Diane	19 Gervais	29 Pierre, Pau
10 Landry	20 Silvère	30 Martial

1 Yvette

2 Ella

3 Joseph

4 Robert

5 Éric

6 Diane

7 What date is Mother's Day?

Question 11

Read the list of times for visiting to caves near Royan in the West of France and answer the questions which follow.

Grottes incroyables à visiter

Visites

- **Du 10 avril au 12 juin :** 14h30, 15h30, 16h30
- **Du 14 juin au 10 juillet :** 10h30, 11h30, 12h30, 14h30, 15h30, 16h30, 17h30
- **Du 11 juillet au 30 août :** 10h30, 10h50, 11h10, 11h30, 11h50, 12h10, 12h30, 13h30, 13h50, 14h10, 14h30, 14h50, 15h10, 15h30, 15h50, 16h10, 16h30, 16h50, 17h10, 17h30, 17h50, 18h10, 18h30
- **Du 31 août au 9 septembre :** 10h30, 11h30, 12h30, 14h30, 15h30, 16h30, 17h30
- **Du 10 septembre au 30 octobre :** 14h30, 15h30, 16h30, 17h30

Du 10 avril au 30 octobre
7 jours sur 7
Toute l'équipe sera heureuse de vous accueillir au 70 avenue de la falaise.

1 Visits begin at 10.30 for **four** months of the year. What are these **four** months?
2 Between which **two** dates is the busiest time, when there are many visits each day?
3 What are the dates when visits are reduced to four per day?
4 When do visits begin each year and on what date do they finish?
5 How many days of the week is the site open to visitors?

Question 12

Lettre symbole ! Rewrite this letter in your copy replacing the symbols with words you have learned.

Besançon, le 17 mars

Chère Sinéad,

Comment vas-tu ? J'espère que toute ta famille va bien. Voici une photo de ma  . À gauche c'est mon , il s'appelle Nicolas. Ma  s'appelle Agnès. J'ai un  qui s'appelle Thibaud, il a  ans. Son anniversaire est le 

. Ma  s'appelle Nadia. Elle a 

ans. Son anniversaire est le 

.

Et moi ? Mon anniversaire est le 

, j'ai 

ans.

Écris-moi et dis-moi quelle est la date de ton . As-tu des frères et sœurs ?

Amitiés,

Chloé

Unité 5

Chez moi !

Civilisation : Le domicile

- Many people in France live in apartments. A building which contains apartments is called '**un immeuble**'. They are mainly found in cities and large towns.

- Some apartments are rented by the local authorities to people on low incomes and these are called '**une H.L.M.**' ('**une Habitation à Loyer Modéré**', *housing at affordable rent*).

- Many French people have a holiday home, often at the seaside, in the countryside or in the mountains. This is called '**une résidence secondaire**'.

5.1 Écoutons maintenant !

Match the person to the place where they live.

d.  un pavillon

a.  une maison

c.  un appartement

e.  une maison de ferme

b.  un studio

Benoît

Nicole

Julie

M. Larchet

Mme Martin

Où se trouve... ?

5.2 Écoutons maintenant !

You will hear people saying where they live in France. Look at the map of France above and write down where each city is located.

Exemple : Nice se trouve au sud-est de la France.

1 Lille se trouve _______________.
2 Strasbourg se trouve _______________.
3 Bordeaux se trouve _______________.
4 Toulouse se trouve _______________.
5 Paris se trouve _______________.
6 Clermont-Ferrand se trouve _______________.

Exercice 1

Look at the map and write in French, in your copy, where the following cities are situated.

1 Dijon 2 Cannes 3 Lourdes 4 Lyon 5 Nantes 6 Vichy

Parlons maintenant !

Ask your partner where these six places are located in Ireland.

Exemple : – Où se trouve Cork ? – Cork se trouve au sud.

1 Où se trouve Belfast ?	**3** Où se trouve Sligo ?	**5** Où se trouve Dublin ?
2 Où se trouve Galway ?	**4** Où se trouve Kerry ?	**6** Où se trouve Athlone ?

Ma maison se trouve...

dans une ville

dans un village

à la campagne

au centre-ville

au bord de la mer

près de l'aéroport

à 10km de Rennes

dans un lotissement

dans la banlieue

Exercice 1

Write where each person lives starting your sentence with '**J'habite...**'.

1 J'habite ______________________________.

2 J'habite ______________________________.

3 J'habite ______________________________.

4 J'habite ______________________________.

5 J'habite ______________________________.

6 J'habite ______________________________.

Civilisation : Écrire une lettre

- When writing a letter in English, you put your full address on the top right-hand side of the page. In French, the full address of the sender is written on the back of the envelope. On the top right-hand corner of the letter, French people simply put the name of their town and the date.

Écoutons maintenant !

5.3

Join the name of the person to the street where they live.

12 AVENUE CHARLES DE GAULLE

22 QUAI LOUIS DURAND

6 Océane

3 Luc

5 Léa

7 PLACE DE LA GARE

9 ALLÉE DE LA PRAIRIE

4 Khalid

1 Christophe

2 Sophie

10 RUE LA FONTAINE

6 BOULEVARD ST MICHEL

5.4 Écoutons maintenant !

Listen to this French '**comptine**'.

Au numéro trois
De la rue Saint-Nicolas
La maison est en carton
L'escalier est en papier
Le locataire est en fil de fer
Le propriétaire en pomme de terre

Exercice 1

Using the same model as the '**comptine**' above, write a poem describing a funny or unusual house. You can suggest a new number and address, funny materials from which the house, the stairs, the tenant and the owner are made! Choose from the new words suggested below or use your '**dictionnaire**' to find other words. Then illustrate your house!

le tissu

le bouton

le chocolat

le glaçon

le beurre

la paille

le sable

la confiture

le verre

Coin grammaire : Plural of nouns ('Le pluriel des noms')

- When you need to make a word plural in English, you generally add an '**s**', e.g. house, house**s**, owner, owner**s**. Likewise in French, most nouns add an '**s**' to make them plural.

Exemples :

la maison ⟶ les maison**s**

l'hôtel ⟶ les hôtel**s**

le garçon ⟶ les garçon**s**

Exercice 1

Write the correct French noun under these pictures.

deux ______________

quatre ______________

trois ______________

deux ______________

six ______________

cinq ______________

- Nouns ending with '**au**' or '**eau**' make the plural by adding an '***x***'.

Exemples :

un gâteau → des gâteau**x** un rideau → des rideau**x**

- Nouns ending with '**al**', change the '**al**' to '**aux**'.

Exemples :

un animal → des animau**x** un cheval → des chevau**x**

- Nouns ending in '**s**', '**x**', or '**z**', do not change at all in the plural.

Exemples :

une souris → deux souris le nez → les nez

- There are a few nouns in French which are usually used only in the plural.

Exemples :

les cheveux

les devoirs

Coin Prononciation: The letters '**s**', '**x**' and '**z**' are not usually pronounced when they come at the end of a French word: 'souri<u>s</u>', 'rideau<u>x</u>', 'animau<u>x</u>', 'ne<u>z</u>'.

Exercice 1

Écrivez les noms suivants au pluriel. Don't forget to change the articles '**le**', '**la**' and '**l'** ' to '**les**'!

le stylo	le bateau	la sœur	l'appartement	le château	l'hôtel
le nez	l'ours	le cheval	la ferme	la maison	le tuyau

Coin dictionnaire : Plural nouns

- Most dictionaries will give some help in showing whether a noun has an irregular plural form. If the plural ends in an irregular way, this is usually shown. Nouns ending in '**x**' in plural will have '**pl ~x**' following the word.

gâte- *préf* v **gâter**.
gâteau, pl **~x** nm **(a)** (*pâtisserie*) cake; (*au restaurant*) gateau. **~ d'anniversaire** birthday cake.

châtain 1 *nm* chestnut-brown. **2** *adj inv cheveux* chestnut (brown); *personne* brown-haired.
château, pl **~x 1** *nm* (*forteresse*) castle; (*résidence royale*) palace, castle; (*manoir, gentilhommière*) mansion, stately home; (*en France*) château.

agneau, pl **~x** *nm* lamb; (*fourrure*) lambskin. (*fig*) **il est un véritable ~** he is as meek as a lamb; (*iro*) **mes ~x** my dears (*iro*); (Rel) ~ pascal paschal lamb; (Rel) **l'~ sans tache** the lamb without stain.

chevaine *nm* = **chevesne**.
cheval, **-aux 1** *nm* **(a)** (*animal*) horse. **carosse à six ~aux** coach and six; **au travail, c'est un vrai ~** he works like a carthorse (*Brit*), he works like a Trojan.

Civilisation : Les maisons

You can see from the photo below that there are some differences between French houses and Irish houses.

- **Les volets :** The windows in a French house will usually have '**des volets**' (*shutters*) outside – these provide shade in sunny weather and protection from the cold in winter.
- **La boîte aux lettres :** French front doors have no letter boxes. The letter box is usually found near the front gate or beside the front door, with '**le nom de famille**' on it.
- **La cave :** Typical French houses have '**une cave**' (*a cellar*). It can be used to store wine – it is dark and cool. However, most people use it for storage, similar to the way in which we use an attic. Most apartment blocks have storage space for all its tenants in the basement.
- **Le grenier :** The attic is often converted for use as an extra room.

La maison

Exercice 1

Write the French word on the labels.

Exercice 2

Qu'est-ce que c'est ? Can you complete the sentences below using one of the words from the box?

porte d'entrée *boîte aux lettres* *garage* *volets* *terrasse*

1 On entre dans la maison par ici. C'est la ______________________.
2 On met les lettres dans la ______________________.
3 On se repose sur la ______________________.
4 Ils protègent les fenêtres. Ce sont les ______________________.
5 On gare la voiture ici. C'est le ______________________.

5.5

Écoutons maintenant !

(a) Dessinez ! Draw '**la maison**' according to the directions you will hear.

(b) Dessinez ! Draw '**le jardin**' according to the directions you will hear.

Les nombres ordinaux !

- When you want to list items in order, you use what are called ordinal numbers, e.g. first, fifth, eighth. In French, apart from '**premier**' (*first*), they all end in '**–ième**'. They are useful when you want to describe where you live in an apartment block, or which '**étage**' (*floor*) a room is on.

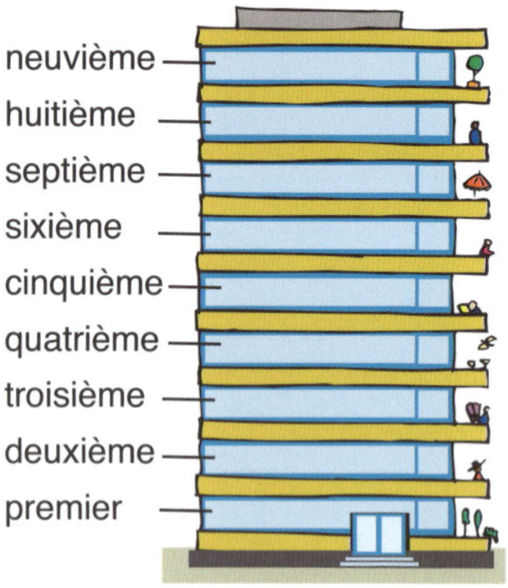

Exercice 1

Match the family to the house.

1 La famille GUILLOT habite dans la cinquième maison.
2 La famille RABIN habite dans la huitième maison.
3 La famille LE PRINCE habite dans la troisième maison.
4 La famille COTTAIS habite dans la première maison.
5 La famille BELLAMY habite dans la septième maison.
6 La famille MEUNIER habite dans la deuxième maison.
7 La famille NICOLAS habite dans la quatrième maison.
8 La famille VICTOR habite dans la sixième maison.

5.6 Écoutons maintenant !

Listen to these people and answer the questions in your copy.

1 On which floor does Mireille live?
2 Where did Jean-Paul come in the race?
3 In which class is Julie?
4 Which birthday is the speaker's little brother celebrating?
5 Marseille is France's ________________ city.
6 Madame Legros won which prize in the Lotto?

Les pièces

5.7 Écoutons maintenant !

Qui habite dans quelle maison ? Listen to Annick, Jean-Paul and Maryse describing their homes and decide who lives in which house.

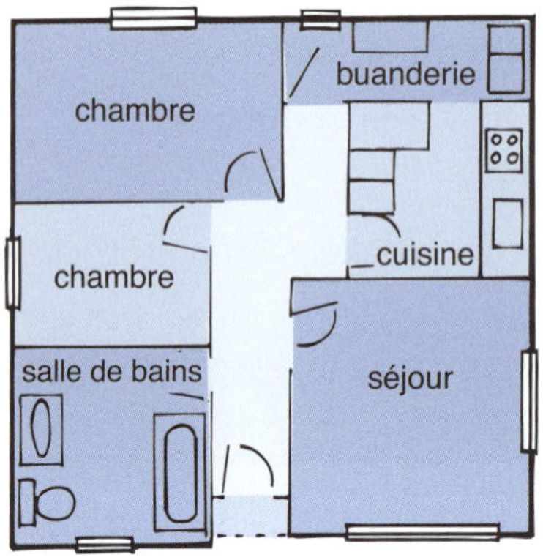

A

Jean-Paul
Havé

____

Maryse
Duclos

____

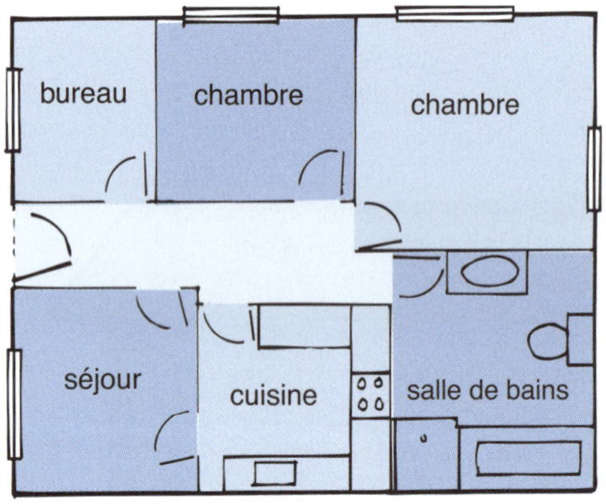

B

Annick
Lambert

____

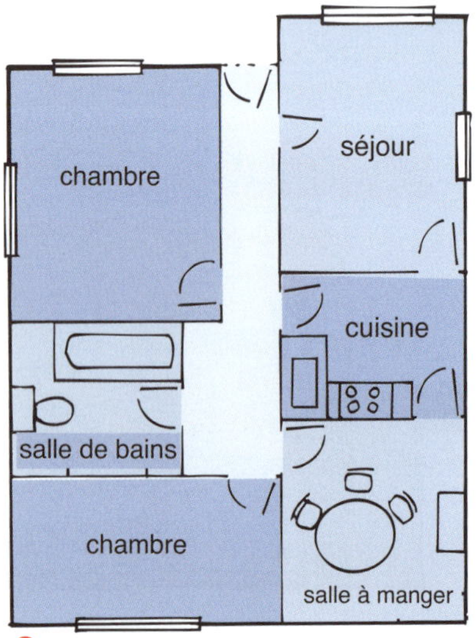

C

Lisons maintenant !

Read the letter sent by Xavier to his Irish '**correspondant**' and answer the questions which follow.

Goven, le 17 août

Cher Andy,

Merci de ta lettre avec les photos de ta famille et ta maison. Ta maison n'a pas de volets comme les maisons en France.

Je vais te décrire ma maison et je joins une photo à ma lettre. J'habite avec mon père et ma mère dans une maison qui est près du village. C'est une maison à deux étages, avec un petit jardin devant et derrière. Il y a des volets bleus et la porte d'entrée est bleue elle aussi.

En bas, il y a une cuisine, une salle à manger, des toilettes et une buanderie. En haut, il y a trois chambres et une salle de bains. Nous avons aussi une cave. Il y a une terrasse derrière la maison.

C'est tout pour l'instant. Écris-moi bientôt.

Amitiés,

Xavier

Exercice 1

Vrai ou faux ? Say whether these statements about Xavier are true or false.

		vrai	faux
1	La maison d'Andy a des volets.		
2	Le jardin de Xavier est grand.		
3	Les volets sont bleus.		
4	La cuisine est en haut.		
5	Xavier habite une maison avec un salon.		
6	Il y a trois chambres dans la maison de Xavier.		
7	La maison de Xavier a une cave.		
8	La terrasse est devant la maison.		

Écrivons maintenant !

Using the letter on the previous page as a guideline, write your own letter to describe your house/apartment to Xavier. You can begin your letter like this:

__________, le ____ ______ 200__

Cher Xavier,

Comment vas-tu ? Merci de ta lettre et de la photo de ta maison. C'est vrai, les maisons en France sont différentes. En Irlande, nous n'avons pas de __________.

J'habite ____________________

Il y a un jardin ____________________

Dans la maison, il y a ____________________

En haut, il y a ____________________

En bas, il y a ____________________

Je joins ____________________

C'est tout pour l'instant.

Amitiés,

Parlons maintenant !

Using the expressions below, ask your partner about his/her house.

– Où se trouve ta maison ?	– Ma maison se trouve dans/au/à la __________.
– Il y a combien de pièces ?	– Il y __________ pièces.
– Il y a combien de chambres ?	– Il y a __________.
– Qu'est-ce qu'il y a en bas ?	– En bas, il y a __________.
– Qu'est-ce qu'il y a en haut ?	– En haut, il y a __________.

Ma chambre

Exercice 1

Sucette de mots ! Trouvez les mots dans la sucette et écrivez la liste.

1 ____________________
2 ____________________
3 ____________________
4 ____________________
5 ____________________
6 ____________________
7 ____________________
8 ____________________
9 ____________________

Exercice 2

Trouvez les mots ! Unscramble these words and include the articles '**le**', '**la**', '**l'** ' or '**les**'.

rubuae	til	marroie	maple	dixearu	iodar-levier
______	______	______	______	______	______

5.8 Écoutons et écrivons maintenant !

Dictée ! Listen to the speaker and write the sentences.

Parlons maintenant !

Trouvez les différences ! Look at the two pictures. Taking it in turn with your partner, say what is and what is not in the two bedrooms.

Exemples : Dans la chambre de Sophie, **il y a** une table et une chaise.
Dans la chambre de Cédric, **il n'y a pas de** radiateur.

Rappel !

- '**Il y a**' means '*there is*' or '*there are*'.
- '**Il n'y a pas de**' means '*there is not*' or '*there are not*'.

Il y a une lampe.

Il n'y a pas de lampe.

Tip: '**Il n'y a pas d'**' is used if the noun following starts with a **vowel**, e.g. '**il n'y a pas d'étagères**'.

la chambre de Sophie

la chambre de Cédric

Exercice 3

Describe your bedroom in French, saying what items are in it. Begin with:

'**Dans ma chambre, il y a…**'

Civilisation : La chambre en France

- Sometimes the French use a bolster pillow called '**le traversin**'. This is a sausage-shaped underpillow covered by the sheet, which stretches across the bed. They often have a large square pillow, '**l'oreiller**' (from the word '**oreille**' meaning *ear*), unlike our rectangular pillow.

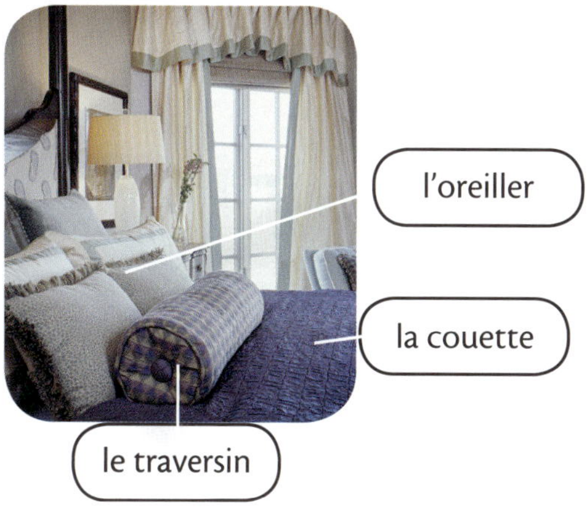

- In summer, it is not unusual to see bedclothes hanging over the windowsill in order to freshen them up, as French windows open fully inwards. This is actually a very healthy thing to do, as sunshine kills house dust-mites.

Le décor dans ma chambre : Quelle couleur ?

Exercice 1

Des transats multicolores ! Can you write the correct colour under each deckchair?

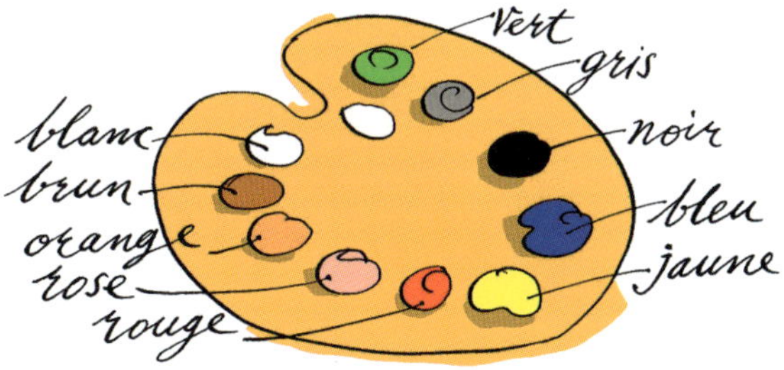

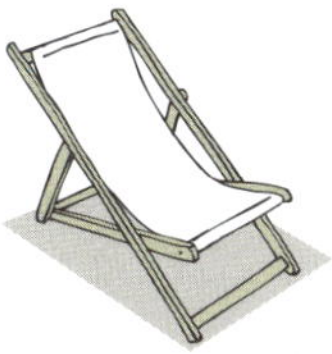

____

____

____

____

____

____

Exercice 2

Les amis de Malou ! Read the details of Malou's friends' bedrooms and fill in the correct name in each box.

1 Victor a une chambre bleue avec un lit bleu.
2 La chambre de Laure est orange.
3 Les rideaux dans la chambre d'Olivier sont gris.
4 La chambre de Thierry a un tapis noir.
5 Elodie a une armoire jaune dans sa chambre.
6 Inès adore le rouge et sa chambre est toute rouge !

Exercice 3

Find the colour of Malou's bedroom. Use the first letter of each name above and write it in the boxes below.

1	2	3	4	5	6

Coin grammaire : Adjectives ('Les adjectifs')

- A describing word in grammar is called an **adjective** (**un adjectif**).
- Colours are adjectives, because they tell us more about the noun they describe, e.g. a blue car or the White House. In English, adjectives do not change their spelling, e.g. the **red** curtains, the **red** door, the **red**-haired girl. In Irish and in French, adjectives have different forms.
- Note how, in Irish, the word for 'black' changes depending on the word it describes.

clár dubh	(because *clár* is masculine)
gruaig dhubh	(because *gruaig* is feminine)
bróga dubha	(because *bróga* is plural)

- In French we say:

'**le tapis noir**'	(because le *tapis* is masculine singular)
'**les rideaux noirs**'	(because *les rideaux* are masculine plural)
'**la porte noire**'	(because *la porte* is feminine singular)
'**les chaises noires**'	(because *les chaises* are feminine plural.)

- Most adjectives in French have **four different forms**:

masculine singular	masculine plural	feminine singular	feminine plural
noir	noir**s**	noir**e**	noir**es**

Exercice 1

Write the grid below in your copy and put in the four forms of the following adjectives: **vert** – **brun** – **bleu** – **gris**

masculine singular	masculine plural	feminine singular	feminine plural

- Some colours have the same form for masculine and feminine. These adjectives already have an 'e' in the masculine form and do not take another 'e' in the feminine forms: '**jaune**', '**rouge**', '**rose**' and '**orange**'.
- You need to know that '**blanc**' (*white*) does not follow the rules: **blanc** – **blancs** – **blanche** – **blanches**.
- So remember, before you use an '**adjectif**', you must check if the noun it is describing is **masculine** or **feminine**, **singular** or **plural**.

5.9 Écoutons maintenant !

(a) In some cases, there is no change in pronunciation in the four forms of the '**adjectif**'. Listen to the following examples.

masculine singular	masculine plural	feminine singular	feminine plural
le livre bleu	les rideaux bleu**s**	la maison bleu**e**	les chaises bleu**es**
le radiateur noir	les bureaux noir**s**	la porte noir**e**	les lampes noir**es**

(b) In other cases, the pronunciation will change when you add the '**e**' to make the feminine form. Listen to the following examples:

the '**d**' in '**grande**'	the '**t**' in '**verte**'	the '**n**' in '**brune**'
the '**t**' in '**petite**'	the '**s**' in '**grise**'	

(c) This is how the four forms of '**blanc**' sound.

masculine singular	feminine singular	masculine plural	feminine plural
blanc	blanch**e**	blanc**s**	blanch**es**

5.10 Écoutons maintenant !

Listen and tick which of the two sounds you hear.

grand	☐	**petit**	☐	**vert**	☐	**brun**	☐	**gris**	☐	**blanc**	☐
grande	☐	**petite**	☐	**verte**	☐	**brune**	☐	**grise**	☐	**blanche**	☐

Exercice 1

In your copy, describe your room naming the colour of each item.

1 Dans ma chambre, l'oreiller est ______.
2 Dans ma chambre, la couette est ______.
3 Dans ma chambre, les draps sont ______.
4 Dans ma chambre, les rideaux sont ______.
5 Dans ma chambre, les murs sont ______.
6 Dans ma chambre, la lampe est ______.

Exercice 2

Make up sentences using one item from each column.

Le canapé		noir.
Les rideaux	est	blancs.
Le tapis	sont	bleu.
Le radiateur		jaunes.
Les murs		blanche.
La porte		rouge.

Civilisation : La cuisine en France

- In French houses, the kitchen and eating areas are often all in one large open space. In apartments, the kitchen can be a '**coin cuisine**', or corner kitchen, with modern fitted cupboards.
- In older country houses, there was often a large wooden press ('**placard**' or '**armoire de cuisine**') where the dishes, cutlery, glass and table cloths were all stored. When a daughter was born, a tree was planted. The wood from the tree was used to make the cupboard when she got married. It was passed from one generation to the next.

La cuisine et la salle à manger

la cuisine

1 des placards
2 une cuisinière
3 un évier
4 un réfrigérateur (frigo)
5 un lave-vaisselle
6 un four à micro-ondes (un micro-ondes)

la salle à manger

7 une table
8 une chaise
9 un buffet
10 une lampe

Exercice 1

Poor Nounours! He has put the price-tags on the wrong items! Can you put the labels on the correct items?

5.11

Écoutons maintenant !

There is a sale in this household goods shop. Can you name the six items which are on special offer this weekend?

5.12

Écoutons maintenant !

(a) and **(b)** Écoutez et dessinez selon les instructions ! Draw the rooms in your copy, putting in the items as you hear them on the CD.

Le salon

Exercice 1

Qu'est-ce que c'est ? Unscramble these words and write them in your copy.

taufileu	apénca	vélétsinoi	quomtete	minécehi	save

Parlons maintenant !

Victor le voleur ! Victor le voleur has visited the house of the Lebrun family and stolen a number of items from their sitting room. Look at the two pictures and see what he has taken! There are five items missing. Tell your partner what is missing!

Coin grammaire : The verb 'faire'

- In **Unité 1** (see page 21), we met a group of verbs called **irregular verbs**. These verbs followed no particular pattern and have to be learned '**par cœur**'. You have already learned '**être**' and '**avoir**'. Here is another **irregular** verb, '**faire**' (*to do/to make*).

5.13 Écoutons maintenant !

Listen to how the verb '**faire**' sounds.

je	fai**s**	*I do/I make*
tu	fai**s**	*you do/you make*
il	fai**t**	*he does/ he makes*
elle	fai**t**	*she does/she makes*
nous	fais**ons**	*we do/we make*
vous	fai**tes**	*you do/you make*
ils	f**ont**	*they do/they make*
elles	f**ont**	*they do/they make*

Did you notice? '**vous faites**' does not end with a '**z**'.

Rappel ! Negative: '**ne... pas**'
Je **ne** fais **pas** mes devoirs. (*I am not doing my homework.*)
Nous **ne** faisons **pas** les lits. (*We don't make our beds.*)

- '**Faire**' is used:

To speak about weather:

To make something:

For certain expressions:

- You will be learning more about the different uses of '**faire**' in a later unit (see page 279).

Exercice 1

Fill in the missing parts of the verb '**faire**' in the grid.

je	
tu	fais
il	
elle	fait
nous	
vous	faites
ils	
elles	font

Les tâches ménagères (Household jobs)

faire le ménage
(*to do the housework*)

faire la vaisselle
(*to do the dishes*)

faire son lit
(*to make the bed*)

faire la cuisine
(*to do the cooking*)

faire la lesssive
(*to do the washing*)

faire le repassage
(*to do the ironing*)

Exercice 1

By taking one item from each house, match the subject with the correct form of the verb '**faire**'. Write the sentences in your copy and translate them into English.

Exemple : Je fais les lits. (*I make the beds.*)

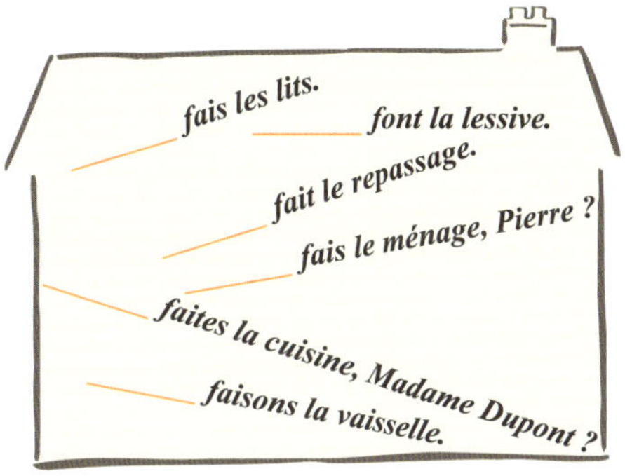

Exercice 2

Choose the correct sentence for each picture.

1 Il fait le lit.
2 Il fait la cuisine.
3 Elle fait le ménage.
4 Elle fait la lessive.
5 Il fait la vaisselle.
6 Elle fait le repassage.

a.

b.

c.

d.

e.

f.

Parlons maintenant !

Est-ce que tu aides à la maison ? Ask your partner the following questions and note their answers.

1 Tu fais ton lit ?
2 Tu fais le repassage ?
3 Tu fais la cuisine ?
4 Tu fais la lessive ?
5 Tu fais la vaisselle ?
6 Ton père fait son lit ?
7 Ta mère fait le repassage ?
8 Qui fait la cuisine ?
9 Ton père fait la lessive ?
10 Ton frère/Ta sœur fait la vaisselle ?

La salle de bains et la buanderie

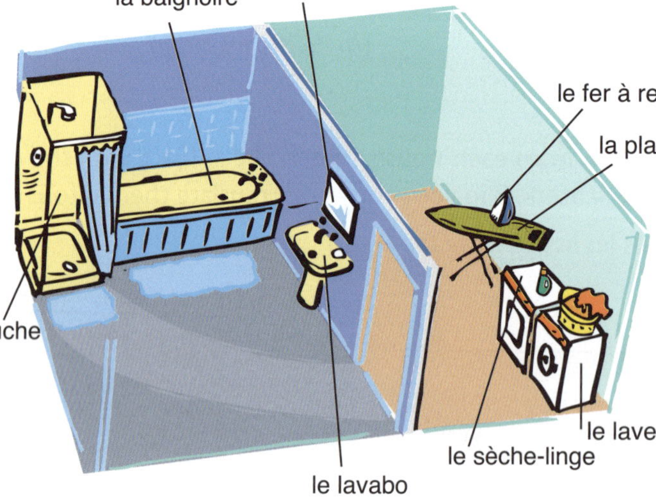

Écrivons maintenant !

Match the actions on the left column with a suitable ending from the right column and write the sentences in your copy.

1 Je me lave	(a) sous la douche.
2 Je me regarde	(b) le fer à repasser.
3 Il lave son short	(c) dans la salle de bains.
4 Elle se baigne	(d) dans le lavabo.
5 Elle fait le repassage sur	(e) dans le lave-linge.
6 Je fais le repassage avec	(f) dans la baignoire.
7 Je me lave les mains	(g) dans le miroir.
8 Je me douche	(h) la table à repasser.
9 Elle fait la vaisselle	(i) dans la salle à manger.
10 Il mange son dîner	(j) dans la cuisine.

Écrivons maintenant !

La maison de la famille Folle ! Look at the unusual house belonging to Félicia Folle, her husband Félix, their children Fantasia and Fulbert and of course Fifi, the pet dog. Some objects are in strange places. List the items in the various rooms in your copy.

Exemple : Dans la salle de bains, il y a une table et des chaises.

Écrivons maintenant !

Lettre symbole ! Écrivez un mot pour chaque symbole. Rewrite the letter into your copy replacing each symbol with the French word.

Sligo, le 10 mai

Cher Vincent,
Comment vas-tu ? Ma nouvelle maison est super. Elle se trouve dans un . En haut, il y a une , trois . En bas, nous avons une , un  et une . Nous avons une  derrière la maison.
J'ai une grande . Il y a un , une grande 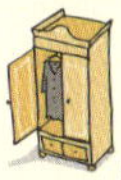. Les rideaux sont  et la couette est . Je fais mes devoirs dans ma chambre.
Et toi ? Est-ce que tu habites un appartement ou une maison ? Comment est ta chambre ?
C'est tout pour l'instant. Écris-moi vite pour décrire ta chambre.

Amitiés,

Eimear

Écrivons maintenant !

Imagine you are Vincent and you have just received the letter from Eimear. Write your reply to her, describing your apartment and in particular your room. Include the following items:

- Where your apartment is situated
- On which floor the apartment is
- Which rooms you have
- What your bedroom is like (furniture and equipment)
- Say you are enclosing a photo of your room (**je joins une photo de ma chambre**)

Comptine

Si j'étais une girafe
Je monterais sans escalier
À la lucarne du grenier.

Communication en classe !

- Ouvrez la porte !
- Fermez la porte !
- Fermez la fenêtre !
- Tirez les rideaux !
- Faites l'exercice 2 !
- Faites vos devoirs !
- Anne, que fais-tu ?
- Faites attention, s'il vous plaît !

Lexique

allée (f.)	*side street*
appartement (m.)	*apartment*
armoire (f.)	*wardrobe*
au bord de	*beside/on the edge of*
avancer	*to go forward*
se baigner	*to take a bath*
baignoire (f.)	*bath*
banlieue (f.)	*suburbs*
barrière (f.)	*gate*
bateau (m.)	*boat*
blanc/blanche	*white*
bleu(e)	*blue*
bouton (m.)	*button*
brun(e)	*brown*
buffet (m.)	*sideboard*
campagne (f.)	*countryside*
canapé (m.)	*sofa*
carton (m.)	*cardboard*
château (m.)	*castle*
cheminée (f.)	*fireplace*
cheveux (m. pl.)	*hair*
coin-cuisine (m.)	*kitchen area*
commode (f.)	*chest-of-drawers*
couette (f.)	*duvet*
cuisinière (f.)	*cooker*
douche (f.)	*shower*
en bas	*downstairs*
en haut	*upstairs*
escalier (m.)	*stairs*
étage (m.)	*floor/storey*
étagère (f.)	*shelf*
évier (m.)	*sink*
fauteuil (m.)	*armchair*
fer à repasser (m.)	*iron*
ferme (f.)	*farm*
fil de fer (m.)	*wire*
four à micro-ondes (m.)	*microwave oven*
frigo (m.)	*fridge*
gâteau (m.)	*cake*
glace (f.)	*ice*
grand(e)	*big*
gris(e)	*grey*
jardin de derrière (m.)	*back garden*
jardin de devant (m.)	*front garden*
jaune	*yellow*
lavabo (m.)	*wash-hand basin*
lave-linge (m.)	*washing-machine*
lave-vaisselle (m.)	*dishwasher*
lit (m.)	*bed*
locataire (m./f.)	*tenant*
lotissement (m.)	*housing estate*
lucarne (f.)	*skylight*
maison (f.)	*house*
mer (f.)	*sea*
micro-ondes (m.)	*microwave*
miroir (m.)	*mirror*
moquette (f.)	*fitted carpet*
mur (m.)	*wall*
noir(e)	*black*
nez (m.)	*nose*
paille (f.)	*straw*
palier (m.)	*landing*
papier (m.)	*paper*
pavillon (m.)	*small town house*
petit(e)	*small*
pièce (f.)	*room*
placard (m.)	*cupboard/press*
place (f.)	*square*
pomme de terre (f.)	*potato*
porte d'entrée (f.)	*hall-door*
près de	*near*
propriétaire (m./f.)	*owner*
radio-réveil (m.)	*radio-alarm*
rideau (m.)	*curtain*
rose	*pink*
rouge	*red*
sable (m.)	*sand*
sèche-linge (m.)	*clothes drier*
souris (f.)	*mouse*
tapis (m.)	*rug*
terrasse (f.)	*patio*
tissu (m.)	*cloth*
toit (m.)	*roof*
transat (m.)	*deckchair*
se trouver	*to be situated*
tuyau (m.)	*pipe*
véranda (f.)	*sun-room/conservatory*
verre (m.)	*glass*
vert(e)	*green*
ville (f.)	*town*

Épreuve

Question 1

Listen to the CD. Three people are talking about where they live. Answer the questions.

Conversation 1 : Solène

1 Solène lives in

(*a*) a house;

(*b*) a studio;

(*c*) an apartment.

2 On which floor does she live?

3 Which of the following does she have?

(*a*) Two bedrooms, a kitchen, a living room and a bathroom;

(*b*) Two bedrooms, a kitchen, a dining room and a bathroom;

(*c*) One bedroom, a kitchen, a living room and a bathroom.

4 Which is her favourite room?

Conversation 2 : Marc

1 Where is Marc's house?

2 Name **two** rooms which he has downstairs.

4 Where is his own bedroom?

5 Where does he have a garden?

Conversation 3 : Benjamin

1 Where is Benjamin's bedroom?

2 Name **two** items he has there.

3 How does he help at home?

4 Who does the cooking?

Question 2

Change the words in brackets into the plural.

1 Nous avons quatre (*chambre*) ____________________ chez nous.

2 Ma chambre a deux (*fenêtre*) ____________________.

3 Maman fait des (*gâteau*) ____________________ superbes.

4 Mon frère a six (*souris*) ____________________ blanches.

5 Il y a quatre (*chaise*) ____________________ dans la salle à manger.

6 Tu aimes les (*animal*) ____________________ ?

7 J'ai deux (*stylo*) ____________________ dans ma trousse.

8 Les (*château*) ____________________ en France sont énormes.

9 Mon père a cinq (*cheval*) ____________________ à la ferme.

10 Dans ma famille, il y a cinq (*personne*) ____________________.

For **help** with this exercise, see pages 125/126.

Question 3

Read this French advertisement for books about house plans. Write in English the names of eight of the books on sale.

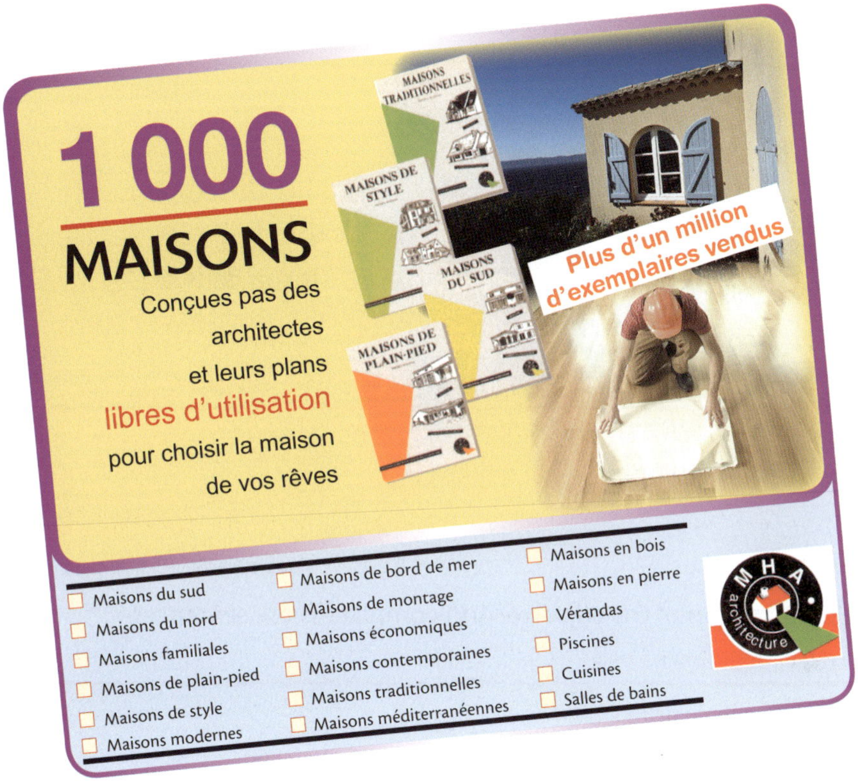

Question 4

Write the correct form of the verb '**faire**'.

1 Marie ______________________ le repassage lundi.
2 Jean et Olivier ______________________ la cuisine samedi.
3 Vous ______________________ la vaisselle ?
4 Je ______________________ le ménage dans ma maison.
5 Nous ______________________ la lessive mardi.
6 Tu ______________________ tes devoirs dans la cuisine ?

For **help** with this exercise, see page 143.

Question 5

Dans quelle pièce ? Listen to these people saying what activity they are doing and in which room they are. Write the sentences below and finish each one.

1 Je regarde la ______________________. Je suis dans le ______________________.
2 Je ______________________ mes devoirs. Je suis dans ma ______________________.
3 Je me ______________________. Je suis dans la ______________________.
4 Je fais la ______________________. Je suis dans la ______________________.
5 Je ______________________ la ______________________. Je suis dans la ______________________.
6 Je ______________________ avec ma ______________________. Je suis dans la ______________________.
7 Je me ______________________. Je suis dans la ______________________.
8 Je fais du ______________________. Je suis dans le ______________________.

Question 6

Choose the correct form of the adjective and complete these sentences.

1 Les murs de ma chambre sont (*bleus/bleues*) ______________________.
2 La porte d'entrée de ma maison est (*vert/verte*) ______________________.
3 Les volets sont (*noirs/noires*) ______________________.
4 Le frigo est (*blanc/blanche*) ______________________.
5 Les rideaux dans le salon sont (*bruns/brunes*) ______________________.
6 Mon livre de français est (*rouge/rouges*) ______________________.
7 Le canapé est (*gris/grise*) ______________________.
8 Les fauteuils sont (*bleus/bleues*) ______________________.

For **help** with this exercise, see pages 139-140.

Question 7

Listen to the conversation between Madame Rimbault and the house painter Simon who are discussing the paint colours for the house. Write the colour chosen under each picture.

rose

bleu

jaune

violet

blanc

rouge

vert

Question 8

Your parents are thinking of buying a holiday home in France. Look at the following ads and write the reference number below.

Appartement de charme rénové. Exposition Sud. Terrasse, 2 chambres, séjour avec cheminée, salle de bains, douche. **Réf. 1543**

Studio au rez-de-chaussée, situé proche commerces. Séjour, cuisine, sdb. **Réf. 1557**

Vue sur le port, **appartement** situé au 3ème étage, quartier calme. 3 chambres, sdb, cuisine/buanderie. Accès à la piscine de la résidence. **Réf. 1569**

Au cœur de la ville, **appartement** au 1er étage, séjour, cuisine, 3 chambres, sdb, douche. **Réf. 1569**

Magnifique appartement avec séjour, 2 chambres, balcons, vue sur la mer, sdb, cuisine aménagée. **Réf. 1573**

Appartement situé au 1er étage d'une résidence. Balcon, 2 chambres, garage en sous-sol. **Réf. 1542**

Which apartment would they buy if they wanted

1 a fireplace in the living-room? __________
2 to be close to the shops? __________
3 to have a garage? __________
4 to have a utility room? __________
5 to have a fitted kitchen? __________

Question 9

Imagine you are an estate agent (**agent immobilier**) in France. Make up advertisements to give to customers who want to buy:

1 A large country house with four bedrooms, a garden, a garage and an attic
2 A modern apartment in the centre of town, on the second floor of a block of flats, with two bedrooms, kitchen/dining area and bathroom
3 A small house on an estate, with one bedroom, a small garden and a cellar

Question 10

Write a short letter to your '**correspondant(e)**' and describe your house, giving the following details:

- You live in a village in a small house with three bedrooms, a sitting room, a kitchen, a bathroom and an attic
- The house has a garden and a garage
- Describe your bedroom
- Ask your '**correspondant(e)**' some questions about his/her house

Unité 6

Les animaux

Civilisation : Les animaux en France

- French people love animals: pets, farm animals, circus animals and animals in the zoo. The rooster/cockerel is the French national emblem. You will see it on the national jerseys of many French sportspeople.
- More than half of all households in France have at least one pet (**un animal domestique**). There are 9.7 million cats (**chats**) and 8.8 million dogs (**chiens**)! There are even shops which cater for clothes and accessories for pets. What surprises many Irish people is that French dogowners quite often take their pets into restaurants and cafés with them, while they eat.

- Families who live in apartments often choose to keep a hamster (**un hamster**), a goldfish (**un poisson rouge**) or a bird (**un oiseau**), as they may be forbidden to have a cat or a dog. It is estimated that there are 28 million pet fish in France!
- Animals feature in many of France's favourite cartoon series.
- There is a wide range of magazines about animals which are popular in France.

6.1 Écoutons maintenant !

Regardez et écoutez ! Match the picture with the animal and practise pronouncing each word.

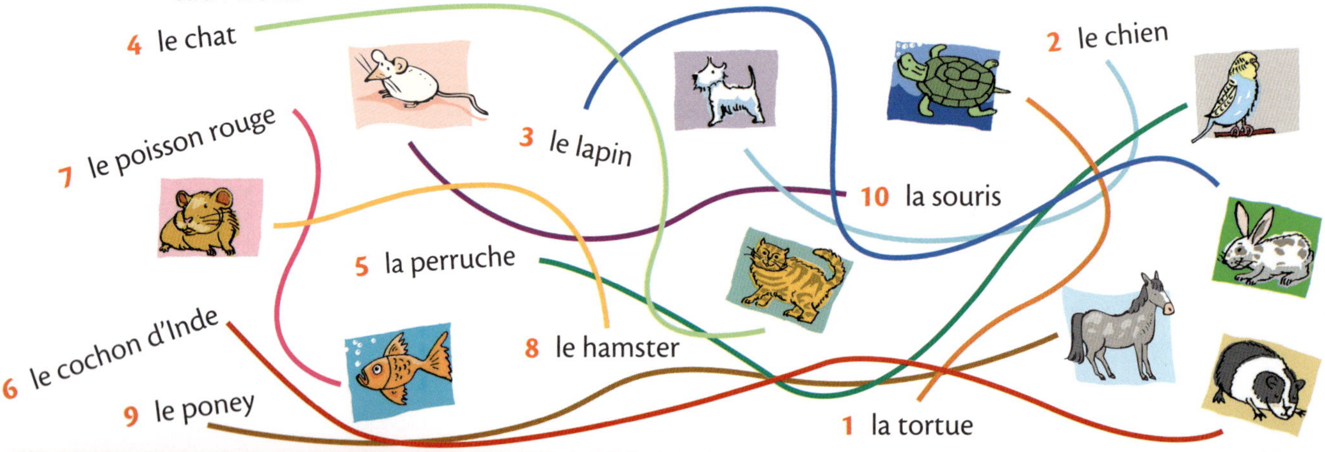

Exercice 1

Faites des paires ! There are many expressions in the French language which involve animals. What do you think the following expressions mean? Join the correct English to its French equivalent. Use your dictionary or '**Lexique**' to help you (see page 178).

what awful weather

my darling

to have a raging temperature

être malin comme un singe

avoir un chat dans la gorge

mon petit chat

to have a frog in your throat

to be very mischievous

an April fool

avoir une fièvre de cheval

poisson d'avril

Quel temps de chien !

Exercice 2

Quels animaux ? Unscramble the words, writing the correct spelling of each animal.

inCeh

taCh

oTuert

Sisour

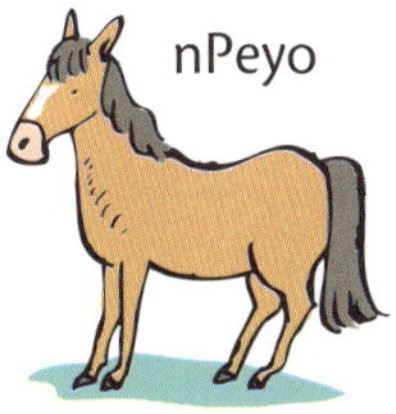

nPeyo

iohConddnec

Exercice 3

(a) À qui sont ces animaux ? Who do these pets belong to? Complete the sentences below.

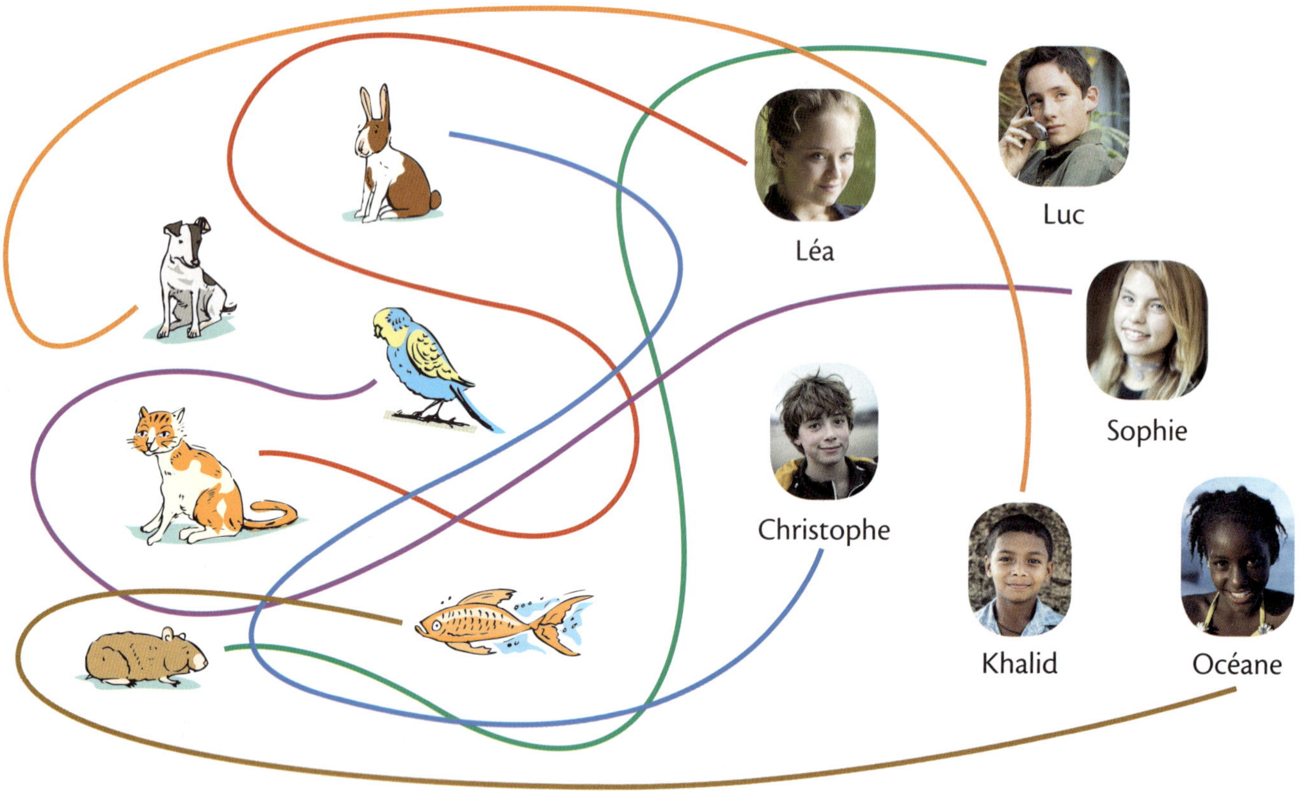

(b) Complete the sentences describing the colour of each pet.

Exemple : Luc a un hamster. Il est brun.

1. Océane a un ______________________. Il est ______________.
2. Léa a un ______________________. Il est ______________ et ______________.
3. Christophe a un ______________________. Il est ______________ et ______________.
4. Khalid a un ______________________. Il est ______________ et ______________.
5. Sophie une ______________________. Elle est ______________ et ______________.

6.2

Écoutons maintenant !

C'est quel animal ? Listen to these six people talking about their pets. Which pet has which name?

1. Charly : ______________________
2. Gurunne : ______________________
3. Gloupie : ______________________
4. Scoubidou : ______________________
5. Tiger : ______________________
6. Diva : ______________________

6.3 Écoutons maintenant !

Écoutez Anne, Clémence, Marc et Manon. Tick ✓ the animals they like and put a cross ✗ for those they do not like.

	chats	chiens	poissons	hamsters	perruches
Anne					
Clémence					
Marc					
Manon					

Coin grammaire : Adjectives ('Les adjectifs')

- When talking about animals, you may need to use adjectives to describe them. In **Unité 5** (see page 139), you learned that, in French, adjectives change their spelling according to the noun they are describing.

Exemples :

le chat noir

la tortue noir**e**

les chiens noir**s**

les perruches noir**es**

- **Remember:** To describe an animal or a pet, you must know whether the noun is masculine or feminine, singular or plural.

Exemples : J'ai **un** chien, **il** est **grand**. — il est grand = *he/it* is big
J'ai **une** tortue, **elle** est **grande**. — elle est grande = *she/it* is big

Further rules for adjectives

- If the adjective ends in '–**eux**', change the '–**eux**' into '–**euse**' to make it feminine.

Exemples : le lion courag**eux** → la souris courag**euse**

les lions courag**eux** → les souris courag**euses**

If the adjective ends in '–**if**', change the '–**if**' into '–**ive**' to make it feminine.

Exemples :

le chien sport**if**	la girafe sport**ive**
les chiens sport**ifs**	les girafes sport**ives**

- Here are a few more **useful adjectives** which follow different patterns.

masculine	feminine	
beau	b**elle**	*beautiful, handsome*
doux	dou**ce**	*soft/gentle*
favori	favor**ite**	*favourite*
long	long**ue**	*long*
mignon	mignon**ne**	*cute*

6.4 Écoutons maintenant !

Listen to these adjectives and tick the box indicating the sound you hear.

actif	☐	active	☐
dangereux	☐	dangereuse	☐
vif	☐	vive	☐
favori	☐	favorite	☐
paresseux	☐	paresseuse	☐
doux	☐	douce	☐
mignon	☐	mignonne	☐
agressif	☐	agressive	☐

Exercice 1

Make up sentences to describe your own pet or an imaginary one using one item from each column. You can use more than one adjective to describe the pet.

Exemple : Mon chien est grand et actif.

	chat		grand(e).
	chien		mignon/onne.
Ma	lapin		petit(e).
Mon	hamster	est	beau/belle.
	souris		noir(e).
	tortue		blanc/he.
	perruche		timide.
	cochon d'Inde		actif/ve.
	poisson rouge		paresseux/euse.
	poney		curieux/euse.

Parlons maintenant !

With your partner, talk about pets.

– Tu as un animal à la maison ?	– Oui, j'ai.../Non, je n'ai pas de...
– De quelle couleur est ton animal ?	– Il/elle est...
– Comment s'appelle-t-il/elle ?	– Il/elle s'appelle...
– Quel animal préfères-tu ?	– Je préfère les…/Mon animal favori est...
– Pourquoi ?	– Il/elle est...
– Tu aimes les chats/les chiens... ?	– Oui, j'aime/j'adore... – Non, je n'aime pas/je déteste...

Lisons maintenant !

Read this text and answer the questions.

Midge, la terreur des dealers

Midge, ce chiot, est un animal exceptionnel. C'est le chien le plus petit de la police américaine.

Depuis cinq mois, Midge a réussi à retrouver la trace de nombreux trafiquants de drogues, qui sont maintenant derrière les barreaux !

1 For which country's police force does Midge work?
2 What is special about her?

Écrivons maintenant !

In your copy, describe the animals using the three sets of details in the green box, as in the following example.

J'ai un chat. Il s'appelle Boule. Il a quatre ans. Il est gris. Il est timide. Il aime dormir dans la buanderie.

1 Dog; Lucky; he is 1 year old; black and brown; he is lazy; lives in the garage.
2 Rabbit; Blanche; she is 2 years old; white; she is beautiful; likes to play; lives in the garden.
3 Mouse; Babe; she is 3 months (**mois**) old; brown and white; she is curious; lives in my bedroom.

Coin grammaire : The verb 'devoir'

- Another useful irregular verb is the verb '**devoir**' which means '*to have to*' or '*must*' do something. Because it is irregular, it does not follow any rule and you must learn it by heart.

6.5 Écoutons maintenant !

Listen to how the verb '**devoir**' sounds in the present tense.

je	d**ois**	nous	dev**ons**
tu	d**ois**	vous	dev**ez**
il	d**oit**	ils	d**oivent**
elle	d**oit**	elles	d**oivent**

Tip: Can you see where you get the word '**les devoirs**' (*homework*) from? You have to do it!

- **Remember:** Le négatif '**ne** ... **pas**'

Je **ne** dois **pas**... ; Nous **ne** devons **pas**...

Exercice 1

Remplissez la grille avec le verbe '**devoir**' (*to have to/must*) au présent.

je	dois	nous	devons
tu		vous	
il		ils	doivent
elle		elles	

Exercice 2

Use the correct form of the verb '**devoir**' in the following sentences.

1. Je ____________ faire mes devoirs.
2. Le professeur ____________ corriger les cahiers.
3. Mon frère ____________ sortir les poubelles.
4. Nous ____________ faire nos lits.
5. Mes parents ____________ travailler le samedi.
6. Tu ____________ finir la lettre pour grand-mère.
7. Vous ____________ arriver à l'heure.
8. Coralie et Mélodie ____________ retourner en France.

6.6

Écoutons maintenant !

Listen to this '**chanson**'. It comes from French-speaking Canada.

Alouette

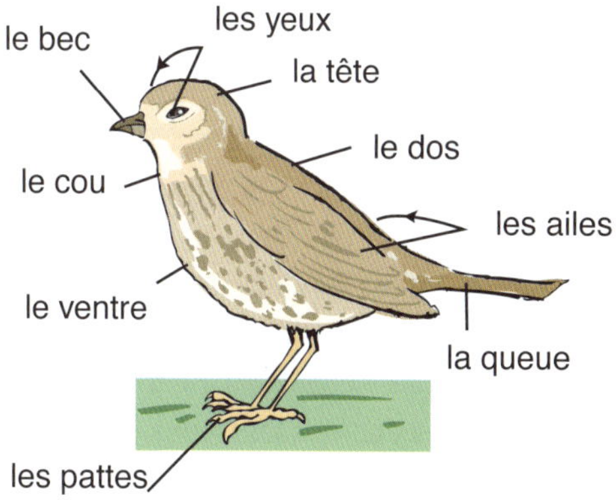

Alouette, gentille alouette,
Alouette, je te plumerai.
Je te plumerai la queue,
je te plumerai la queue.
et la queue, et la queue,
et le dos, et le dos,
et le cou et le cou,
et la tête, et la tête,
et le bec, et le bec,
Alouette, alouette,
Alouette, gentille alouette, alouette, je te plumerai.
Alouette, gentille alouette, alouette, je te plumerai.

Civilisation : La ferme

- Besides providing food products for its own large population, France is Western Europe's largest agricultural producer and one of the world's main exporters of farm produce.
- In 2005, there were 1.1 million people involved in agriculture in France. 54% of the area of France is agricultural land. The French are the largest producers of cereals in the EU.
- As a leading wine producer (second in the world after Italy), the cultivation of vines in vineyards (**les vignobles**) is very important for France.
- Cows and goats are important in the production of cheeses and other milk-based products.

un vignoble

La cour de ferme

les chèvres (f.)

le taureau

les moutons (m.)

les cochons (m.)

les oies (f.)

la poule

le canard

les vaches (f.)

les dindes (f.)

Lisons maintenant !

Lisez cet article et répondez aux questions.

Cochons bouclés et moutons à quatre cornes

Venez faire une promenade à la ferme du Tessonet pour découvrir qu'il existe vraiment des chèvres aux cornes torsadées (Italie), des cochons à laine (Hongrie) et des moutons à quatre cornes (Angleterre). Si vous apportez du pain sec, vous sympathiserez vite avec l'un des cinquante animaux présentés. Les plus jeunes pourront aussi faire leur baptême de poney !

1 Which of the following animals is mentioned in this text: *(a)* cows; *(b)* pigs; *(c)* horses.
2 Where do the goats come from?
3 How many animals are there in all on this farm?

Lisons maintenant !

Lisez cet article et répondez aux questions. The following article is about a stay on a farm.

Une semaine à la ferme

Partez le matin soigner les lapins, les poules, les pigeons, les ânes et les chèvres. L'après-midi, baladez-vous à dos de poney dans la campagne. Le soir, après le feu de camp et les crêpes de Nadine, il est tout à fait recommandé de faire une bataille de polochons !

De 6 à 12 ans. Tarif : 270€ la semaine, du dimanche 18h au samedi avant midi.

Nadine et Marc Ferret, La Ferme d'Autrefois

1. How long is each stay for?
2. Name **two** animals you can find on this farm?
3. What is the activity offered in the afternoon?
4. What does Nadine prepare for you to eat each evening?

Écoutons maintenant !

6.7

Listen to Robert describing his holiday on the farm.

Kerry le 15 juin

Salut Kévin !

Me voici à la ferme de mon oncle Matthew, près de Tralee. Je suis ici pour une semaine avec ma famille. Je m'amuse bien à la ferme. J'aime aider mon oncle. J'adore les animaux. Il y a des moutons, un taureau, des vaches et des poules. Je n'aime pas le taureau. Il est dangereux !

À bientôt,

Robert

Kévin Dupont
11 rue de la gare
35580 Guignen
FRANCE

Exercice 1

Find the French for the following expressions in Robert's postcard on the previous page.

1 Hi: ____________________.
2 Here I am: ____________________.
3 on the farm: ____________________.
4 I am here for a week: ____________________.
5 with my family: ____________________.
6 I am enjoying myself: ____________________.
7 I like helping: ____________________.
8 there are: ____________________.
9 I don't like: ____________________.
10 See you soon: ____________________.

Écrivons maintenant !

(a) Can you complete the gaps in the following postcard from Laoise to Marine?

Wexford, le 4 juillet

Salut Marine !

Me voici à la ____________ de mon oncle John à Wexford.
Je ____________ ici pour deux ____________ avec ____________ sœur.
Je m'____________ bien à la ferme. Il y a des ____________ des ____________ et un ____________.
Je n'aime pas ____________. J'adore aider mon oncle.

À ____________
Laoise

Marine Sinaud
4, rue Émile Loubet
69000 Lyon
FRANCE

(b) Write a postcard to your '**correspondant(e)**' from a farm in Ireland.

- Say whose farm it is
- Say how long you are staying and who is with you
- Say what animals there are on the farm
- Say what animals you like
- Say which animal you don't like

Coin grammaire : Verbs ending in '–re'

- You have already learned about regular '–**er**' and '–**ir**' verbs. The **third group** of verbs we need to look at is regular '–**re**' verbs.
- There are **two steps**:

Step 1: **Take** away the '–**re**'. What is left is the stem.

Step 2: **Add** the following endings to the stem.

je	–**s**	nous	–**ons**
tu	–**s**	vous	–**ez**
il	–	ils	–**ent**
elle	–	elles	–**ent**

- You need to learn these endings '**par cœur**' (*by heart*)!

Example of an '–re' verb

- This is what the present tense of the verb '**vendre**' (*to sell*) looks like.

je	vend**s**	nous	vend**ons**
tu	vend**s**	vous	vend**ez**
il	vend	ils	vend**ent**
elle	vend	elles	vend**ent**

6.8

Écoutons maintenant !

- Listen to what the present tense of the verb '**vendre**' sounds like.

Le négatif 'ne ... pas'

Roger **ne** vend **pas** sa maison. *Roger is not selling his house.*

Mon chien **ne** mord **pas** les enfants. *My dog doesn't bite children.*

Exercice 1

Complétez la grille avec le verbe '**mordre**' (*to bite*).

je	mords
tu	
il	
elle	mord
nous	
vous	mordez
ils	
elles	mordent

Exercice 2

Remplissez la grille avec le verbe '**perdre**' (*to lose*).

je	
tu	
il	
elle	
nous	
vous	
ils	
elles	

Exercice 3

Write the correct form of the following '**–re**' verbs and translate the sentences into English. Check their meaning in your dictionary or '**Lexique**' (see pages 178-179).

1 Guillaume (*tondre*) ________________ la pelouse chaque samedi.
2 Je (*perdre*) ________________ mon chat de temps en temps.
3 Cécile (*vendre*) ________________ son cochon d'Inde.
4 Les souris (*mordre*) ________________ les biscuits.
5 Le chien (*rendre*) ________________ l'os à Lucie.
6 Les fermiers (*vendre*) ________________ les canards.
7 Le poney (*attendre*) ________________ sa nourriture.
8 Le hamster (*descendre*) ________________ l'escalier.

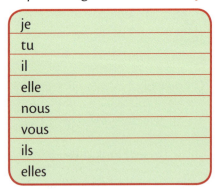

6.9 Écoutons maintenant !

Écoutez le CD et remplissez les blancs ci-dessous.

Je m'appelle Régine Béton. Mon mari et moi avons ______ ______ en Mayenne, en France. À la ferme, nous avons des __________, deux __________ et des ___________. Mes amis viennent avec leurs enfants au printemps voir les petits animaux, comme les ________. Nous avons trois ___________. Le week-end, nous proposons des balades à ___________ pour les enfants.

6.10 Écoutons maintenant !

Des comptines ! Écoutez et lisez.

Un lapin dans le jardin
mange du petit pain
avec son beau copain.

Un mouton et sa mère
sont en plein air
avec leur bergère.

Un grand taureau noir
dans la grande patinoire
s'amuse du matin au soir.

Exercice 1

Can you write a little rhyme like the rhymes above? Use the words in the speech bubbles to help you.

1 Un poisson dans la ______________________
est un nageur ______________________
comme son vieux ______________________.

2 Un cochon qui est ______________________
mange un bonbon chaque ______________________
dans la basse ______________________.

super, père, mer

cour, jour, lourd

Coin grammaire : Possession ('Les possessifs')

In English, when you want to say that things belong to someone, you use an apostrophe '**'s**', e.g. Shona'**s** bike, Shane'**s** copy. In French, you don't use an apostrophe.

- If you want to say who owns something, you use the preposition '**de**' (*of*).

le chat **de** Nadia ⟶ *Nadia's cat (the cat of Nadia)*

les vaches **de** Marc ⟶ *Mark's cows (the cows of Mark)*

Exercice 1

Translate the following sentences into French.

1 Julie's dog	2 Paul's goldfish	3 Suzanne's tortoise
4 Valérie's chickens	5 Kevin's turkeys	6 Luc's cats

- If the person's name begins with a vowel, you use '**d'** ':

le lapin **d'**Anne ⟶ *Anne's rabbit*

- What happens when you do not have a person's name? What do you do when you want to say 'the girl's cat' or 'the boy's cat' or 'the children's pets'?

le chat **de la** fille ⟶ *the cat of the girl/the girl's cat*
le chat **du** garçon ⟶ *the cat of the boy/the boy's cat*
les animaux **des** enfants ⟶ *the animals of the children/the children's animals*

- '**De la**' is used because the noun '**fille**' is feminine.
- '**Du**' is used because the noun '**garçon**' is masculine.
- '**Des**' is used because the noun '**enfants**' is plural.
- If the owner starts with a vowel or silent '**h**' masculine or feminine, '**de l'** ' is used.

Exemples : le chien **de l'**enfant ; le chat **de l'**homme

6.11

Écoutons maintenant !

Complete the missing word in each of these sentences. Write them in your copy and translate them into English.

1 Le cheval ______________ garçon.	2 Le lapin ______________ fille.
3 Le chat ______________ élève.	4 Les vaches ______________ fermiers.
5 La cage ______________ perruche.	6 Les portes ______________ maisons.
7 Le chien ______________ enfant.	8 Les becs ______________ oiseaux.

Exercice 2

Traduisez les phrases suivantes en français.

Exemple : *the mother's horse* → le cheval de la mère

1 the mother's horse ______________________

2 the boy's dog ______________________

3 the grandad's rabbit ______________________

4 the farmer's sheep ______________________

5 the nephew's cat ______________________

6 the children's hamster ______________________

7 the girls' ponies ______________________

8 the teacher's mouse ______________________

Le zoo : Au zoo, je vois…

- Voici les animaux du zoo.

le crocodile

l'éléphant (m.)

la girafe

le lion

le singe

l'ours blanc

le perroquet

le rhinocéros

le serpent

le tigre

Lisons maintenant !

PARC ANIMALIER

Promenade de 2,5 km dans la nature à la rencontre des animaux du parc.

1 repas au restaurant '***La Cage***' = 1 entrée gratuite au parc.

Ouvert tous les jours de 10h00 à 18h00 du 01 mai au 31 octobre.

Remise par personne sur présentation de ce coupon d'une valeur de 1,00 €.

1 What is the distance of the walk through this animal park?

2 Which of these animals are pictured here (tick the grid)?

les singes	les tigres	les lions	les ours	les perroquets

3 If you buy a meal in the restaurant '**La Cage**', what discount do you get?

Coin grammaire : The verb 'voir'

- When you are writing, another useful verb is '**voir**' (*to see*). It is an **irregular verb**.

6.12 Écoutons maintenant !

Listen to how the verb '**voir**' sounds.

je	vois
tu	vois
il	voit
elle	voit
nous	voyons
vous	voyez
ils	voient
elles	voient

Remember : le négatif '**ne... pas**'

Je **ne** vois **pas** de souris au zoo. — *I don't see mice in the zoo.*
Nous **ne** voyons **pas** de lions dans une ferme irlandaise. — *We don't see lions on an Irish farm.*

Exercice 1

Remplissez la grille ci-dessous.

je	vois
tu	
il	
elle	voit
nous	
vous	
ils	
elles	voient

Coin Prononciation : The letters '**oi**' in French are pronounced like the start of the English word '**wha**t' without the 't' : 'vois', 'trois', 'dois', 'oie', 'oiseau'.

Exercice 2

Une journée au zoo ! Complétez les phrases suivantes en utilisant le verbe '**voir**'.

Je ____________ les perroquets.

Louise ____________ l'éléphant.

Nous ____________ les serpents.

Tu vois ____________ la girafe ?

Luc et Paul ____________ les singes.

Vous ____________ le rhinocéros ?

Quel temps fait-il ?

- When you are on a day out, the weather will be a very important part of the day. Here are some phrases you will need to talk about the weather.

Il fait beau.

Il fait mauvais.

Il fait chaud.

Il fait froid.

Il fait soleil.

Il pleut.

Exercice 1

Finish the following sentences with the correct weather phrase.

1 Quand je suis au Pôle Nord, il ____________________.
2 Quand je suis à la plage, il ____________________.
3 Les canards aiment quand il ____________________.
4 Mon chat dort dans le jardin quand il ____________________.
5 Patrick met le linge dehors quand il ____________________.
6 Je n'aime pas quand il ____________________.

Exercice 2

Here are some phrases from postcards with weather symbols. Write out the weather phrase for each symbol.

1 Me voici en vacances. Il fait ______________ .

2 Je suis au bord de la mer en France. Comme il fait ______________  !

3 Nous sommes en montagne, je m'amuse mais il fait ______________ .

4 Ma famille et moi sommes à Paris, il fait chaud mais il ______________ .

5 Salut de Monaco dans le sud de la France, il ______________ .

6 Bonjour de Normandie ! Me voici à la ferme de mon correspondant, il ______ ______ .

Un petit quiz !

Find the answers to the following quiz.

1 Un chat a : *(a)* deux pattes ; *(b)* six pattes ; *(c)* quatre pattes ? ☐

2 Une girafe habite : *(a)* en Afrique ; *(b)* dans une cage ; *(c)* au bord de la mer. ☐

3 Quel animal habite dans la jungle ? *(a)* le poney ; *(b)* le tigre ; *(c)* le hamster. ☐

4 Quel animal adore les carottes ? *(a)* le lapin ; *(b)* la souris ; *(c)* le serpent. ☐

5 Quel animal nous donne des yaourts ? *(a)* le canard ; *(b)* la vache ; *(c)* la dinde. ☐

Exercice 3

Faites des paires ! Many well-known films featuring animals have been popular in France. Can you match the French titles to the English titles?

1	*Le livre de la jungle*	(a)	*Flushed away*
2	*Les cent un dalmatiens*	(b)	*101 Dalmatians*
3	*Souris City*	(c)	*The Lady and the Tramp*
4	*La panthère rose*	(d)	*Happy Feet*
5	*La belle et le clochard*	(e)	*Jaws*
6	*Le Roi Lion*	(f)	*The Lion King*
7	*Les petits pieds du bonheur*	(g)	*Jungle Book*
8	*Les dents de la mer*	(h)	*The Pink Panther*

1 = **g**	2 =	3 =	4 =	5 =	6 =	7 =	8 =

Exercice 4

Lisez la liste des films ci-dessous. Quel animal est la star de chaque film ?

Exemple : une souris = *Petit Stuart*

1	un cochon	______	4	un chien saint-bernard	______
2	un chien colley	______	5	un tigre	______
3	un gorille	______	6	un cheval	______

Écrivons maintenant !

(a) Lettre-symbole ! Remplacez les symboles par des mots dans la lettre ci-dessous.

Paris, le 4 juin

Chère Cian,

J'espère que tu vas bien. Comment va ton nouveau  ? Comment s'appelle-t-il ? Moi, j'adore les chiens. Mais nous habitons en appartement et ce n'est pas pratique.

dernier je suis allé au zoo avec mes amis. Il a fait  . C'était fantastique !

Au zoo, il y a des  , des  et des  . Mes animaux favoris sont les  . Ils sont amusants. Je n'aime pas les  , ils sont dangereux ! Mon amie Julie adore les  . Ils sont si paresseux ! Ils adorent dormir dans l'eau. Théo adore les  . Ils sont mignons.

Il y a un zoo près de chez toi ? Tu vas souvent voir les animaux ?

C'est tout pour l'instant.

Amitiés,

Louis

(b) You are visiting the zoo. Write a postcard to your French friend Tony.

- Say where you are and with whom
- Say what the weather is like
- Say which animals you like
- Say which animals you don't like

Communication en classe !

- Je ne comprends pas.
- Attendez un instant, s'il vous plaît !
- Je rends les cahiers maintenant.
- Vous devez finir l'exercice 2 ce soir.
- Nous devons écrire ça dans les cahiers.
- Quel temps fait-il ?
- Il fait beau aujourd'hui.
- Il fait mauvais aujourd'hui.
- Il pleut.

Lexique

actif/ive	*active, lively*
agressif/ive	*aggressive*
aider	*to help*
alouette (f.)	*lark*
amusant(e)	*funny*
âne (m.)	*donkey*
animal/aux (m.)	*animal/s*
animal domestique (m.)	*pet*
attendre	*to wait for*
aveugle (m./f.)	*blind person*
balade (f.)	*stroll/walk*
barreaux (m. pl.)	*bars*
bassecour (f.)	*farmyard*
berger/ère (m./f.)	*shepherd(ess)*
bonheur (m.)	*happiness*
bouclé(e)	*curly*
campagne (f.)	*countryside*
canard (m.)	*duck*
chat (m.)	*cat (male)*
cheval/aux (m.)	*horse/s*
chèvre (f.)	*goat*
chien (m.)	*dog*
chiot (m.)	*puppy*
cochon (m.)	*pig*
cochon d'Inde (m.)	*guinea pig*
copain/copine	*pal*
corne (f.)	*horn*
corriger	*to correct*
cour (f.)	*yard*
courageux/euse	*brave*
crêpes (f.pl.)	*pancakes*
dangereux/euse	*dangerous*
dent (f.)	*tooth*
de temps en temps	*from time to time*
descendre	*to go down*
dinde (m.)	*turkey*
dormir	*to sleep*
faire beau	*to be fine*
faire chaud	*to be warm*
faire soleil	*to be sunny*
faire froid	*to be cold*
faire mauvais	*to be bad*
fermier/ière	*farmer*
feu (m.)	*fire*
fièvre (f.)	*temperature/ fever*
gorge (f.)	*throat*
gourmand/e	*greedy*
gratuit(e)	*free*
heureux/euse	*happy*
jungle (f.)	*jungle*
laine (f.)	*wool*
lapin (m.)	*rabbit*
lourd(e)	*heavy*
malin/igne	*smart/cunning*
mordre	*to bite*
moitié (f.)	*half*
mouton (m.)	*sheep*
nez (m.)	*nose*
nourriture (f.)	*food*
oie (f.)	*goose*
oiseau (m.)	*bird*
os (m.)	*bone*
ours (m.)	*bear*
pain (m.)	*bread*
paresseux/euse	*lazy*
perdre	*to lose*
perruche (f.)	*budgie*
pied (m.)	*foot*
plage (f.)	*beach*
pleut (il)	*it is raining*
plume (f.)	*feather*
poisson (m.)	*fish*
poisson rouge (m.)	*goldfish*
polochon (m.)	*bolster*
poney (m.)	*pony*
poule (f.)	*hen*

proposer	*to offer/suggest*
raconter	*to tell*
rendre	*to return*
repas (m.)	*meal*
retrouver	*to find*
roi (m.)	*king*
serpent (m.)	*snake*
singe (m.)	*monkey*
soigner	*to mind*
souris (f.)	*mouse*
taureau (m.)	*bull*
temps (m.)	*weather*
timide	*shy*
tondre la pelouse	*to cut the grass*
torsadé(e)	*twisted/coiled*
tortue (f.)	*tortoise/turtle*
vache (f.)	*cow*
vedette (f.)	*star/celebrity*
vendre	*to sell*
vif/vive	*lively*
yeux (m. pl.) (œil sg.)	*eyes*

Épreuve

Question 1

Read the article below and answer the questions which follow.

50% La moitié des familles françaises ont un animal à la maison : poissons, oiseaux, tortues, lapins et bien sûr chats et chiens sont les animaux préférés des Français.

Il y a plus de chiens en France que d'enfants : 27 millions en tout !

1. How many families in France have pets?
2. Which of the following animals are **not** mentioned in this article:
   (a) dogs; *(b)* budgies; *(c)* rabbits; *(d)* cats. ☐
3. Which of the following statements is true?
   (a) There are 27 million children in Paris. *(b)* There are 27 million dogs in Paris.
   (c) There are 27 million dogs in France. *(d)* There are 27 million children in France. ☐

Question 2

Listen to Martin and answer the following questions in your copy.

1 What is Martin's favourite animal?
2 Why can't he have this animal as a pet?
3 What did his father buy for his birthday?
4 Where in the house does he keep his pet?
5 What pet does his sister have?
6 Name **one** thing he says about his sister's pet.

Question 3

Mots croisés ! Fill in the grid below.

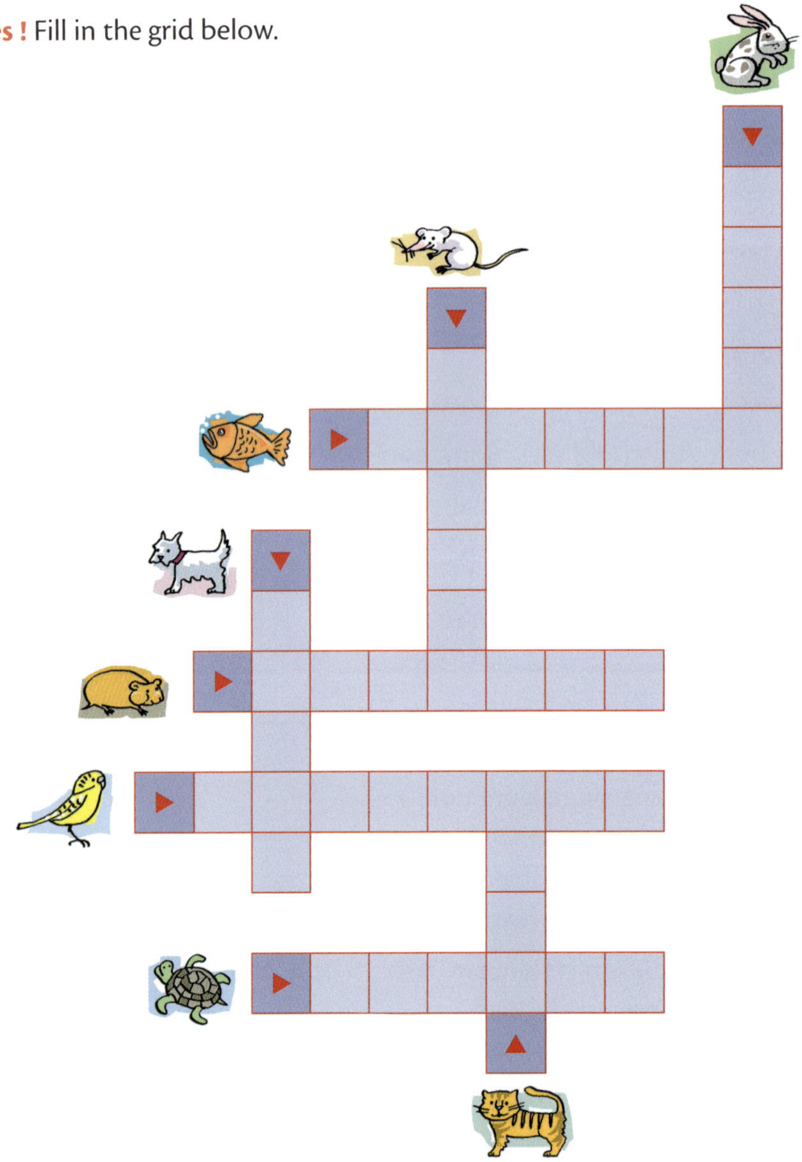

Question 4

Listen and fill in the correct form of the adjective in these sentences. (Don't forget you will not hear the letter '**s**', if the adjective is plural!)

1 Mon petit chat est vraiment (*mignon*) ________________.
2 La girafe est intelligente et (*doux*) ________________.
3 Ma tortue est très (*paresseux*) ________________.
4 Ma perruche chante quand elle est (*heureux*) ________________.
5 Les petites chèvres sont très (*actif*) ________________.
6 Le lion est un animal (*courageux*) ________________.
7 Les poissons rouges sont très (*actif*) ________________.
8 Les vaches ne sont pas (*agressif*) ________________.

For **help** with this exercise, see pages 159-160.

Question 5

Complétez les phrases suivantes comme dans l'exemple ci-dessous.

Exemple : Le chat ______ femme. → Le chat de la femme.

1 La souris __________ enfant.
2 Le cheval __________ homme.
3 Le chien __________ Pierre.
4 Le lapin __________ garçon.
5 Le poisson rouge ______ Henri.
6 Les cochons ________ fermier.
7 Les vaches ________ Catherine.
8 Le chiot ________ enfants.
9 La queue ________ chat.
10 Les ailes __________ perruche.

For **help** with this exercise, see page 170.

Question 6

Faites des paires comme dans l'exemple ci-dessous. Écrivez vos réponses dans votre cahier.

1 éléphant → (c)	(a) animal marin
2 taureau	(b) animal de basse-cour
3 alouette	(c) animal de cirque
4 poisson	(d) animal domestique
5 poulet	(e) animal de la jungle
6 singe	(f) animal de ferme
7 chat	(g) oiseau

Question 7

Listen to these people talking about animals and answer the questions.

1 **Étiennette**

Her pet: ____________________

Age: ____________________

One detail about the pet's appearance: ____________________

2 **Jean-Luc**

Number of animals he has: ____________________

His favourite animal: ____________________

Why? ____________________

3 **Jasmine**

Her job: ____________________

Animals she deals with: ____________________

Animal she doesn't like: ____________________

Question 8

Choose the correct form of the verb for each sentence.

1. Le serpent (*mord/morde/mordent*) ____________________ le petit garçon.
2. Marie (*perds/perd/perdons*) ____________________ souvent ses stylos.
3. Le fermier (*tond/tonds/tondez*) ____________________ ses moutons.
4. Mes enfants, nous (*attendons/attendez/attendent*) ____________________ le bus ici.
5. David, Julie ! Vous (*vends/vendez /vendent*) ____________________ votre chien ?
6. Les chèvres (*descends/descend/descendent*) ____________________ la montagne.

For **help** with this exercise, see page 167.

Question 9

Can you make the names of eight animals by joining the syllables from the boxes below? Write them in your copy.

che–	–afe	tor–	–ard
–reau	–tue	mou–	pou–
ser–	–let	–val	tau–
–ton	can–	gir–	–pent

Unité 7

Bon appétit !

Civilisation : À table !

- French people take great care in preparing and enjoying their food. In a recent survey (2006), 76% said they go regularly to the market to buy fresh food. Mealtimes are very important. In the evening most families try to eat together (**manger en famille**). In a French household, you will always find bread (**le pain**) on the table. Cheese, if it is on the menu, is eaten before dessert. The idea that French people regularly eat snails (**les escargots**) or frogs' legs (**les cuisses de grenouille**) is not true at all. In fact, you might only have these items on a special occasion.

- There are many traditional French dishes which come from different regions of France:
  - la bouillabaisse (*Marseille*)
  - la quiche lorraine (*Lorraine*)
  - le bœuf bourguignon (*Bourgogne*)
  - le cassoulet (*Languedoc*)
  - la salade niçoise (*Nice*)
  - les moules à la crème (*Nord-Pas de Calais*)
  - les crêpes bretonnes (*Bretagne*)
  - la choucroute (*Alsace*)

Can you find the recipes for some of these dishes ?

- Food from other countries is very popular in France. Examples of these are '**le couscous**' from North Africa, '**les nouilles**' from China or '**les pâtes**' from Italy.

Coin Prononciation : Don't forget that the letters 'd' and 't' at the end of French words are not pronounced: 'pla**t**', 'chocola**t**', 'croissan**t**', 'lai**t**', 'desser**t**', 'chau**d**', 'froi**d**', 'gran**d**', 'pren**d**'.

Civilisation : Le petit-déjeuner

- Breakfast (**le petit-déjeuner**) is very simple and no one cooks at this time. Drinks are usually served in a bowl (**le bol**) . Adults generally have coffee (**le café**) with bread (**le pain**) or '**le croissant**'. Children have a bowl of hot chocolate (**le chocolat chaud**) with bread and jam or with sweet cake-type bread (**la brioche**). Breakfast cereals were not traditionally eaten in France, but nowadays they are popular with children and adults.

7.1

Écoutons maintenant !

Faites des paires ! Link the picture of the food item to the correct word, while listening to the CD.

3 

2 

la confiture
le beurre
la tartine
le pain

4 

1 

6 

7 

le chocolat chaud
le lait
le thé
le jus d'orange

5 

8 

11 

12 

le miel
le croissant
les céréales
le sucre

9 

10 

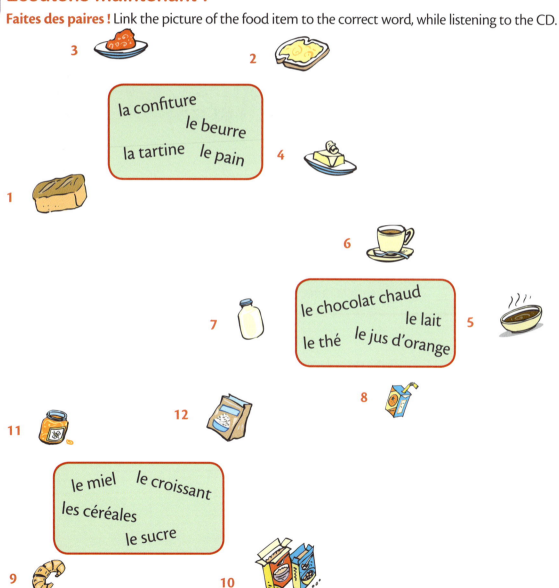

La famille Folle au petit-déjeuner !

Exercice 1

Look at the illustration above and complete the following sentences.

1	Le ________________ est dans l'évier.	4	La ________________ est sur le placard.
2	Le ________________ est dans le lave-vaisselle.	5	La ________________ est dans le micro-ondes.
3	Le ________________ est sous la table.	6	Le ____________ d'____________ est dans la cage.

7.2

Écoutons maintenant !

Qu'est-ce qu'ils mangent ? Écoutez et cochez la bonne case.

	du pain	du beurre	du miel	un croissant	du chocolat chaud	du thé	du café au lait
Luc							
Océane							
Christophe							
Sophie							
Khalid							
Léa							

Coin grammaire: The verb 'boire'

- You already know the verb '**manger**' (*to eat*). It is now useful to learn the verb '**boire**' (*to drink*). '**Boire**' is an **irregular verb**, so it must be learned '**par cœur**' (*by heart*).

Écoutons maintenant !

7.3

Listen to how the verb '**boire**' sounds.

je	bois	nous	buvons
tu	bois	vous	buvez
il	boit	ils	boivent
elle	boit	elles	boivent

Exercice 1

Use the correct form of '**boire**' to complete the following sentences.

1 Carine ___________ du lait.
2 Le matin, je ___________ du chocolat chaud.
3 Nous ne ___________ pas dans la salle de classe.
4 Ils ___________ du thé au restaurant.
5 Tu ___________ du café ?
6 Mathilde et Élodie ___________ du jus d'orange.

Civilisation : Le déjeuner

- On the whole, French children do not snack as frequently as we do. Sweets (**les bonbons**), fizzy drinks (**les boissons gazeuses**) and packets of crisps (**les chips**) are not generally eaten in school. Very few schools would have a school shop where such snacks can be bought. On the other hand, all schools have a school canteen, where a full lunch (**le déjeuner**) is available.
- Lunch is an important meal in France. Students go to the school canteen for a 3-course meal: '**une entrée, un plat principal et un dessert**'. The state pays a certain amount towards the cost of the food, so it is not expensive for students to eat a healthy school meal every day.
- In warm weather, a typical starter would be salad or '**pâté**', followed by a meat option with vegetables and fruits or yoghurt for dessert. In cold weather, soup (**la soupe**) would be on the menu as a starter, followed by a casserole, roast meat or a fish option, followed by a warm dessert of apple tart or a warm pie. Students drink lots of water (**l'eau**) and eat fresh bread (**le pain**) with their meal.
- Salad is usually eaten with fresh crusty bread, such as '**une baguette**'.

La viande

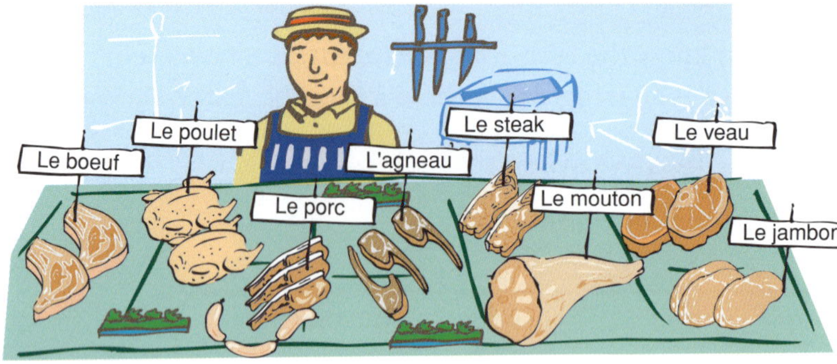

Le plat principal

- Here are some main courses from the school menu.

Lundi	*Sauté de porc*
	Cuisse de poulet
Mardi	*Escalope de dinde*
	Saumon sauce hollandaise
Mercredi	*Quiche lorraine*
	Blanquette de veau
Jeudi	*Rôti de boeuf*
	Côtelette d'agneau
Vendredi	*Poulet rôti*
	Omelette aux champignons

Exercice 1

1. On Monday, there is (*a*) pork or chicken; (*b*) pork or turkey; (*c*) pork or beef. ☐
2. On Tuesday, there is (*a*) chicken; (*b*) turkey; (*c*) duck. ☐
3. On Wednesday, which meat is on the menu? (*a*) lamb; (*b*) beef; (*c*) veal. ☐
4. What type of chops are on Thursday's menu? (*a*) pork; (*b*) lamb; (*c*) veal. ☐
5. How is the chicken on Friday cooked? (*a*) roasted; (*b*) fried; (*c*) boiled. ☐

7.4 Écoutons maintenant !

Cochez la bonne case ! Listen to these five students saying which type of meat they like and dislike. Use a ✓ for what they like and a ✘ for what they dislike.

	beef	lamb	chicken	ham	veal
Sandrine					
Raphaël					
Zoé					
Thomas					
Narissa					

Les légumes

Coin grammaire : Qu'est-ce que c'est ?

- Mathilde is shopping at the market with her mother.

- When Mathilde's mother wanted to point out or name something that was **singular** she used the little phrase '**c'est**'. When something was **plural**, she used '**ce sont**'.

Exercice 1

Fill in the blanks in these sentences using '**c'est**' or '**ce sont**'.

1 Qu'est-ce que c'est ? ______________ des tomates. 

2 Paul, qu'est-ce que c'est ? ______________ une pomme de terre. 

3 Monsieur, c'est quoi ça ? ______________ des champignons. 

4 ______________ des petits pois. 

5 ______________ un poivron vert. 

- The negative of '**c'est**' is '**ce n'est pas**'. The negative of '**ce sont**' is '**ce ne sont pas**'.

Parlons maintenant !

Faites un sondage ! En groupes de trois ou quatre élèves, posez les questions suivantes à tour de rôle. Faites un bilan des résultats.

1 Tu aimes quelle soupe ?	(*a*) la soupe aux champignons ; (*b*) la soupe à l'oignon ; (*c*) la soupe à la tomate.
2 Sur les pizzas, qu'est-ce que tu préfères ?	(*a*) les poivrons ; (*b*) les champignons ; (*c*) les oignons.
3 Avec le poulet rôti, quel légume est-ce que tu préfères ?	(*a*) les petits pois ; (*b*) le brocoli ; (*c*) les haricots verts.
4 Tu manges des pommes de terre…	(*a*) tous les jours ; (*b*) deux/trois fois par semaine ; (*c*) le dimanche ?
5 Tu n'aimes pas quel légume ?	(*a*) le chou ; (*b*) l'ail ; (*c*) le chou-fleur.

Écrivons maintenant !

(a) In your copy, write out in English the daily menus in the collège St Joseph.

Lundi
Potage à la tomate
Steak-frites
Haricots verts

Mardi
Quiche aux oignons
Omelette au fromage
Petits pois

Mercredi
Potage aux champignons
Cassoulet de porc
Carottes

Jeudi
Salade de tomates
Poulet rôti
Purée de pommes de terre

Vendredi
Carottes râpées
Agneau
Frites

(b) Write a menu in French for one day in a school canteen.

7.5

Écoutons maintenant !

Quel est ton plat préféré ? Écoutez ces deux conversations à la cantine et répondez aux questions qui suivent.

Conversation 1	Conversation 2
1 Name **one** thing Anne-Julie does not like.	1 Why is Delphine pleased with today's menu?
2 Which is Tony's favourite dish?	2 What does Fabienne not like about today's menu?
3 Why does Anne-Julie like Friday's menu?	3 What is her favourite type of soup?

Civilisation : Le goûter

- After school, French school children like to have a snack to keep them going until dinner. This is called '**le goûter**'. Usually, it is taken at home, but older students may go to the local café. At home, one might eat '**des biscuits**', '**une tartine**', '**une barre de céréales**', '**un yaourt**' or '**des fruits**'.
- On a cold day, '**un chocolat chaud**' might be a good choice of drink. Otherwise, '**un jus de fruit**' (*fruit juice*), '**de l'eau minérale**' or simply a glass of milk (**un verre de lait**) might be a good choice.

7.6 Écoutons maintenant !

Listen to the following six people describe what they have chosen for '**le goûter**' today. Can you say who chooses which snack?

Léa

Khalid

Luc

Sophie

Christophe

Océane

a.  ____________________

b.  ____________________

c.  ____________________

d.  ____________________

e.  ____________________

f.  ____________________

Exercice 1

Describe what each person had for their snack, based on the information above.

Exemple : Océane mange ____________________ et elle boit un ____________________.

Parlons maintenant !

What do you like to eat when you come home from school? Discuss with your partner.

– Est-ce que tu manges quelque chose quand tu rentres de l'école ?
– Oui, je mange/je bois …
– Non, je ne mange rien.

– Qu'est-ce que tu préfères manger après l'école ?
– Je préfère …

– Tu aimes … ?
– Oui, j'aime …
– Non, je n'aime pas/je déteste …

Civilisation : Au café

- The café plays a very important role in the life of a French teenager. It is a meeting place to chat, discuss, have a laugh or play a game of '**le baby-foot**' , '**le flipper**' (*pinball*) or sometimes '**les échecs**' . Students can go there after school, particularly on Wednesday afternoons, when they have no classes, or on Saturdays, when they are out for a day's shopping.

CAFÉ DES SPORTS

Plats		Boissons chaudes	
Pizza du jour *grande*	3,00€	Café	1,80€
petite	2,00€	Expresso	1,75€
Croque-monsieur	2,50€	Cappuccino	2,25€
Croque-madame	2,90€	Chocolat chaud	2,00€
Sandwich *jambon/beurre*	2,30€	Thé	1,80€
jambon/fromage	2,80€	Milk-shake fraise	2,00€
végétarien	2,20€	Milk-shake banane	2,00€
Frites *grande portion*	2,30€		
petite portion	1,80€		
Gaufre	1,20€		
Crêpe au sucre	1,60€	**Boissons froides**	
Crêpe au chocolat	1,80€	Eau minérale 50 cl.	1,20€
Crêpe à la confiture	1,75€	Orangina 50 cl.	1,50€
Hamburger	2,30€	Coca-cola 50 cl.	1,50€
Hot-dog	2,20€	Jus de fruits 50 cl.	1,80€

7.7 Écoutons maintenant !

Fill in the gaps in the following conversations which take place in a café.

Conversation 1

Nicolas :	J'ai faim ! Je prends un ___________ et une grande portion de ___________.
Laurie :	Moi, je préfère un sandwich au ___________. Qu'est-ce que tu vas boire ?
Nicolas :	Je voudrais un milk-shake à la ___________.
Laurie :	Oh ! Nicolas ! Tu es gourmand ! Moi, je vais prendre un jus ___________.
Nicolas :	Garçon !

Conversation 2

Manon :	Quelle journée ! Je suis fatiguée !
Luc :	Moi aussi. Je suis fatigué, et j'ai ___________ !
Manon :	Moi, j'ai soif ! Il fait ___________. Je vais prendre un ___________.
Luc :	Et moi, je voudrais une crêpe à la confiture.
Manon :	Et comme boisson ?
Luc :	Je vais prendre un ___________. Tu vas manger quelque chose ?
Manon :	Non, merci. Seulement la ___________. Garçon !

Coin grammaire : The verb 'vouloir'

- When ordering or choosing food, the verb '**vouloir**' (*to want/to wish*) is most useful. It is another irregular verb and must be learned '**par cœur**'!

7.8 Écoutons maintenant !

Listen to the '**présent**' of the verb '**vouloir**'.

je	ve**ux**
tu	ve**ux**
il	ve**ut**
elle	ve**ut**
nous	voul**ons**
vous	voul**ez**
ils	ve**ulent**
elles	ve**ulent**

Exercice 1

Remplissez la grille avec le verbe **vouloir** au présent.

je	veux
tu	
il	
elle	
nous	voulons
vous	
ils	
elles	veulent

- The '**négatif**' of '**vouloir**' is made, as usual, by putting '**ne**' in front of the verb and '**pas**' after.

Exercice 2

Faites des paires !

Exercice 3

Here are six people talking in a café. Write the sentences in your copy in the correct order.

Exemple : Je un veux hamburger. → Je veux un hamburger.

Tip: It is very useful to learn the phrase '**Je voudrais...**' (*I would like...*) at this stage. It is a form of the verb '**vouloir**' which you will learn next year.

1 crêpe une veux Tu manger ?

2 boisson une chaude voulez Vous ?

3 boire Je veux un fruits de jus.

4 veut sœur payer l'addition Ma.

5 manger Les enfants des yaourts veulent.

Parlons maintenant !

Qu'est-ce que tu dis au café ? Practise ordering the following items in a restaurant.

1 2 3 4 5 6

Exemple : **1** Je voudrais un café et une crêpe à la confiture, s'il vous plaît.

Coin grammaire : Partitive article ('l'article partitif')

- '**L'article partitif**' (*some* or *any*) is used in French when you want to indicate that there is an indefinite quantity of an item. The little bear is saying '*I eat cereal!*' but he doesn't say how much. He says '*I want jam*', but again he doesn't say how much. In English, we quite often leave out the 'some' or 'any'. It **must always be used in French**.

Exemples :	Tu prends **du** lait ?	*Do you take milk?*
	Tu veux **de la** confiture ?	*Do you want some jam?*

- '**L'article partitif**' changes in French depending on the **gender** (masculine or feminine) and **number** (singular or plural) of the noun which follows it.

Exemples :	**du**	before **masculine singular** nouns	→ Il mange **du** chocolat.
	de la	before **feminine singular** nouns	→ Elle mange **de la** confiture.
	de l'	before **singular** vowels starting with a **vowel** or **silent 'h'**	→ Tu bois **de l'**eau minérale ?
	des	before all **plural** nouns	→ Vous mangez **des** sandwichs.

Exercice 1

Remplissez les blancs avec '**du**', '**de la**', '**de l'** ' or '**des**'.

1 Tu veux _________ croissants ?
2 Amélie adore boire _________ eau minérale.
3 Paul boit _________ jus d'orange.
4 Maman veut _________ café.
5 Nous voulons _________ confiture.
6 Vous voulez _________ frites ?
7 Je prends _________ viande.
8 Ils veulent _________ oignons dans l'omelette.

Les fruits

une pomme

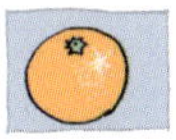
une orange

une pêche

une banane

une poire

une fraise

une framboise

une cerise

une prune

un pamplemousse

une noisette

une pistache

la menthe

le cassis

un abricot

un ananas

un citron

un melon

le raisin

Exercice 1

Can you find ten fruits in the ice cream cone?

Write them down in your copy.

Chez le glacier

- Another nice snack food is ice cream (**la glace**). Although French people do not eat as much ice cream as some countries, in 2005, €1.6 billion worth of ice cream was sold. This means that on average, each French person ate 6.3 litres of ice cream!

Quel parfum ?

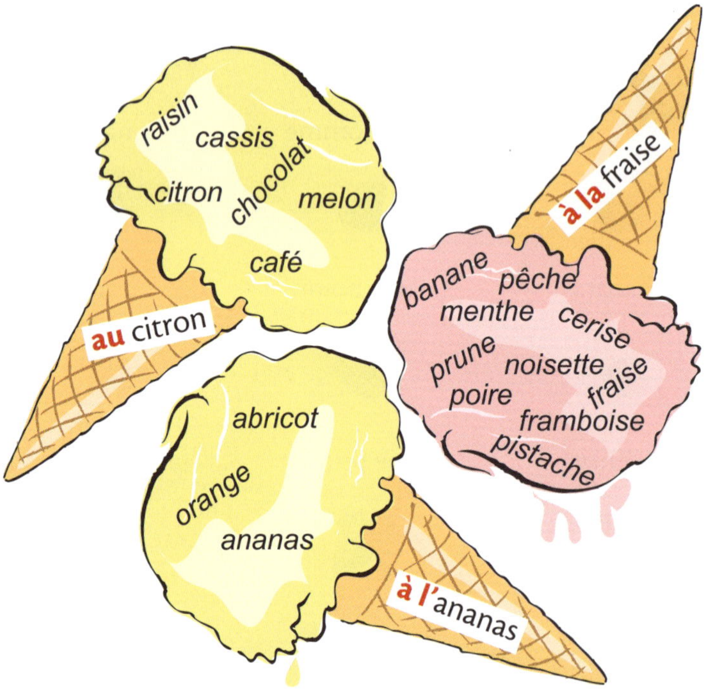

Can you see?

- If the fruit flavour is masculine, you use '**au**'.
- If the fruit flavour is feminine, you use '**à la**'.
- If the fruit flavour starts with a vowel, you use '**à l'** '.

7.9

Écoutons maintenant !

Qui parle ? Listen to these six people ordering an ice cream. Who orders which ice cream?

Exercice 1

Complétez les phrases suivantes comme dans l'exemple ci-dessous.

Exemple : Je voudrais une glace… → Je voudrais une glace à la pêche.

1 Maman veut une glace ______________________.
2 David veut une glace ______________________.
3 Elle préfère une glace ______________________.
4 Il veut une glace ______________________.
5 Céline veut une glace ______________________.
6 Tu veux une glace ______________________ ?
7 Je veux bien une glace ______________________.
8 Vous voulez une glace ______________________ ?

Parlons maintenant !

With your partner, take turns ordering ice creams of various flavours. Use the following conversation as your model.

– Tu veux une glace ?	– Oui, je veux bien.
– Quel parfum ?	– Une glace au chocolat, s'il te plaît.
– Une simple ou une double ?	– Une simple.
– Voilà.	– Merci.

Lisons maintenant !

Read the following recipe and answer the questions which follow.

Milk shake à la framboise

Préparation : 5 minutes
Niveau de difficulté : facile
Pour 4 personnes

Méthode

- Lavez les framboises et séchez-les bien.
- Mettez tous les ingrédients dans un mixeur et mélangez.
- Servez dans des verres et décorez avec un peu de menthe.

Ingrédients

- 150 g framboises
- 2 boules de glace vanille
- 2 dl de lait

1. Which fruit is used in this milk-shake?
2. What piece of kitchen equipment do you use to combine the ingredients?
3. What ice cream flavour should you use?
4. How should it be served (**one** point)?

Coin grammaire : The verb 'mettre'

- At this stage, you have learned a number of **irregular verbs**. Here is another irregular verb: '**mettre**' (*to put/to put on*). Again, this verb must be learned '**par cœur**' (*by heart*).
- The expression '**mettre le couvert**' means '*to set the table*'.

7.10

Écoutons maintenant !

Listen to how the verb '**mettre**' sounds.

je	met**s**
tu	met**s**
il	met
elle	met
nous	me**ttons**
vous	me**ttez**
ils	me**ttent**
elles	me**ttent**

Rappel ! Le négatif 'ne … pas'. Je ne mets pas de confiture dans mon yaourt. Loïc et Pierre ne mettent pas de sucre sur leurs crêpes.

Exercice 1

Remplissez la grille ci-dessous avec le verbe '**mettre**'.

je	mets
tu	
il	
elle	met
nous	
vous	mettez
ils	
elles	mettent

Mettre la table

7.11 Écoutons maintenant !

Listen to these items in French and number them in the order you hear them.

le sel et le poivre ☐

la tasse ☐

la soucoupe ☐

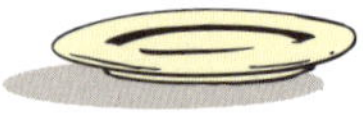
l'assiette ☐

la cuillère ☐

la serviette ☐

le couteau ☐

le verre ☐

la carafe d'eau ☐

la fourchette ☐

Exercice 2

Write six sentences about setting the table. Choose a word from each circle below.

Exemple : Je mets un verre sur la table.

7.12 Écoutons maintenant !

Listen to the following three sets of directions and draw what you hear described!

Lisons maintenant !

Look at these advertisements and answer the questions which follow.

Mugs avec cuillères

Faïence, 3 coloris assortis

14,50 €

les 6 mugs + 6 cuillères

Tasses à café

12,50 €

Verres à thé

Plusieurs motifs disponibles

2,95 € le verre

Ensemble de couverts

6 cuillères à soupe, 6 fourchettes,
6 couteaux, 6 cuillères à café

Disponible en rouge, vert et bleu : **20,00 €**

Sucriers

Plusieurs couleurs

13 x 15 cm : **12 €**

1 Apart from the mugs, what else do you get for €14.50?
2 What type of cups are available for €12.50?
3 What drink are the items at €2.95 designed to hold?
4 What should go in the containers which are priced at €12?
5 Apart from green, in what colours are the cutlery sets available?

Les quantités

- If you want to read a French recipe, you will need to know the expressions for quantities. Weight in France is expressed in '**kilos**' and liquids are measured in '**litres**'. Here are some of the most common other measurements.

a. une cuillerée à soupe

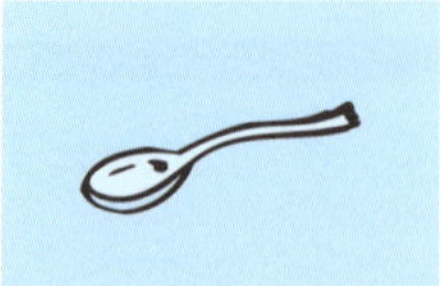

b. une cuillerée à café

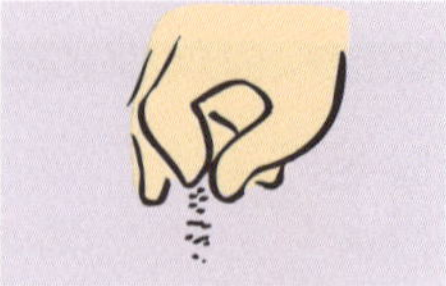

c. une pincée

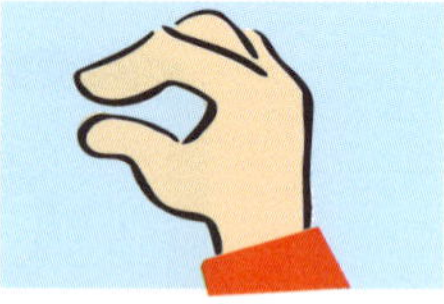

d. un peu

e. un demi-litre

f. une tasse

g. une bouteille

h. un verre

7.13 Écoutons maintenant !

Listen to these five people preparing various dishes for dinner and answer the questions.

1. How much milk does Luc's mother need?
2. How much mint is used in this recipe?
3. How much water does Joël's mother need?
4. How much salt does Julie put in this dish?
5. How much chocolate does papa need to decorate this dessert?

Civilisation : Le dîner

- The evening meal (**le dîner**) is an important part of French daily life. The family usually sits down to eat a three course dinner with a starter, a main course and a dessert. Parents might have a glass of wine with their meal. The children drink mineral water, '**l'eau minérale**'.
- Bread (**le pain**) is always on the table – it helps to mop up the nice sauces! There may be cheese after the main course and a salad. Everyone in the family helps preparing the meal or setting the table.
- For a special occasion, French families go to '**le restaurant**'. There are lots of different types of restaurants in every French town. You will find the menu outside all restaurants, with the prices clearly stated. Quite often, there is '**un plat du jour**', a special dish of the day.

Le poisson

- Fish is often on the menu in France and it is popular when people eat out. Here are some types of fish which you might find on the menu.

le saumon

la truite

le cabillaud

le merlan

les moules

les fruits de mer

le thon

les sardines

Lisons maintenant !

Read these advertisements for fish and answer the questions which follow.

Promo Poisson

Du mardi 4 au samedi 8 avril

TRUITE
Elevée en France
Pyrénées
Le kilo :
6,30 €

MAQUEREAU
Pêché en
ATLANTIQUE
NORD-EST
La pièce :
0,75 €

FILET DE CABILLAUD
Pêché en OCÉAN
PACIFIQUE ou
ATLANTIQUE NORD-EST
Le kilo :
8,90 €

FILET DE MERLAN
Pêché en ATLANTIQUE
NORD-EST
Le kilo :
10,90 €

1 Where does the mackerel come from?

2 The cost of a kilo of whiting fillets is (*a*) €8.90;
(*b*) €10.90;
(*c*) €0.75.

3 Name the **two** areas the cod comes from?

Civilisation : Le fromage

- Cheese is popular after the main course and France is famous for its cheeses. There are over 300 different cheeses! You can see some of these cheeses in the supermarket: '**brie**', '**camembert**', '**roquefort**', '**gruyère**'. Goat's cheese (**le fromage de chèvre**) is very popular in salads and it is sometimes heated under the grill.
- Cheeses are produced in different regions of France. For example, '**camembert**' cheese traditionally comes from '**Normandie**'.

Civilisation : Les desserts

- No meal would be complete without a dessert and the French are no different to us. Many of the words for desserts which we use come from the French, e.g. '**mousse**', '**profiteroles**', '**sorbet**', '**gâteau**', '**crème caramel**' or '**meringues**'.
- Quite often, on a Sunday or special day, the dessert will be bought in a cake shop (**une pâtisserie**).

- Look at these words for popular French desserts.

la salade de fruits

le yaourt

la tarte aux pommes

la tarte aux poires

la tarte au citron

le gâteau

la mousse au chocolat

la crème caramel

la crème brûlée

les crêpes

les profiteroles

les sorbets

les glaces

l'île flottante

la meringue

Lisons maintenant !

Lisez le menu de desserts ci-dessous et répondez aux questions qui suivent.

Les desserts

Mousse *(au chocolat, au citron, à l'orange, à la fraise)*	3,75€
Crème caramel	3,75€
Salade de fruits	3,50€
Tarte aux pommes *(nature, avec crème ou boule de glace)*	3,75€
Profiteroles au chocolat	4,50€
Coupe Maison *(glace cerise, chocolat noir, coulis de fruits rouges)*	5,00€
Glaces et sorbets *(deux parfums au choix : vanille, chocolat, pêche, cerise, cassis, citron)*	5,50€
Pêche Melba *(glace pêche et vanille, pêche, crème, coulis de fruits)*	5,50€

1 Mousse is available in which of the following flavours: (*a*) pineapple; (*b*) raspberry; (*c*) lemon; or (*d*) mint ? ☐

2 What can you have with your apple tart?

3 What kinds of ice cream are used in 'la Coupe Maison'?

4 If you order ice cream, you may choose how many flavours?

5 What are the **three** main ingredients of 'la Pêche Melba'?

Lisons maintenant !

Lisez cette publicité pour le '**Restaurant du Soleil**' et répondez aux questions qui suivent.

Restaurant
du Soleil
Formule d'été
1 BUFFET + PLAT
10,00 €

1 de nos Plats du Jour
+
1 Buffet au choix
(entrée ou fromages
ou desserts)

Prix net – Sans boisson

Valable pendant les mois de
juin, juillet et août

1. What choice do you have to make?
2. What is not included in this offer?
3. When is this special offer available?

Quiz !

Can you work out the foods and drinks in the quiz? Use the clues to help you.

This **L** – French word for vegetables.
This **E** – something to drink, it can be sparkling or still.
This **S** – something to eat, on a cold day as a starter to your meal.
This **R** – the fruit used to make wine.
This **E** – a French word for starter.
This **P** – a vegetable which Irish people eat a great deal of.
This **A** – a type of meat which comes from a lamb.
This **S** – used to flavour food. Too much is bad for you!

Écrivons maintenant !

(a) Lettre-symbole ! Remplacez les symboles par les mots appropriés.

Nice, le 13 novembre 2007

Cher Eoghan,

Merci de ta lettre et des photos de ta famille. J'aime bien les photos au restaurant.

Tu m'as demandé de parler un peu de la cuisine française dans cette lettre.

Le matin, pour le petit-déjeuner, je bois du  ____________ et je mange du 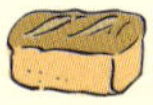 ____________ avec du beurre et de la  ____________.

À midi, je mange à la cantine. Pour commencer, il y a de la  ____________ ou de la  ____________. Comme plat principal, je préfère du  ____________ car je n'aime pas la viande. Pour le dessert, il y a normalement des  ____________, un  ____________ ou une  ____________.

Chez moi, papa et maman font la cuisine. Papa prépare le dîner le vendredi.

Il y a des  ____________ rôties et du  ____________ avec des  ____________.

Qui fait la cuisine chez toi ? Qu'est-ce que vous mangez en Irlande ? Quel est ton plat préféré ? Écris-moi bientôt avec tes réponses.

Amitiés,

Philippe

(b) Pretend you are Eoghan and write your reply to Philippe. Use the '**lettre-symbole**' above as a guide and the vocabulary you have learned in this unit.

Écrivons maintenant !

Write to a French-speaking friend, Mathieu/Mathilde, and include the following points.

- You are staying with a French family in Rennes
- The weather is very good
- You go to school and eat lunch in the canteen
- You go to the Café des Sports for a snack after classes
- You love the ice cream (mention your favourite flavour)

Communication en classe !

- Mettez le chewing-gum à la poubelle tout de suite !
- Mettez les cahiers sur ma table, s'il vous plaît !
- Mettez les papiers dans la poubelle !
- Ne mangez pas en classe !
- Ne buvez pas en classe !
- Il est interdit de boire en classe !
- Il est interdit de manger en classe !
- Allez à la cantine !

Lexique

abricot (m.)	*apricot*
addition (f.)	*bill*
agneau (m.)	*lamb*
ail (m.)	*garlic*
ananas (m.)	*pineapple*
avec	*with*
avoir faim	*to be hungry*
avoir soif	*to be thirsty*
banane (f.)	*banana*
barre de céréales (f.)	*cereal bar*
beurre (m.)	*butter*
bœuf (m.)	*beef*
boisson (f.)	*drink*
bon appétit	*enjoy your meal*
bouillabaisse (f.)	*fish stew*
bouteille (f.)	*bottle*
boule (f.)	*scoop*
brocoli (m.)	*broccoli*
côtelette (f.)	*chop*
confiture (f.)	*jam*
céréales (m. pl.)	*cereals*
cabillaud (m.)	*cod*
carotte (f.)	*carrot*
cassis (m.)	*blackcurrant*
cassoulet (m.)	*pork and bean casserole*
cerise (f.)	*cherry*
champignon (m.)	*mushroom*
chou (m.)	*cabbage*
chou-fleur (m.)	*cauliflower*
citron (m.)	*lemon*
crème brûlée (f.)	*baked cream custard*
crêpe (f.)	*pancake*
croque-madame (m.)	*toasted ham, egg and cheese sandwich*
croque-monsieur (m.)	*toasted ham and cheese sandwich*
crudités (f. pl.)	*raw salad vegetables*
dessert (m.)	*dessert*
dinde (f.)	*turkey*
disponible	*available*

eau minérale (f.)	*mineral water*
entrée (f.)	*starter*
farine (f.)	*flour*
fraise (f.)	*strawberry*
framboise (f.)	*raspberry*
frites (f. pl.)	*chips*
fromage (m.)	*cheese*
fruits de mer (m. pl.)	*seafood*
gâteau (m.)	*cake*
gaufre (f.)	*waffle*
goûter	*to taste*
haricots verts (m.pl.)	*French beans*
hors d'œuvre (m.)	*starter*
jambon (m.)	*ham*
jus (m.)	*juice*
lait (m.)	*milk*
laitue (f.)	*lettuce*
légume (m.)	*vegetable*
maquereau (m.)	*mackerel*
marché (m.)	*market*
melon (m.)	*melon*
menthe (f.)	*mint*
merlan (m.)	*whiting*
midi (m.)	*midday*
miel (m.)	*honey*
moules (f. pl.)	*mussels*
mouton m.)	*mutton*
nape (f.)	*table-cloth*
noisette (f.)	*hazelnut*
nouilles (f. pl.)	*noodles*
œuf (m.)	*egg*
oignon (m.)	*onion*
orange (f.)	*orange*
pamplemousse (m.)	*grapefruit*
parfum (m.)	*flavour*
pâté (m.)	*pâté*
plat du jour (m.)	*dish of the day*
pâtes (f. pl.)	*pasta*
pêche (f.)	*peach*
petits pois (m. pl.)	*peas*
peu de (m.)	*little of*
pincée (f.)	*pinch*
pistache (f.)	*pistachio nut*
plat principal (m.)	*main course*
poire (f.)	*pear*
poisson (m.)	*fish*
poivre (m.)	*pepper*
porc (m.)	*pork*
poivron (m.)	*pepper (fruit)*
pomme de terre (f.)	*potato*
pomme (f.)	*apple*
potage (m.)	*vegetable soup*
poulet (m.)	*chicken*
prune (f.)	*plum*
quiche (f.)	*savoury quiche*
raisin (m.)	*grape*
recette (f.)	*recipe*
riz (m.)	*rice*
rôti (m.)	*roast*
salade de fruits (f.)	*fruit salad*
sans	*without*
saumon (m.)	*salmon*
sel (m.)	*salt*
sucre (m.)	*sugar*
tartine (f.)	*slice of bread*
thon (m.)	*tuna*
tomate (f.)	*tomato*
tranche (f.)	*slice*
truite (f.)	*trout*
valable	*valid*
veau (m.)	*veal*
viande (f.)	*meat*
yaourt (m.)	*yoghurt*

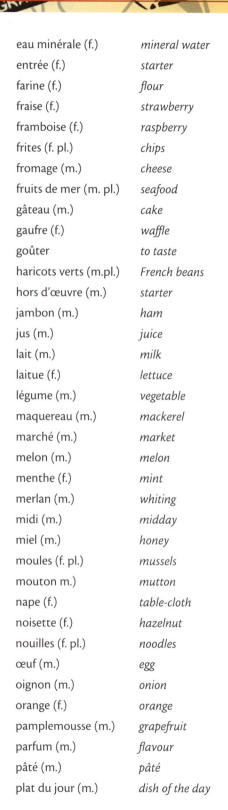

Épreuve

Question 1

(a) Write out what Delphine has for breakfast.

(b) Write out what Marc has for Saturday lunch.

Question 2

Can you find these words for crockery and cutlery?

Q	K	D	X	C	Q	E	R	E	W	U	K	I	A	F
A	S	C	I	I	M	R	H	D	P	Z	V	S	Q	G
N	T	E	N	O	F	R	T	L	T	P	S	B	I	T
F	O	U	R	C	H	E	T	T	E	I	A	X	P	U
J	J	U	V	V	N	V	K	M	E	O	D	N	G	C
W	Z	P	B	F	I	R	J	T	H	B	U	K	G	U
G	F	J	Y	Q	Z	E	T	K	C	U	C	W	O	I
W	J	Q	X	E	Q	E	T	J	D	L	J	F	W	L
P	C	S	Q	X	P	W	K	T	G	A	P	M	L	L
H	I	P	F	Y	Z	E	B	W	E	A	Y	Q	T	E
T	T	F	I	H	Q	L	F	B	E	K	V	F	C	R
T	N	W	A	M	E	W	P	K	T	N	V	I	I	E
X	Q	I	H	D	R	G	V	L	C	L	I	N	F	P
M	L	U	A	E	T	U	O	C	T	O	I	E	B	G
T	N	G	G	W	X	B	G	E	T	O	Q	D	W	Q

ASSIETTE
CUILLERE
SERVIETTE
BOL
FOURCHETTE
VERRE
COUTEAU
NAPPE

Question 3

Plats préférés ! Read this article and answer the questions which follow.

- Selon un sondage en janvier 2006, les Français continuent à aimer les plats traditionnels. Voici les résultats :

1 la blanquette de veau 

2 le couscous 

3 les moules-frites 

4 la côte de bœuf 

5 le bœuf bourguignon 

6 le gigot d'agneau 

- Et leurs desserts préférés ? En tête, on trouve :

1 la salade de fruits 

2 l'île flottante 

3 la tarte tatin 

4 la mousse au chocolat 

5 les profiteroles 

- Un autre fait intéressant : les Français préfèrent la cuisine française (77%). 7% des Français aiment la cuisine italienne et 5% la cuisine chinoise.

1 In what month was this survey carried out?
2 What did the survey reveal about the French attitudes to traditional foods?
3 What type of meat is used in the most popular dish?
4 What type of dessert is the most popular?
5 Apart from French food, what type of cooking comes next?

Question 4

Listen to Sylvie, Marie-Claire and Ali speaking about what they like to eat and answer the following questions.

Sylvie

1 What type of cooking is her favourite?
2 Name **two** ingredients in her favourite salad.
3 What is her favourite dessert?

Marie-Claire

1 Name **two** fruits she likes.
2 Which of the following ingredients is in cassoulet?
   (a) beans;
   (b) peas; ☐
   (c) carrots;
   (d) potatoes.
3 What is her favourite snack food.

Ali

1 Name **one** fast food he likes?
2 Apart from oranges, which fruit does he like?
3 What is his favourite dessert?

Question 5

Change the verbs in brackets into their correct form.

1 Je (*boire*) ________ du jus de pamplemousse.
2 Sophie (*mettre*) ________ la table.
3 Louis et Charles (*vouloir*) ________ un coca.
4 Nous (*boire*) ne ________ pas d'alcool.
5 Vous (*mettre*) ________ les verres ici.
6 Lucie (*vouloir*) ________ du lait.
7 Je (*mettre*) ________ de la confiture sur mon pain.
8 Tu (*boire*) ________ du thé ?
9 Elles (*mettre*) ________ les tasses dans le placard.
10 Nous (*vouloir*) ________ une glace.

For **help** with this exercise, see pages 187, 194 and 201.

Question 6

Lisez la recette suivante pour le croque-monsieur et répondez aux questions qui suivent.

Le croque-monsieur

Ingrédients

- 4 tranches de pain
- 4 tranches de jambon
- 100g de fromage (gruyère)
- sel, poivre
- mayonnaise

Instructions

- Tartiner chaque tranche de pain avec la mayonnaise.
- Poser 1 tranche de jambon, du sel, du poivre sur chaque tranche de pain.
- Couvrir chaque tranche avec une tranche de fromage.
- Mettre les croque-monsieur dix minutes dans un four assez chaud.

1 Which of the following ingredients is **not** included in this recipe?
(*a*) bread; (*b*) cheese; (*c*) salami; (*d*) salt. ☐
2 Besides pepper, what other seasoning is used?
3 For how long do you cook the croque-monsieur?

Question 7

This is a recipe for a '**salade de carottes à l'orange**', which is being given out on a local radio station. Listen and fill in the gaps with the correct ingredients.

You need: ____________ carrots; 2 ____________; 1 ____________ of olive oil; juice of half a ____________; 4 leaves of ____________ and 1 ____________ of salt.

Question 8

For **help** with this exercise, see page 189.

Can you name these items? Don't forget to use the correct form of '**c'est**' or '**ce sont**'!

1  ________

2  ________

3  ________

4  ________

5  ________

6  ________

7  ________

8  ________

Question 9

Read this recipe and answer the questions which follow.

Les crêpes

Pour 24 crêpes environ

- 250 g de farine de froment
- 4 œufs
- 175 g de sucre
- 3 sachets de sucre vanillé
- ¾ l. de lait frais
- environ 50g de beurre demi-sel pour la cuisson
- 1 pincée de sel
- 4 cuillerées à soupe d'huile

Préparation : quinze minutes

1 How long does it take to prepare this recipe?

2 Tick the ingredients which are needed for this recipe.

flour		**butter**	
porridge oats		**sugar**	
eggs		**salt**	
water		**pepper**	
milk		**cream**	

Question 10

Carte postale ! You are on holidays in France in '**Provence**' with your family. Write a postcard to your French-speaking friend Nikki including the following information.

- You are on holidays with your family
- The weather is fine and sunny
- You are having a good time (**s'amuser**)
- Mention some French foods which you love
- Mention **one** food you don't like

Question 11

Listen to these announcements in a supermarket about their special offers for this week and answer the questions.

1. Name **one** of the flavours in which the lasagne is available.
2. How many slices of ham are available for €3.30?
3. What price is the packet of turkey slices?
4. Name **one** type of fish available in the product called **L'Assiette Bleue**.
5. What type of grapes are on offer?

Unité 8

Mon quartier

Civilisation : Le marché

- French people are interested in the food they eat and in buying fresh food. In recent years, many people have been growing organic food products (**les produits biologiques**). Nearly every town and village in France has a market. Some of these are held every day. In smaller towns, the market is held once or twice a week. Besides fruits and vegetables, fish, poultry, eggs, cheeses, honey, olive oils, fruit juices and flowers may be on sale.

Lisons maintenant !

Read the following dialogues and decide who owns which stall.

1 Bonjour ! Je m'appelle Jean Bonnet. J'achète mes produits aux fermiers de la région. Mes clients aiment les petits pois, les choux-fleurs et les champignons frais.

2 Bonjour ! Je suis Marguerite Rocher. Mes frères élèvent des canards, des poulets et des oies. Nous avons aussi des œufs. J'adore venir au marché.

3 Bonjour, Je m'appelle Jean-François Ménard. J'achète mes poissons et fruits de mer aux pêcheurs du port de Brest. Le produit le plus populaire ? Les moules !

4 Bonjour ! Je m'appelle Joséphine Plessis. Je viens sur ce marché pour vendre le lait des vaches et des chèvres. Les clients aiment bien les fromages biologiques.

5 Bonjour ! Moi, je suis Isabelle Fournier. Je viens sur ce marché le week-end. En général, mes bouquets viennent d'un horticulteur de la région.

Exercice 1

Quel marchand ? Here is a list of goods. Which stall holder would you go to in order to buy each item?

1 kilo de carottes	→	Je vais chez le marchand de ________________.
1 morceau de brie	→	Je vais chez le marchand de ________________.
1 crabe	→	Je vais chez le marchand de ________________.
6 œufs	→	Je vais chez le marchand de ________________.
1 dizaine de roses	→	Je vais chez le marchand de ________________.
1 saumon	→	Je vais chez le marchand de ________________.
6 poires	→	Je vais chez le marchand de ________________.
2 cuisses de canard	→	Je vais chez le marchand de ________________.

Coin grammaire : The verb 'venir'

- When the stall holders were talking about the market (see page 218), they used '**viens**' and '**viennent**'. These are parts of '**le présent**' (*present tense*) of the verb '**venir**' (*to come*). It is an irregular verb and so you need to learn it '**par cœur**' (*by heart*).

8.1

Écoutons maintenant !

Look and listen to the verb '**venir**'.

je	vi**ens**
tu	vi**ens**
il	vi**ent**
elle	vi**ent**
nous	ven**ons**
vous	ven**ez**
ils	vi**ennent**
elles	vi**ennent**

Exercice 1

Can you complete these sentences by using the correct part of the verb '**venir**'?

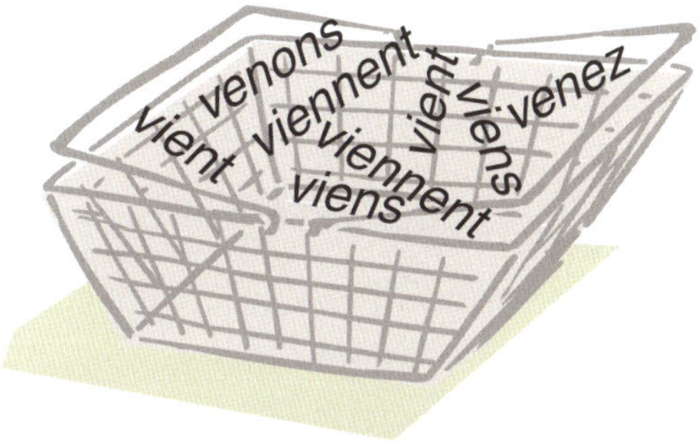

1. Il ________________ de Nice.
2. Je ________________ de Lille.
3. Nous ________________ de Rennes.
4. Elles ________________ de Toulouse.
5. Tu ________________ de Nantes.
6. Elle ________________ de Strasbourg.
7. Vous ________________ de Perpignan.
8. Ils ________________ de Dijon.

Encore des nombres !

- You have already learned numbers as far as **60** (see **Unités 2** and **4**). Now that you are going shopping, it is time to move on to some bigger numbers. As the numbers get larger in French, they vary a little in the pattern you learned until now.

8.2

Écoutons maintenant !

Listen and look at the numbers from **60** to **80**.

soixante	**60**		
soixante et un	**61**	**soixante et onze**	**71**
soixante-deux	**62**	**soixante-douze**	**72**
soixante-trois	**63**	**soixante-treize**	**73**
soixante-quatre	**64**	**soixante-quatorze**	**74**
soixante-cinq	**65**	**soixante-quinze**	**75**
soixante-six	**66**	**soixante-seize**	**76**
soixante-sept	**67**	**soixante-dix-sept**	**77**
soixante-huit	**68**	**soixante-dix-huit**	**78**
soixante-neuf	**69**	**soixante-dix-neuf**	**79**
soixante-dix	**70**	**quatre-vingts**	**80**

- As you can see, there is no word for **70** in French. You say *'60-10'*.
- Nor is there any word for **80**. You say *'four twenties'*!

Exercice 1

Write the following numbers in French in your copy.

61 – 63 – 67 – 70 – 71 – 74 – 76 – 80

Coin Prononciation : The letters 'er' at the end of a French word are pronounced like 'aye': 'laiti**er**', 'fermi**er**', 'épici**er**', 'boulang**er**'. The letters 'ère' at the end of a French word are pronounced like 'air': 'laiti**ère**', 'fermi**ère**', 'épici**ère**', 'boulang**ère**'.

La monnaie

- '**L'argent**' is the French word for money. It comes from the Latin word for silver, 'argentum'. France is a member of the European Union, so French people use the Euro as we do. However, because the word for 100 is '**cent**', they use '**centimes**' when they want to talk about cents. Money comes in '**billets**' (*notes*) and '**pièces**' (*coins*). '**La monnaie**' is the word for small change.

Exercice 1

Reliez les bulles avec les images ! These six people have been clearing out their pockets and find the following amounts of small change. Can you work out who has which amount of money?

Marc

Valérie

Manon

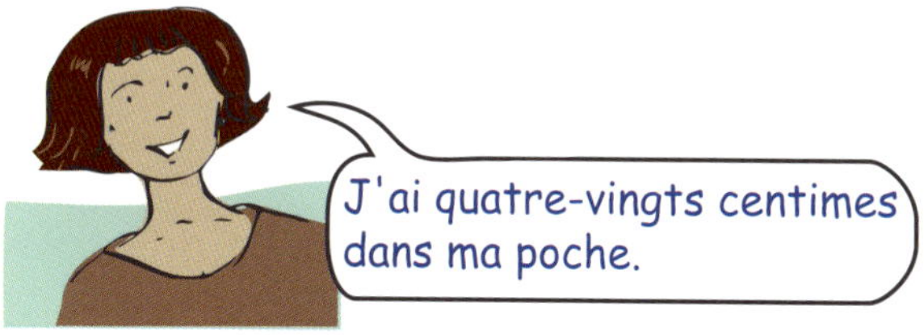

Lucie

Richard

Philippe

(a)  ________

(b)  ________

(c)  ________

(d)  ________

(e)  ________

(f)  ________

8.3

Écoutons maintenant !

Listen to these five people buying items at the market. How much does each person spend?

1 ________ 2 ________ 3 ________ 4 ________ 5 ________

GRAMMAIRE

Les quantités

- Like most European countries, France uses the **metric system** for weights and measures. '**Kilos**' and '**grammes**' are used for weight, while '**litres**' are used for liquids.

- Some other **useful measures** are:

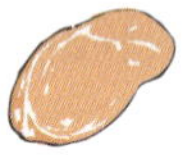

une tranche de...

un paquet de...

un pot de...

une livre de...

une tête de...

une boîte de...

un morceau de...

une demi-douzaine de...

- When using expressions of quantity such as these, notice that they are always followed by '**de**'.

Exemples : un morceau **de** fromage ; un paquet **de** biscuits ; 250 g **de** cerises.

- If the noun which follows the expression of quantity begins with a vowel or silent '**h**', '**de**' is shortened to '**d'** '.

Exemples : un kilo **d'**oignons ; 50 grammes **d'**herbes de Provence.

8.4

Écoutons maintenant !

Listen to these four people at the market buying items. Can you say how much of each item they buy?

1 ______________ chou
______________ pommes de terre

2 ______________ œufs
______________ pâté de canard

3 ______________ de yaourt
______________ fromage de chèvre

4 ______________ jus de pomme
______________ huile d'olive

Parlons maintenant !

You and your partner can take turns being the customer and the stall holder. Ask the price of the following items and give the answer.

Exemple **:** – Combien coûtent les tomates ? – Les tomates coûtent 2,60 € le kilo.

2,60 €
le kilo

1		______________	1,20 € le demi-kilo
2		______________	6,50 € la pièce
3		______________	1,50 € la pièce
4		______________	10,75 € le kilo
5		______________	3,50 € le pot
6		______________	3,60 € le kilo
7		______________	2,80 € le kilo
8		______________	5,00 € la douzaine

Civilisation : Les magasins du quartier

- As well as going to the market, French people often use their local shops for everyday shopping. Shops open early in the morning, in particular the baker, who may be open from 6.30am to bring fresh bread to the customers. Most shops in France do not open on Sundays. A small number, which provide essential items, open for a short time on Sunday mornings.

La boulangerie

- You are all probably familiar with the French baguette, as it is available in many shops in Ireland. The word 'baguette' actually means the leg of a chair! There is a narrower bread stick, '**une ficelle**', which means a piece of string.

Lisons maintenant !

Read what each person says to the baker and join them with the correct shopping basket.

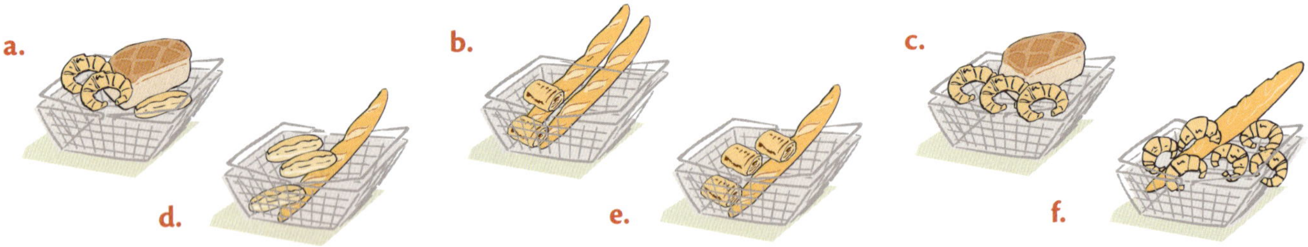

La boucherie

8.5

Écoutons maintenant !

Remplissez les blancs ! Fill in the gaps in the following conversation between Mme Roux and Monsieur Lebœuf, '**le boucher**' (*the butcher*).

Boucher :	Bonjour, Madame Roux. Je peux vous aider ?
Mme Roux :	Bonjour, Monsieur Lebœuf. Un kilo de __________ haché, s'il vous plaît.
Boucher :	Bien. Un ______________ de steak haché. C'est tout, Madame Roux ?
Mme Roux :	Non. Je veux de la viande pour ce week-end. Un gigot ______________, je crois.
Boucher :	Le gigot d'agneau est bon, Madame. Mais j'ai aussi du ______________. Il est excellent en ce moment.
Mme Roux :	Mmm… du veau... Vous avez des ______________ ?
Boucher :	Oui. Les voilà. Vous en voulez combien ?
Mme Roux :	__________, s'il vous plaît. Elles sont grandes.
Boucher :	Un kilo de steak haché, 7,50 € et quatre escalopes de veau, __________. Ça fait 15,70 €, s'il vous plaît.
Mme Roux :	Voilà, Monsieur Lebœuf : 20,00 €.
Boucher :	Et voilà votre __________ : 4,30 €.

L'épicerie

- '**L'épicerie**' is the local grocery shop. It is useful when you want to buy small amounts of food or do not want the hassle of going to the big supermarket. In a small town, customers are known to the shopkeeper (**l'épicier**/**l'épicière**) and they might feel they are getting a more personal service.

8.6

Écoutons maintenant !

Nounours range les rayons ! Nounours is working on Saturdays in his local corner shop. He is supposed to stock the shelves. He must put the following items on the correct shelf. Can you help him? Listen and put the correct word on the space provided on the shelves.

For this exercise you need to learn some new prepositions:

sous	Les oignons sont **sous** les carottes.	*The onions are under the carrots.*
à côté du/de la/des	Les bananes sont **à côté des** poires.	*The bananas are beside the pears.*
au-dessus du/de la/des	Les ananas sont **au-dessus des** pommes.	*The pineapples are above the apples.*

la farine

le sucre

le thé

le thon

les chips

la confiture

le beurre

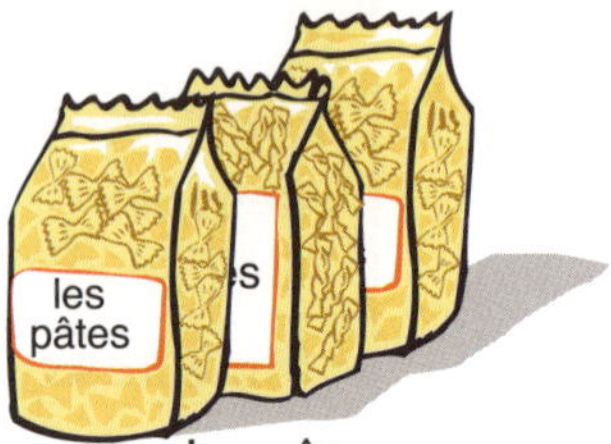

les pâtes

La charcuterie

- '**La charcuterie**' in France is where you go to buy prepared meals, cold meats and salads. If you can solve the following exercise, you will find a list of items which you can buy in a '**charcuterie**'.

Exercice 1

Cherchez l'intrus ! Find the odd item in the following lists.

1 *(a)* une quiche ; *(b)* un bifteck ; *(c)* une côtelette de porc ; *(d)* un gigot d'agneau.

2 *(a)* des courgettes ; *(b)* du pâté ; *(c)* des petits pois ; *(d)* des haricots verts.

3 *(a)* des pommes ; *(b)* du jambon cuit ; *(c)* des poires ; *(d)* des ananas.

4 *(a)* des éclairs ; *(b)* des profiteroles ; *(c)* un gâteau au chocolat ; *(d)* une terrine de saumon.

5 *(a)* du saucisson ; *(b)* du sucre ; *(c)* du lait ; *(d)* du thé.

6 *(a)* une salade de fruits ; *(b)* une mousse au citron ; *(c)* une salade de riz au crabe ; (d) une tarte aux pommes.

7 *(a)* des pommes de terre ; *(b)* une salade de carottes ; *(c)* des petits pois ; *(d)* un chou-fleur.

8 *(a)* une tarte au citron ; *(b)* une tarte aux poires ; *(c)* une tarte au fromage de chèvre ; *(d)* une tarte aux pommes.

Lisons maintenant !

Look at these items and answer the questions which follow.

Promo

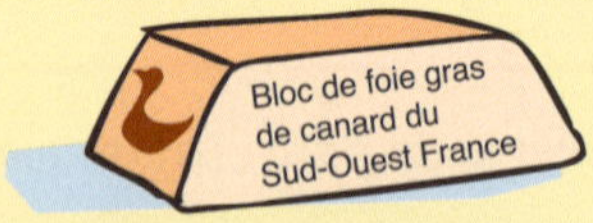

Produit de France.
300g minimum
8,90 €

La plaque de 8 tranches.
300g minimum
8,99 €

Produit de France.
Le pot de 300g
0,99 €

La barquette de 2 tranches (soit 100g).
Produit de France, préparé à partir de viande de veau en provenance des pays de l'UE
1,67 €

Le plat cuisiné pour une personne = 300g
Origine France
3,50 €

La pièce de 300g
+ 10% gratuit = 330g
Produit de France
4,75 €

1 This item comes from Scotland. ____________
2 This item is designed for one person. ____________
3 This item gives you a bonus 10% extra. ____________
4 This item comes in 2-slice packs. ____________
5 This item is from South-West France. ____________

8.7

La pâtisserie

Écoutons maintenant !

Listen to these people talking about which type of cake they like and which they do not like. Tick the boxes as follows: if the person likes the cake, put a tick ✓. If they don't like it, put a cross ✘.

	les tartes aux pommes	le gâteau au chocolat	la tarte au citron	les madeleines	le gâteau aux fruits de la forêt	les éclairs
Solène						
Hervé						
Erwan						
Guy						
Yvette						

Le supermarché

- Besides shopping in small local shops, French people visit large supermarkets to do their weekly shopping. These are usually situated on the outskirts of towns. A hypermarket is known as '**une grande surface**' and can be part of a shopping centre (**le centre commercial**).

Dans le supermarché SuperPro !

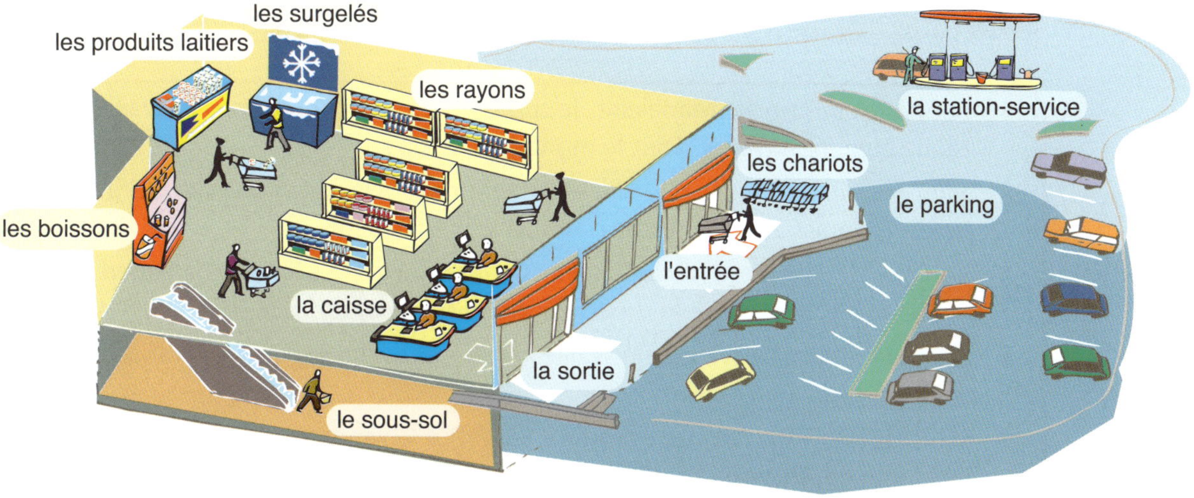

8.8 Écoutons maintenant !

Faites des paires ! Listen to these words and link them to the item mentioned. The first one is done for you.

1 *les surgelés*
2 *le parking*
3 *les produits laitiers*
4 *les boissons*
5 *le chariot*
6 *la caisse*
7 *l'entrée*
8 *la sortie*
9 *les rayons*
10 *le sous-sol*

1

Lisons maintenant !

Read about five people who work at '**SuperPro**'. Write their names under their place of work.

1 Bonjour. Je m'appelle Madeleine. Je suis employée de SuperPro. Je travaille à la caisse. J'aime bien mon travail. Tout le monde est sympa.

2 Salut ! Je suis Jérôme. Je travaille le samedi matin à la station service de SuperPro. Je suis pompiste. Je n'aime pas travailler quand il pleut.

3 Bonjour ! Je m'appelle Michel du Plessis. Je travaille tous les jours à SuperPro. Je suis vigile. Je surveille le supermarché. Je suis toujours à la sortie du magasin.

4 Salut ! Je m'appelle Sylvie. Je travaille le week-end ici à SuperPro. Je range les produits sur les rayons. Le travail est ennuyeux.

5 Salut ! Je suis Tony. Moi, je travaille à SuperPro le vendredi soir et le samedi. C'est moi qui surveille les chariots. Je les range près de l'entrée.

Lisons maintenant !

Read these special offers and answer the questions which follow.

100% jus de fruits pressés, orange ou pomme.
Le carton de 1 litre = 1,15 litres :
2,45 €

Spécialité au soja 100% végétal aux parfums de fruits (ananas, pêche, abricot) ou au chocolat.
Le lot de 4 pots de 100g :
1,59 €

Le lot de 6 pots :
2,99 €

Œufs datés du jour de ponte.
Le plateau de vingt œufs :
3,49 €

La boîte de dix steaks :
6,15 €

1. What flavours are available in the fruit juice offer?
2. The yogurts are available in which of these flavours? (circle your answer)
   (a) Strawberry; *(b)* Raspberry; *(c)* Pineapple.
3. What do you get for €2.99?
4. What gift do you get with the tray of eggs?
5. How many burgers are in the pack?

Lisons maintenant !

Read these two receipts and answer the questions which follow.

carrefour
Rennes
Tél. : 02. 99. 08. 24. 13

GLACE	4,50
PETITS POIS	3,75
AGNEAU	5,30
CITRONS	1,25
STEAK HACHÉS SURGELÉS	4,90

Auchan
Le Val d'Europe
Tél. : 01. 89. 56. 76. 23

LAIT	2,75
PAIN	1,85
POIRES	3,60
CAMEMBERT	2,90

1 Name **two** frozen products the customer bought in Carrefour?
2 What type of meat was bought in Carrefour?
3 Which of the following items was **not** bought in Auchan? ☐
(a) bread; *(b)* pears; *(c)* apples; *(d)* cheese.

8.9 Écoutons maintenant !

Listen to these special offers and fill in the details in the grid.

	shelf	product	quantity	price
annonce 1				
annonce 2				
annonce 3				
annonce 4				
annonce 5				

Coin grammaire : The future ('le futur proche')

GRAMMAIRE

- So far, you have learned about '**le présent**' (*present tense*) of verbs. Sometimes, you want to be able to say what you are going to do in the future. In order to do this, you can use '**le futur proche**'. It is not too difficult to do this.
- Read the following sentences and then look at their translation in English.

Je **vais** manger dans un restaurant.	*I am going to eat in a restaurant.*
Il **va** acheter des tomates.	*He is going to buy tomatoes.*
Nous **allons** boire une boisson froide.	*We are going to drink a cold drink.*
Ils **vont** parler au professeur.	*They are going to speak to the teacher.*

- Can you see that, in English, you use the verb 'to go' to make these sentences? The same pattern happens in French.

Formation

- To make '**le futur proche**', you use '**le présent**' of the verb '**aller**' + '**l'infinitif**' of the verb you need to use.

Exemples : Je **vais** + mang**er** une quiche.
Tu **vas** + fini**r** à quelle heure ?
Elles **vont** + vend**re** la maison.

Rappel ! '**L'infinitif**' is the part of the verb you find in your '**dictionnaire**' or '**lexique**'. Find the verb '**aller**' on page 73.

Useful phrases to talk about the future

ce soir	*this evening*	demain soir	*tomorrow evening*	la semaine prochaine	*next week*
demain	*tomorrow*	plus tard	*later on*	le week-end prochain	*next weekend*

Exercice 1

Can you complete these sentences and say what they mean in English? Write them out in your copy.

Exemple : manger : Je **vais** mang**er** à la maison dimanche.

1 travailler : Je __________ __________ au supermarché samedi.
2 venir : Il __________ __________ à Dublin ce soir.
3 rester : Elle __________ __________ chez ses parents.
4 visiter : Nous __________ __________ le zoo le week-end prochain.
5 voir : Vous __________ __________ un bon film demain soir.
6 choisir : Les parents __________ __________ un gâteau pour Suzanne.
7 organiser : Tu __________ __________ une excursion pour la semaine prochaine ?
8 être : Je __________ __________ à Paris plus tard.

Civilisation: Le restaurant

 Nearly every town and village in France has a local restaurant or café where families eat out for special occasions. Many local restaurants are small, family-run businesses. They offer local dishes at very good prices. This means that eating out tends to be cheaper than in Ireland.

Dîner au restaurant

• When booking a table, you are asked for your name which you need to be able to spell.

Écoutons maintenant!

Écoutez et répétez les lettres de l'alphabet en français.

Rappel! You have learned the French alphabet in Unité 1 (see page 14). Listen to it again to remind yourself of how it sounds.

abcdefghijklmnopqrstuvwxyz.

• In Amélie's neighbourhood, there are some restaurants where the family go for special occasions such as birthdays, holidays and other celebrations.

Écoutons maintenant!

Amélie is organising a meal in the local restaurant to celebrate her mother's birthday. Listen to her conversation and fill in the details in the grid below.

	détails
Table for how many?	
Day and date?	
Time?	
Family name?	

Écoutons maintenant!

Here are five people making bookings for meals in the restaurant. Write the name of each family in your copy.

Commander un repas (Ordering a meal)

Je suis votre serveur pour ce soir.
Et je suis votre serveuse.

Vous désirez ?
Je vais prendre ...

♦ This is how the waiter/waitress asks you if you are ready to order.

Pour commencer ? Comme entrée ?
Pour commencer/ Comme entrée, je vais prendre ...

♦ Here you are asked what you would like as a starter.

Et comme plat principal ? Et avec ça ?
Comme plat principal, le bœuf. Une salade verte/des frites/ des haricots verts...

♦ Next comes your main course.

Pour le dessert ?
Une île flottante/ une tarte tatin/ une salade de fruits. Je vais prendre du fromage.

♦ You might like to order a dessert.

Et comme boisson ?
De l'eau minérale, s'il vous plaît. Du vin rouge/blanc, s'il vous plaît.

♦ Finally, the waiter needs to know what you would like to drink.

8.13

Écoutons maintenant !

Marcel is dining out and gives his order to the waiter. Listen to this conversation and write in your copy what Marcel is going to eat.

Exercice 1

Faites des paires! Amélie is in the restaurant for the family dinner. She is ordering her food. Here are the phrases she uses. Match the beginning of the phrase with the correct ending.

- 1 Pour commencer...
- 2 Ensuite, comme plat principal...
- 3 Et avec ça, je voudrais...
- 4 Comme dessert...
- 5 Comme boisson, je voudrais...
- (a) une carafe d'eau.
- (b) une mousse au chocolat.
- (c) le poulet rôti.
- (d) des frites.
- (e) je vais prendre le pâté maison.

Parlons maintenant!

With your partner, take turns at being the waiter/waitress and customer. You can use the phrases above and the menu in the next exercise.

Lisons maintenant!

Here are the menus for each day at **Le Restaurant Marcel** (they are closed on Mondays). Read the menus and then tick the box for the day that each food is on the menu.

Mardi Salade de tomates Rosbif carottes Glace van<u>ille/fraise/cassis</u> Mercredi Œufs mayonnaise Poulet Normandie Crème caramel Jeudi Soupe à l'oignon Gigot d'agneau Tarte aux pommes

Vendredi Pâté de campagne Omelette aux champignons Gâteau au chocolat Samedi Crudités Côtelettes de porc Forêt noire Dimanche Quiche au jambon Escalope de veau Mousse au citron

	Tuesday	Wednesday	Thursday	Friday	Saturday	Sunday
pork chops						
onion soup						
veal						
raw vegetables						
chicken						
ice cream						
mushrooms						
lamb						
apple tart						
lemon mousse

Lisons maintenant !

Les restaurants ! You are on holidays and you want to eat in one of these restaurants.

1

LA RASCASSE

BAR - BRASSERIE - RESTAURANT

Fruits de mer et poissons
Glaces faites maison
Salle de restaurant avec terrasse
72, av. de la mer
Tél. : 02. 13. 78. 41. 53

2

Le Miramar

Restaurant – Bar – Brasserie

Spécialités :
homards, langoustines
61, rue de la gare maritime
Tél. : 02. 13. 96. 77. 78

3

La Marine

Spécialité de moules à la normande

Desserts faits maison
Ouvert tous les jours
à toute heure
45, rue de la plage
Tél. : 02. 13. 22. 61. 97

4

Hôtel-Restaurant de la Mer

Vue panoramique
sur le port et la mer
Spécialités de poissons
et de fruits de mer
Crêpes savoureuses/sucrées
Pizzas sur place ou à emporter
5, rue de la Libération
Tél. : 02. 13. 98. 76. 22

5

Le Channel

Hôte-Restaurant

Spécialités : poissons, crabes, langoustines
Nouveau : salon privé (20 personnes)
Ouvert 7 jours sur 7
43, av. de la mer
Tél. : 02. 13. 17. 18. 43

6

Le Corsaire

Restaurant traditionnel
Soupe de poissons
Fruits de mer
Carte variée
17, av. du port
Tél. : 02. 13. 10. 69. 95

Write the name of the restaurant you would go to

1 if you want to eat mussels: ____________________
2 if you wanted to eat crab: ____________________
3 if you want pancakes: ____________________
4 if you want home-made ice cream: ____________________
5 if you want fish soup: ____________________

Écrivons maintenant !

You are on holidays in Antibes. Send a postcard to your French penfriend, Julien/Julie, in which you say:

- you are staying in Antibes in the south of France with your family
- the weather is fine and sunny
- you go to the market each day (**tous les jours**)
- some of the things you buy there
- you are going to visit Nice next Saturday

Communication en classe !

- Venez ici avec vos cahiers !
- Je viens tout de suite, Madame.
- Je vais donner vos devoirs maintenant. Sortez vos carnets !
- Nous allons écrire une dictée maintenant.
- Vous allez avoir un petit test demain.
- Ouvrez vos livres à la page soixante-douze !
- L'exercice est à la page 80.
- Mettez les cartables sous les chaises !
- Killian, va t'asseoir à côté de Rory.

Lexique

barquette de (f.)	*plastic pack of*
biologique	*organic*
boisson (f.)	*drink*
boîte (f.)	*tin/can/box*
boucher/ère (m./f.)	*butcher*
boucherie (f.)	*butcher's shop*
boulanger/ère (m./f.)	*baker*
boulangerie (f.)	*bakery shop*
bouquet de (m.)	*bunch of*
bouteille (de) (f.)	*bottle*
caisse (f.)	*the cash desk/ check-out*
carte (f.)	*menu*
charcuterie (f.)	*pork butcher/ delicatessen*
chariot (m.)	*trolley*
chips (f. pl.)	*crisps*
client(e) (m./f.)	*customer*
commander	*to order a meal*
côtelette (f.)	*chop*
coûter	*to cost*
cuisse (f.)	*leg/thigh*
cuit(e)	*cooked*
désirer	*to want*

douzaine de (f.)	*dozen of*
Écosse (f.)	*Scotland*
entrée (f.)	*entrance*
épicerie (f.)	*grocery shop*
épicier/ère (m./f.)	*grocer*
épinards (m. pl.)	*spinach*
escalope (f.)	*chop*
essence (f.)	*petrol*
exotique	*exotic/unusual*
farine (f.)	*flour*
fleur (f.)	*flower*
frais/fraîche	*fresh*
jus de fruit pressé (m.)	*squeezed fruit juice*
fruits de la forêt (m. pl.)	*fruit of the forest*
fruits de mer (m. pl.)	*seafood*
gâteau (m.)	*cake*
gigot d'agneau (m.)	*leg of lamb*
gratuit(e)	*free*
huile d'olive (f.)	*olive oil*
laitier/ère	*dairy*
langoustine (f.)	*prawn*
litre de (m.)	*litre of*
livre de (f.)	*pound of*
lot (de) (m.)	*pack of*
madeleine (f.)	*small sponge cake*
marchand(e)	*seller/trader*
marché (m.)	*market*
morceau de	*piece of*
moules (f. pl.)	*mussels*
paquet de (m.)	*packet of*
parking (m.)	*carpark*
pâtes (m. pl.)	*pasta*
pâtisserie (f.)	*cake shop*
pâtissier/ère (m./f.)	*pastry cook*
payer	*to pay for*
pêcheur/euse (m./f.)	*fisherman/woman*
petit pain (m.)	*bread roll*
pièce (f.)	*coin/room*
plat cuisiné (m.)	*ready cooked meal*
plateau de (m.)	*tray of*
pompiste (m./f.)	*petrol pump server*
pot (m.)	*jar/pot*
produit (m.)	*product*
prochain(e)	*next*
ranger	*to tidy*
reçu (m.)	*receipt*
saucisse (f.)	*sausage*
saucisson (m.)	*sausage (salami)*
saumon fumé (m.)	*smoked salmon*
serveur/euse (m./f.)	*waiter/waitress*
sortie (f.)	*exit*
sous-sol (m.)	*basement*
steak haché (m.)	*minced beef*
sucre (m.)	*sugar*
surgelé(e)	*frozen*
tarte (f.)	*tart*
tête de (f.)	*head of*
thon (m.)	*tuna*
toujours	*always*
tous les jours	*everyday*
tout le monde	*everybody*
tranche de (f.)	*slice of*
volaille (f.)	*poultry*
vigile (m./f.)	*security guard*

Épreuve

Question 1

Read this shopping list and say which trader in the market the person needs to visit.

Question 2

Listen and decide what each of these six people buy.

1 ______________	2 ______________	3 ______________
4 ______________	5 ______________	6 ______________

Question 3

Fifi the poodle was hungry and munched this shopping list.
Can you help Madame LaFolle put her shopping list back together?

Question 4

Use the correct form of '**venir**' in these sentences.

1 Mon ami ______________ chez moi demain.
2 Ma mère ______________ de Waterford.
3 Nous ______________ avec Julie.
4 Je ______________ en car scolaire.
5 Est-ce que vous ______________ au cinéma ?
6 Mes parents ______________ de Cork.
7 Nous allons au zoo. Tu ______________ aussi ?
8 Graziella et Elida ______________ d'Italie.

For **help** with this exercise, **see page 219.**

Question 5

Choisissez la bonne réponse !

1 **You are in a French supermarket and wish to find the basement. Which sign do you look for?**
(a) surgelés ; *(b)* sous-sol ; *(c)* sortie ; *(d)* basse-cour. ☐

2 **You want to buy some frozen pastry in the supermarket. Which sign do you look for?**
(a) essence ; *(b)* pâté ; *(c)* surgelés ; *(d)* sortie. ☐

3 **You want to buy some mineral water in the supermarket, which sign do you look for?**
(a) boissons ; *(b)* buvette ; *(c)* entrée ; *(d)* plats congelés. ☐

4 **You want to buy vegetables, in which section of the supermarket would you find them?**
(a) surgelés ; *(b)* confiserie ; *(c)* boucherie ; *(d)* légumes. ☐

5 **Which sign leads you to the trolleys?**
(a) escalier ; *(b)* chariots ; *(c)* parking ; *(d)* trains. ☐

For **help** with this exercise, **see pages 229-230.**

Question 6

Listen to these announcements in a supermarket. What is on offer and what is the price?

	item	price
1		
2		
3		
4		
5		
6		

Question 7

Find the 12 words in this word-search. Look them up and write them in your copy.

ADDITION
COMMANDER
MENU
RESERVER
ANNIVERSAIRE
DESSERT
PLAT PRINCIPAL
SERVEUR
BOISSON
ENTREE
REPAS
SERVEUSE

A	I	W	G	W	P	X	X	D	T	S	P	P	U	B
D	O	I	Y	Q	O	W	E	W	P	Z	L	B	N	O
R	E	F	P	W	A	S	Z	K	R	A	J	Q	E	I
E	Z	B	X	G	S	R	J	G	T	S	P	W	M	S
V	C	O	B	E	K	V	P	P	T	P	A	A	N	S
R	E	E	R	I	A	S	R	E	V	I	N	N	A	O
E	E	T	S	Q	C	I	Q	D	M	U	V	Y	F	N
S	V	D	H	E	N	V	N	Q	K	H	E	X	X	Y
E	A	W	N	C	R	O	S	E	R	V	E	U	S	E
R	L	P	I	A	I	V	A	A	S	W	N	E	N	B
G	E	P	E	T	M	D	E	Q	U	H	E	S	C	F
P	A	A	I	R	V	M	H	U	Q	X	G	Y	C	Q
L	X	D	S	Z	U	I	O	Y	R	Z	T	U	W	K
G	D	G	U	Z	O	I	V	C	E	E	R	T	N	E
A	J	M	W	P	I	Y	K	J	Y	Q	G	K	E	X

Question 8

You and your friend are visiting an Irish town/city for the day. Send a postcard to your French penfriend, Christophe/Christine in which you say

- where you are and with whom
- the weather is cold and its raining
- you are going to visit the market
- you are going to buy a plant for your Mam
- you are going to see your grandparents next weekend

Question 9

The pupils of the class of 5ème in the collège Marcel Pagnol write to their friends in St Patrick's Community School, Ballymichael about their local town. Listen and fill in the gaps, using the following words.

fleurs – chips – supermarché – vendredi – magasins – restaurant – gâteaux – fruits et légumes – courses – épicerie – poissons – boucherie

St Julien-sur-Seine, le 27 octobre

Chers amis de St Patrick,

Merci de votre lettre, que le professeur Monsieur Legros a reçue. C'est intéressant ! Les repas en Irlande sont un peu différents. Vous mangez plus de friandises et de chips que nous !

Maintenant, nous allons décrire les magasins du quartier. Nous habitons une petite ville, St Julien. Il y a un marché le ________________. Il y a des marchands de ________________, un marchand de volaille, un marchand de ________________ et un marchand de produits laitiers. La mère de Magali vend des ________________ et des plantes.

Dans la ville, il y a des magasins. Il y a une ________________. C'est le magasin du père de Suzanne. À côté, il y a une boulangerie-pâtisserie. C'est le magasin des parents de Cédric. Nous adorons acheter des ________________ dans ce magasin. En ville, il y a aussi une petite ________________ où nous allons acheter des bonbons et des ________________ après l'école. Les parents de Julien ont un petit ________________, qui s'appelle 'Chez Barbara'.

À deux kilomètres de la ville, il y a une grande surface avec un ________________ qui s'appelle 'Super A'. Nous allons faire les ________________ là-bas le samedi.

C'est tout pour l'instant.

Écrivez-nous bientôt avec une description des ________________ de la ville de Ballymichael.

Amitiés de toute la classe de 5ème du Collège Marcel Pagnol.

Mélanie Bernard
Romain Musset

Unité 9

En ville

Civilisation : Les villes françaises

- Many small French towns have a traditional layout, with the church, '**l'église**', at the centre and all streets and buildings leading from this central point. The church square is usually called '**la place de l'église**'. '**Une place**' is the French word for '*a square*', which can be a bit confusing.

- Another public building which can cause confusion is '**l'hôtel de ville**', which is not a hotel at all! In large towns, it is the town hall, where '**le conseil municipal**' (*town council*) has its offices. It is also called '**la mairie**'. All French towns have a mayor (**le maire**/**la mairesse**) elected by the local population. Among the mayor's duties is that of marrying couples. All French marriages must be carried out by the mayor, so you may sometimes see bridal celebrations outside this building. Couples then walk to the church, if they wish to have a religious service as well.

- If you want information about the local town you need to visit the tourist information office, '**l'office du tourisme**', sometimes called '**le syndicat d'initiative**'. You can get '**un plan**' (*a town map*) and find out what there is to see and do in the town.
- In many French towns, even small ones, you will often find a sports centre (**un centre sportif**), a youth centre (**la Maison des Jeunes et de la Culture, MJC**) and a swimming pool (**une piscine**). These will be provided by '**le conseil municipal**'. The costs are mostly met from local taxes, which all householders in the area pay.

Coin Prononciation : The letters '**an**' and '**en**' in French are usually pronounced as the English sound '**ong**': 'b**an**que', 'boul**an**ger', 'fr**an**çais', 'ag**en**t', 'pr**en**d', '**en**'.

9.1

Écoutons maintenant !

Write the number on the building as you hear its name called out. They are numbered 1 to 14.

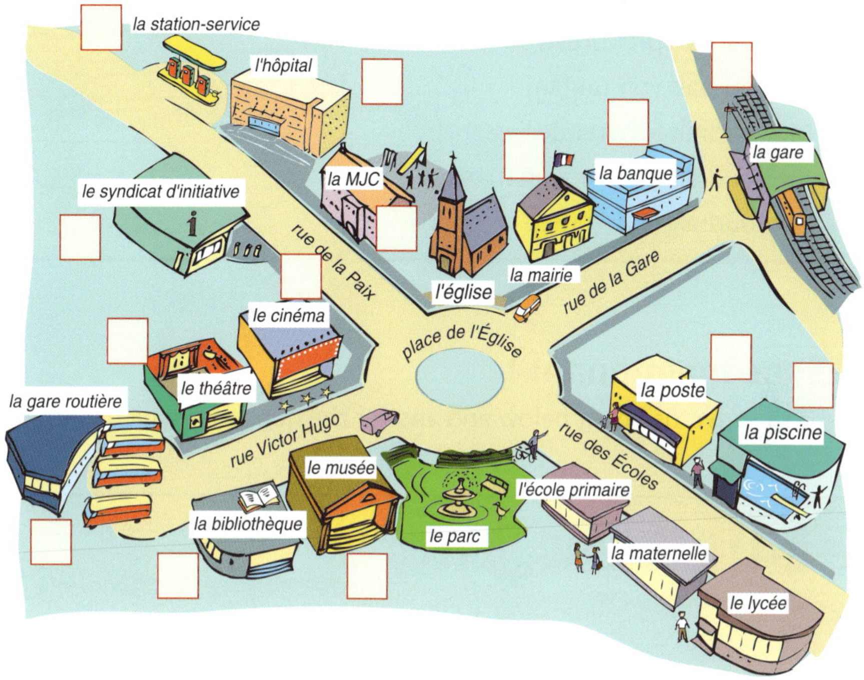

Exercice 1

Où est-ce qu'ils veulent aller ? Six visitors from abroad are visiting St Julien-sur-Seine. Where do they want to go? Complete the sentences below in your copy.

1 Hildegard veut voir...
2 Brad veut aller à ...
3 Luiza veut trouver...
4 Sven veut visiter ...
5 Mikko veut trouver ...
6 Juan veut aller à ...

Exercice 2

Where would I go for the following items?

1 Je voudrais un plan de la ville : Le ____________________
2 Je voudrais prendre le bus : La ____________________
3 Je voudrais voir un film : Le ____________________
4 Je voudrais acheter de l'essence : La ____________________
5 Je voudrais assister à un mariage : La ____________________
6 Je voudrais voir Roméo et Juliette : Le ____________________

Lisons maintenant !

Read the advertisement below and answer the questions which follow.

Le Musée St. Jean

Situé au centre de Saint-Julien-sur-Seine, à côté de l'église

Horaires

- Ouvert tous les jours (sauf lundi) de 10h00 à 18h00
- Fermé à l'heure du déjeuner de 12h00 à 14h00

Tarifs

- Adultes **8,00 €**
- Enfants (jusqu'à seize ans) **4,00 €**
- Enfants (moins de cinq ans) **gratuit**

Tél. : 00. 34. 76. 54. 78

1 The museum is situated near which other building?
2 What can you visit in the museum besides the café?
3 When is the museum closed?
4 What is the closing time of the museum?
5 Who can visit the museum for free?

9.2 Écoutons maintenant !

Can you complete the following street plan?

Rappel ! Don't forget your prepositions! '**à côté de**' (*beside*) and '**entre**' (*between*).

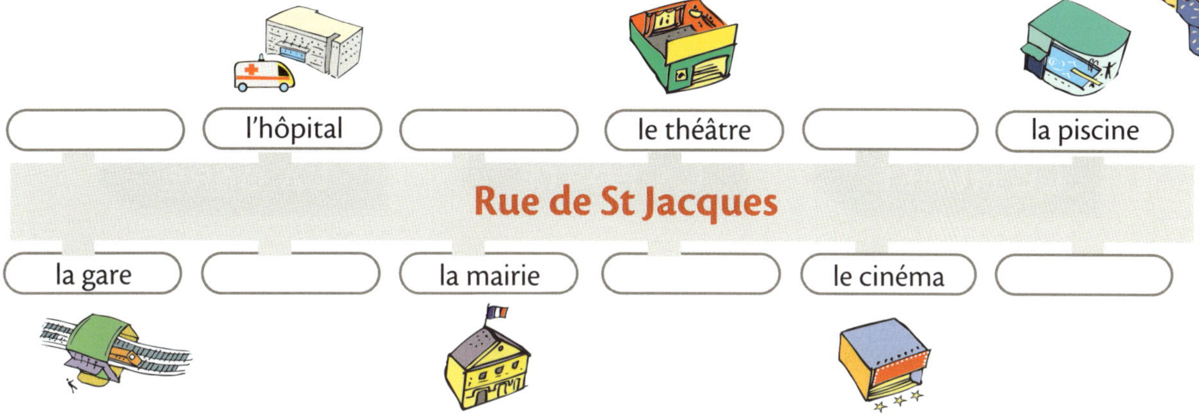

Lisons maintenant !

Study the key to the map of Rennes (**la légende**) and find the places suggested below. Write the answers in your copy.

1 This **P** is where you will find the post office.
2 This **G** is the railway station.
3 This **H** is the town hall.
4 This **J** is a famous park in Rennes.
5 This **C** is a very important church.
6 This **E** is the museum of ecology in Rennes.
7 This **C** now houses the tourist office.
8 This **M** is home of the history of Brittany.

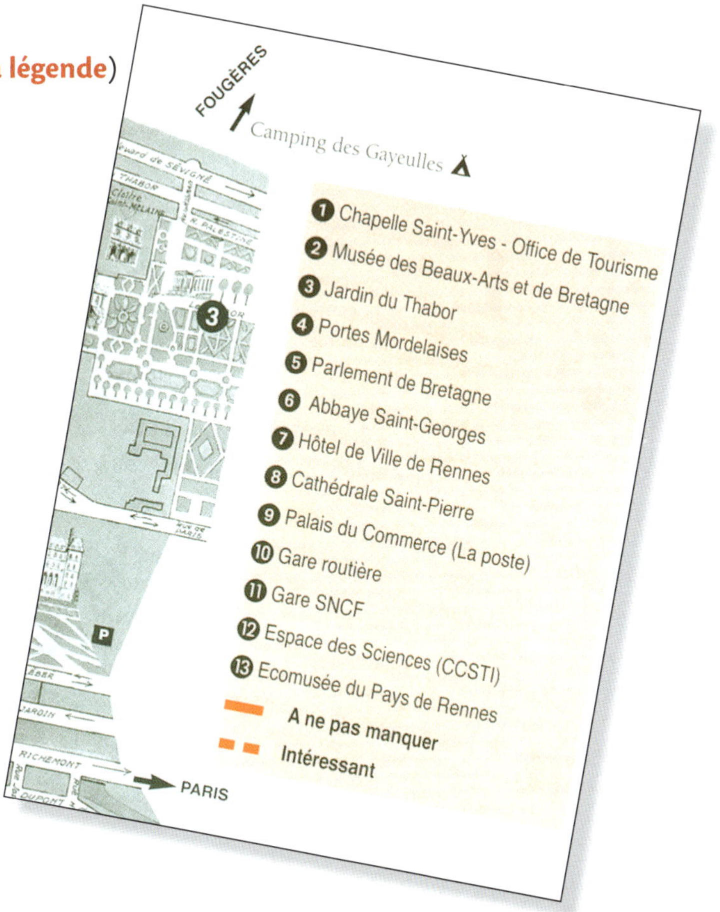

Les directions !

C'est à droite ou à gauche ?

Exercice 1

Read the signposts above and complete these sentences.

Exemple : Le musée est à droite.

1 La gare routière est ______________________.
2 La poste est ______________________.
3 L'hôtel de ville est ______________________.
4 Le musée est ______________________.
5 La gare est ______________________.
6 L'église est ______________________.

Parlons et écrivons maintenant !

Pick various items or people in your classroom and say whether they are on the right-hand side or left-hand side. Make at least six sentences. Then, write them below.

Exemples : La porte est à droite de la classe. | Shona est à gauche de John.

1 ______________________ **2** ______________________

3 ______________________ **4** ______________________

5 ______________________ **6** ______________________

Où se trouve la banque, s'il vous plaît ?

- Finding your way around a French town can be easy, once you know how to ask the **correct questions** and know the main street directions. Don't forget, you always use the **polite** form of the verb when speaking to someone you do not know ('–**ez**' ending).

Va/Allez à gauche.

Tourne(z) à droite.

Continue(z) tout droit.

Prends/Prenez la première rue à droite.

Prends/Prenez la deuxième rue à gauche.

For **help** with ordinal numbers, see page 130.

9.3

Écoutons et lisons maintenant !

Listen and read the following conversations to see the phrases you need.

Conversation 1

Hildegard : **Excusez-moi**, Monsieur. **Où se trouve** la banque, s'il vous plaît ?
Passant : La banque se trouve place de l'église. **Continuez tout droit**.
Hildegard : Merci, Monsieur.
Passant : Je vous en prie.

Conversation 2

Sven : **Pardon**, Madame. Où se trouve la bibliothèque, s'il vous plaît ?
Passante : La bibliothèque se trouve place du marché. **Prenez la première rue à gauche**.
Sven : La première rue à gauche.
Passante : Oui, c'est ça.
Sven : Merci. Au revoir.

Conversation 3

Natascha : Excusez-moi, Monsieur. Où se trouve la poste, s'il vous plaît ?
Passant : La poste ? C'est rue de la Libération. **Tournez à droite**.
Natascha: Merci beaucoup, Monsieur.

- As you can see, there are **two useful phrases** when you want to attract someone's attention:

Excusez-moi, Madame/Monsieur/Mademoiselle !

Pardon, Monsieur/Madame/Mademoiselle !

- If you are speaking to a policeman, you would say '**Monsieur**/**Madame l'Agent**'.

Parlons maintenant !

With your partner, practise the following conversations.

Exemple :

Continuez tout droit.

Fille :	Excusez-moi, Monsieur l'Agent, où se trouve la piscine, s'il vous plaît ?
Policier :	**La piscine** ? **Continuez tout droit**.
Fille :	Merci, Monsieur.

Coin grammaire : The imperative ('L'impératif')

- You will have noticed in '**Communication en classe**' throughout the book and in the previous conversations, that the instructions given do not use the word '**vous**'.

Sortez vos livres et vos cahiers !	**Tournez** à droite !
Écoutez le CD !	**Tournez** à gauche !
Ne **parlez** pas !	**Continuez** tout droit !

- The form used for these instructions is known as the '**l'impératif**' (*imperative*). The old Latin name for the emperor was 'imperator' and what he said had to be done! Hence the name of this form.

Formation

- You use the second person of the verb in '**le présent**', but **without** the '**tu**' or '**vous**' pronoun. This applies even to irregular verbs, except '**avoir**' and '**être**'. However, with '–**er**' verbs including '**aller**', drop the '**s**' from the second person singular.

verb group	présent			impératif
'–**er**' verbs (including '**aller**')	**Tu** parles.	→	~~Tu~~ parle~~s~~	**Parle** !
	Tu vas à la gare.	→	~~Tu~~ va~~s~~ à la gare.	**Va** à la gare !
'–**ir**' verbs (including irregular verbs)	**Tu** finis tes devoirs.	→	~~Tu~~ finis tes devoirs.	**Finis** tes devoirs !
	Vous remplissez le sac.	→	~~Vous~~ remplissez le sac.	**Remplissez** le sac !
'–**re**' verbs (including irregular verbs)	**Tu** vends ton vélo.	→	~~Tu~~ vends ton vélo.	**Vends** ton vélo !
	Vous faites les devoirs.	→	~~Vous~~ faites les devoirs.	**Faites** les devoirs !

Exemples :

singular speaking to one person (someone you know well)	**plural** speaking to a group of people or being polite
Bois !	Buvez !
Mange !	Mangez !
Finis !	Finissez !
Vends !	Vendez !

Exercice 1

Bonne santé ! Here is a chart from a doctor's surgery in the town. Write the imperative of the verb in the following sentences. Use the plural form!

Exercice 2

Write '**l'impératif**' of the following verbs in the singular and the plural in your copy.

1 Fermer	______/______	la porte !	2 Tourner	______/______	à droite !
3 Continuer	______/______	le long de la rue !	4 Aller	______/______	à gauche
5 Traverser	______/______	la rue !	6 Finir	______/______	l'exercice deux !
7 Écouter	______/______	les instructions !	8 Attendre	______/______	le bus !

The negative of the imperative ('l'impératif au négatif')

- To make the negative form of '**l'impératif**', you put '**ne**' before and '**pas**' after the verb as usual.
- Don't forget that '**ne**' becomes '**n'** ' before a verb beginning with a **vowel** or **silent** '**h**'.

Exercice 1

Write the following sentences in the negative.

1 Mangez dans la salle de classe !
2 Faites cet exercice !
3 Donne la pomme à Julie !
4 Parlez en classe !
5 Ouvrez la porte du magasin !
6 Tournez à droite !

Civilisation : Les magasins

- As in Ireland, shopping in big stores and shopping centres is popular in the larger French towns and cities, but smaller towns still have individual shops which continue a family trade handed down from generation to generation. In **Unité 8**, we saw that most '**quartiers**' (*local areas*) still have shops such as '**une boulangerie**', '**une boucherie**' or '**une épicerie**'.
- A large shop is called '**un magasin**', while a small shop is called '**une boutique**'. This applies to **all** small shops, not just clothes shops as in Ireland.
- Here are some of the shops you might find in a small town.

la boucherie

la poissonnerie

la boulangerie

la bijouterie

la pharmacie

la librairie-papeterie

l'épicerie

le/la fleuriste

le coiffeur/la coiffeuse

la pâtisserie

le bureau de tabac

le/la photographe

9.4 Écoutons maintenant !

Faire du shopping ! A group of students from St Patrick's Community School are in St Julien-sur-Seine. Listen to what they wish to buy and where they are told to go to buy the item.

	what they wish to buy	which shop they will go to
1		
2		
3		
4		
5		

Lisons maintenant !

Vrai ou faux ? Look at the following illustrations and say whether the statements below are true or false. Tick your answer.

	vrai	faux
1 La pâtisserie est à côté de la boucherie.		
2 Le photographe est entre la librairie et la banque.		
3 Le tabac est à côté de la banque.		
4 Il y a une librairie à côté de la poissonnerie.		
5 La banque est entre le bureau de tabac et le photographe.		
6 Il y a une fleuriste entre la charcuterie et la mairie.		

Lisons maintenant !

Read these advertisements for shops in St Julien-sur-Seine and answer the questions.

Librairie Ancienne et Moderne
Romans - Livres poches - Textes
24-26, rue St Pierre
Vente/Achat livres anciens et curieux
Ouvert: lundi 13h30/19h00
mardi/samedi : 9h30/12h30, 13h30/19h00
Tél. *: +33.(0)2. 31. 38. 63. 68*

Petit Chou
45, rue de l'église
Légumes/Fruits biologiques
Produits laitiers biologiques
Ouvert : lundi/samedi : 08h30/17h00
Tél. : +33. (0)2. 31. 84. 91. 71

Le Rex
17, rue Leclerc
Cinéma de luxe
6 salles climatisées au coeur de la ville
Ouvert tous les jours
Tél. :+33. (0)2. 31. 97. 91. 76

Laperche et Fils
Tabac -
Presse -
Papeterie
6, place du marché
Ouvert tous les jours
Dimanche : 08h00/12h00
Tél. : +33. (0)2. 31. 66. 88. 22

Cave St Julien
Cuisine traditionnelle
Vente vins -
Boissons normandes
Fermée le dimanche
Tél. :+33. (0)2. 31. 20. 83. 53

Bons Moments
Chocolatier artisanal
depuis 150 ans
23,rue de la gare
Fermé le dimanche
Tél. : +33. (0)2. 31. 58. 20. 24

L'Arlequin
Bar - Crêperie - Restaurant
12, place de l'église
Ouvert tous les jours sauf le lundi
Service non-stop !
Tél. : +33. (0)2. 31. 59. 13. 94

La Sirène
8, rue des écoles
piscine privée
Bassin : samedi de 9h00 à 18h30
Dimanche matin de 9h00 à 12h30
Tél. : +33. (0)2. 31. 84. 22. 28

Write down where you would go if you wanted

1. to buy some special chocolates: ______________________
2. to buy a book: ______________________
3. to buy a magazine: ______________________
4. to buy organic food: ______________________
5. to go to the cinema: ______________________
6. to visit the swimming pool: ______________________

Exercice 1

Faites des paires ! Faites correspondre les articles suivants avec le bon magasin, comme dans l'exemple ci-dessous.

b. la librairie/papeterie

8 

6 

3 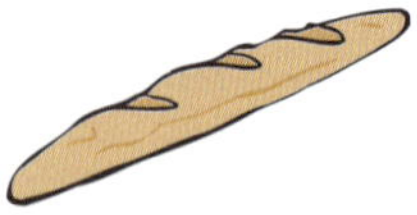

a. la pâtisserie

c. la charcuterie

4 

f. la boucherie

1 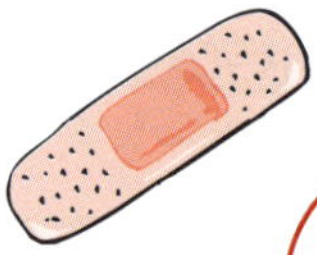

e. la boulangerie

5 

i. la poissonnerie

g. la bijouterie

2 

h. la pharmacie

7 

Exercice 2

Créons une ville française ! Now that you have learned the names of the various buildings and shops in a French town, why not create one in your own classroom?

- Each student or pair of students can choose a particular shop or building.
- Use A3 sheets of paper.
- Draw and colour your shop/building.
- Don't forget to put the name on top.
- When all of the pictures are complete, hang them up around your classroom wall.
- Don't forget to give your town a French name!

Coin dictionnaire : Gender of nouns

boucher[2] *nm* (*lit, fig*) butcher.
bouchère *nf* (woman) butcher; (*épouse*) butcher's wife.
boucherie *nf* (*magasin*) butcher's (shop); (*métier*) butchery (trade); (*fig*) slaughter.

fleuriste *nmf* (*personne*) florist; (*boutique*) florist's (shop).
fleuron *nm* [*couronne*] floweret; [*bâtiment*] finial; (*fig*) [*collection*] jewel.

photogénique *adj* photogenic.
photographe *nmf* (*artiste*) photographer; (*commerçant*) camera dealer. **vous trouverez cet article chez un ~** you will find this item at a camera shop.
photographie *nf* **(a)** (*art*) photography. **faire de la ~** (*comme passe-temps*) to take photographs.

libraire *nmf* bookseller. **~-éditeur** publisher and bookseller.
librairie *nf* **(a)** (*magasin*) bookshop. **~ d'art** art bookshop; **~-papeterie** bookseller's and stationer's shop.

- It is difficult to know in French whether a noun is **masculine** or **feminine** unless there is an obvious gender hint in the word itself, as in '**la fille**' or '**le garçon**'. Some endings can sometimes help to indicate the **gender** of words. The following endings usually indicate that the noun is feminine:

–elle	**–ienne**	**–ière**
–ette	**–euse**	**–onne**

- A good dictionary will give extra information about each word entry such as whether or not there is a '**masculin**' and a '**féminin**' form of the same word. For example, there are two forms in French for the word '**boucher**' (*butcher*) depending on whether the butcher is a man or a woman.
- In the case of '**fleuriste**', '**photographe**' and '**libraire**', you will notice that there is only one word but the dictionary entry tells us that this is a noun which can be masculine and feminine 'n. m/f'. For the female florist, you say '**la fleuriste**' and for the male '**le fleuriste**'.
- For the female photographer you say '**la photographe**' and for the male '**le photographe**'.
- For the female bookseller, you say '**la libraire**' and for the male '**le libraire**'.

Coin grammaire : The preposition 'à' (*to, at* or *in*)

- You have already learned some phrases where you use this preposition:

Je vais **à** Paris. J'écris une lettre **à** Marie.
Ma maison se trouve **à** Waterford.

- However, when you want to use this preposition with the word '*the*' ('**le**', '**la**', '**l'**' or '**les**'), you will find that there are **four** different forms:

à + le	→	**au**	Nous allons **au** cinéma.
à + la	→	**à la**	Nous attendons le train **à la** gare.
à + l'	→	**à l'**	Le bus va **à l'**Hôtel de Ville.
à + les	→	**aux**	Vous parlez **aux** enfants.

Exercice 1

Fill in the correct form of the preposition '**à**' in the following sentences.

1 Je voudrais aller __________ théâtre.
2 Paul attend Suzanne __________ gare routière.
3 Nous allons __________ marché samedi.
4 Vous devez aller __________ pharmacie pour acheter du sparadrap.
5 Pour acheter des légumes, allez __________ marché.
6 Les enfants veulent aller __________ piscine.
7 Tu veux parler __________ adultes ?
8 Le petit enfant doit aller __________ hôpital.

- When you want to say that you are going to a particular shop, you can do so in **two** ways:

(a) You can use the **name** of the particular shop:

Je vais **à la boucherie**. | Je vais **à l'épicerie**.

(b) You can use the **preposition** '**chez**', which means '*to the shop of*':

Je vais **chez le boucher**. | Je vais **chez le boulanger**.

Encore des prépositions !

- To help give street directions the following prepositions will help.

La mairie est **en face de** l'église.

Le supermarché est **près du** café.

La poste est **au coin de** la place.

L'école est **au bout de** la rue.

L'homme se promène **le long du** parc.

Exercice 1

Fill in the following sentences with the missing preposition.

1 La boucherie est ____________________ de la rue.

2 Le cinéma est ____________________ du théâtre.

3 Le port est ____________________ de la gare.

4 La dame se promène ____________________ de la plage.

5 La bibliothèque est ____________________ de la rue.

9.5

Écoutons maintenant !

Une dictée ! Listen and write the six sentences you hear in your copy and translate them.

Encore des directions !

Pour aller à la piscine ?

- As well as using '**Où se trouve**... ?', you can use the phrase '**Pour aller**... ?' (*How do I get to?*).

Parlons maintenant !

Travaillez à deux ! You are asked to give directions to the following places in town. You and your partner take turns playing the role of visitor and local person who gives directions.

Exemple : – **Pour aller** au supermarché, s'il vous plaît ?
– Allez tout droit, et prenez la deuxième rue à droite.
– C'est à gauche/C'est au bout de la rue.

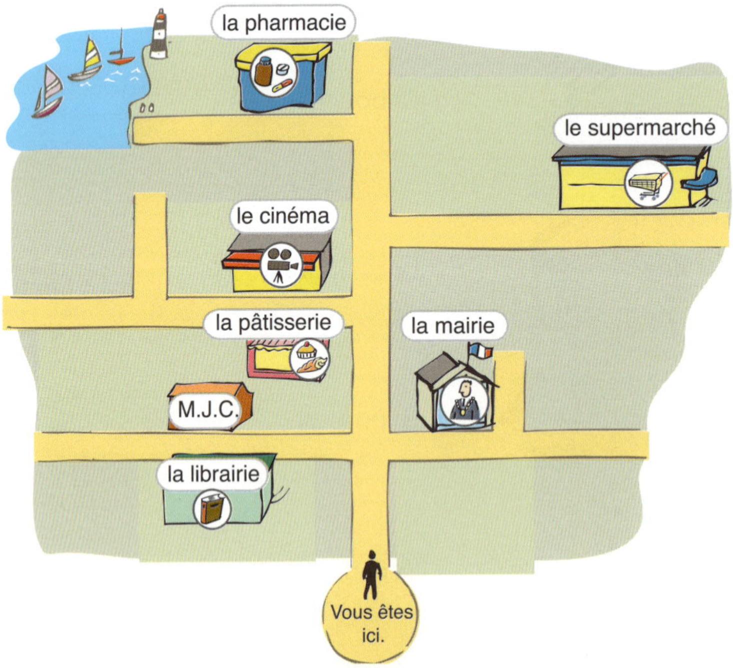

1 Pour aller à la MJC, s'il vous plaît ?
2 Pour aller à la mairie, s'il vous plaît ?
3 Pour aller au cinéma, s'il vous plaît ?
4 Pour aller à la pharmacie, s'il vous plaît ?
5 Pour aller à la pâtisserie, s'il vous plaît ?

Encore des nombres !

9.6 Écoutons maintenant !

Voici les nombres de **80** à **100**. Listen and repeat.

quatre-vingts	80	quatre-vingt-dix	90
quatre-vingt-un	81	quatre-vingt-onze	91
quatre-vingt-deux	82	quatre-vingt-douze	92
quatre-vingt-trois	83	quatre-vingt-treize	93
quatre-vingt-quatre	84	quatre-vingt-quatorze	94
quatre-vingt-cinq	85	quatre-vingt-quinze	95
quatre-vingt-six	86	quatre-vingt-seize	96
quatre-vingt-sept	87	quatre-vingt-dix-sept	97
quatre-vingt-huit	88	quatre-vingt-dix-huit	98
quatre-vingt-neuf	89	quatre-vingt-dix-neuf	99
		cent	100

Cent (100)

- The word '**cent**' takes an '**s**' to make it plural, provided it is not followed by another number.

Exemple : Il y a deux cent**s** maisons dans le lotissement.
Il y a huit cent**s** élèves dans l'école.

Mais ! Il y a trois cent cinquante filles dans le lycée.
Ça fait quatre cent douze euros en tout.

9.7 Écoutons maintenant !

Cochez la bonne case ! Listen and tick which number you hear.

quatorze	quatre-vingts	quatre-vingt-un	quatre-vingt-deux	quatre-vingt-trois	quatre-vingt-quatre	quatre-vingt-cinq	quatre-vingt-six	quatre-vingt-dix-sept	quatre-vingt-huit
quatre	quarante	quatre-vingt-onze	quatre-vingt-douze	quatre-vingt-treize	quatre-vingt-quatorze	quatre-vingt-quinze	quatre-vingt-seize	quarante-sept	quatre-vingt-dix-huit

Exercice 1

Write the following numbers in French in your copy.

100 96 94 85 98
87 89 90 82 92

Coin civilisation : Les grands magasins

- Most French towns have large department stores which sell a variety of clothes and other goods. '**Monoprix**', '**les Galeries Lafayette**' and '**le Printemps**' are well-known French chains. Stores such as '**Sisley**', '**Benneton**', '**H&M**', and '**Zara**' are all familiar names in France nowadays. French clothes chains include '**Pinkie**', '**Jennyfer**', '**Jules**' and '**Célio**'. The large music and electrical chain '**la FNAC**' has an outlet in most large French towns. Most of these shops have websites you can visit.

9.8 Écoutons maintenant !

The pupils from St Patrick's Community School are getting ready to go home and want to do some shopping, '**faire du shopping**', for presents for their families. Listen to the following conversations.

Conversation 1
1 What does Killian want to buy for his sister?
2 What colour is the item he buys?

Conversation 2
1 Which of the following does Orla say her mother would like?
(*a*) a bracelet;
(*b*) some French perfume;
(*c*) a coffee-maker.
2 On which floor of the store will she be able to buy the present?

Conversation 3
1 What does Hannah say about her brother?
2 In which shop will she get his present?

Conversation 4
1 When is Robert's dad celebrating his birthday?
2 What present will he get for his dad?

Conversation 5
1 Who does Ruth want to buy a present for?
2 What gift does Sophie suggest?

Coin grammaire : The verb '**préférer**'

- During the conversations in the last exercise, the verb '**préférer**' was used several times. This is a very useful verb to know, when you have to make choices.
- This '–**er**' verb is slightly different in '**le présent**'. In all parts **except** the '**nous**' and '**vous**' **forms**, there is a slight spelling change. Look out for the '**accent grave**' on the **second syllable**.

9.9

Écoutons maintenant !

- Listen and repeat '**le présent**' of the verb '**préférer**'.

Rappel !
Les accents page 14.

je	préf**ère**
tu	préf**ère**
il	préf**ère**
elle	préf**ère**
nous	préfér**ons**
vous	préfér**ez**
ils	préf**èrent**
elles	préf**èrent**

Exercice 1

Remplissez la grille avec le verbe '**préférer**'.

- The verb '**préférer**' is not usually used in the negative form; it would sound funny to be saying 'I don't prefer!'

je	
tu	préfères
il	
elle	
nous	
vous	préférez
ils	
elles	

Exercice 2

Remplissez les blancs dans les phrases suivantes.

1 Quand Élise veut un livre, elle pr____f____re aller à la librairie.
2 Nous préf____r____ns acheter des timbres au bureau de tabac.
3 Jean-Pierre et Claire pr____fèr____nt aller au syndicat d'initiative quand ils arrivent en ville.
4 Monsieur Clavel pr____fèr____ visiter les musées en ville.
5 Est-ce que tu pr____f____res aller à la place ou au parc ?
6 Est-ce que vous pr____fèr____z rester chez des amis ou à l'hôtel ?

9.10 Écoutons maintenant !

Cochez la bonne case ! Listen to these three people describing the place where they live and tick off the places each one mentions.

	Laillé	Lyon	St Julien-sur-Seine
bakery			
bank			
butcher's			
castle			
chemist			
church			
hairdresser			
library			
museum			
railway station			
restaurant			
stadium			
swimming-pool			

Civilisation : Bienvenue à Paris, la capitale de la France

- Paris, the capital of France, is a world centre for fashion design. Many of the famous fashion houses (**les maisons de couture**) are located in Paris, founded by such designers of high fashion (**la haute couture**) as '**Yves Saint Laurent**', '**Christian Dior**', '**Pierre Cardin**', '**Givenchy**', '**Jean-Paul Gaultier**' or '**Chanel**'. These designers each have their own boutiques. Famous department stores in Paris are '**Les Galeries Lafayette**' and '**Le Printemps**'.

les galeries Lafayette

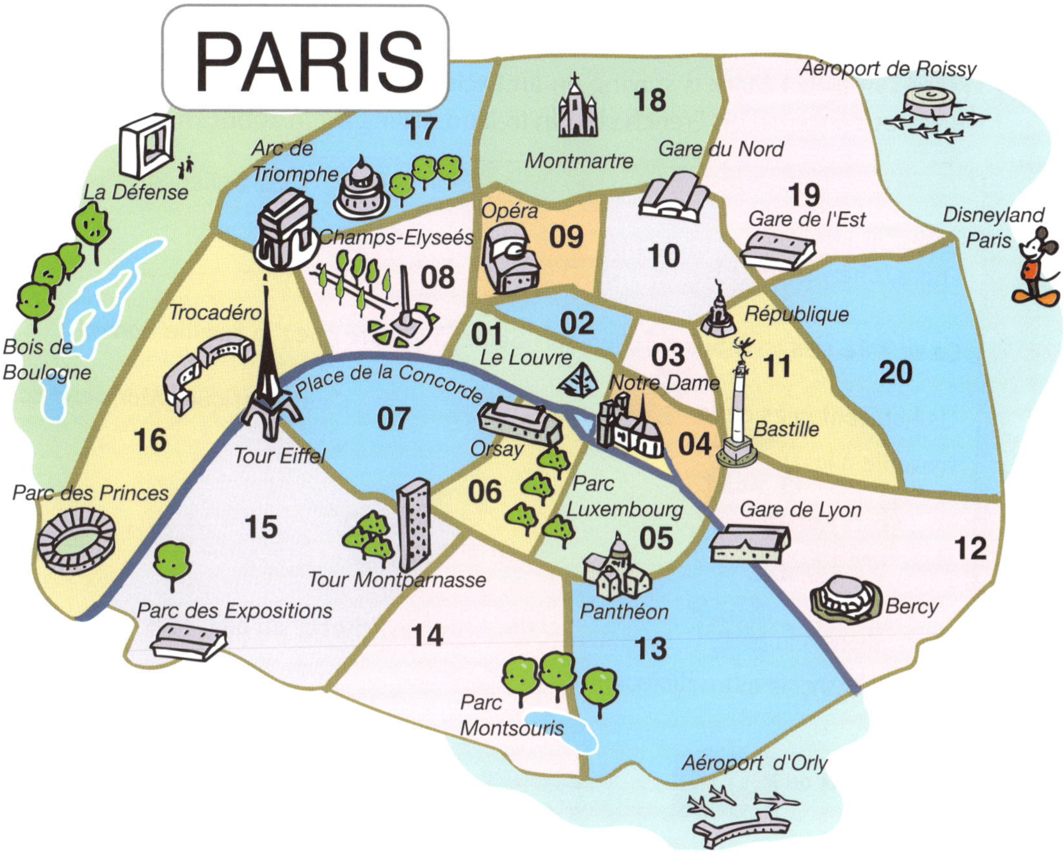

- The various divisions of the city are called '**arrondissements**', with the sixteenth, '**le seizième arrondissement**', being the most chic area in which to live. The arrondissements are laid out in a snail-like shape, with those furthest away from the centre having the higher numbers. Suburban areas of Paris and many other large French towns are called '**les banlieues**'.

Exercice 1

Petit Dossier ! You can do a small project on a district of Paris or any French town of your choice – perhaps somewhere you have already visited.

Écrivons maintenant !

Killian writes a postcard to his French teacher Mr O'Riordan from St Julien-sur-Seine. In it he says

- The weather is fine and he is enjoying himself
- The town is nice and has a youth club, a swimming-pool and a museum
- He is visiting the castle today
- He is going to see the market tomorrow

Écrivons maintenant !

Lettre-symbole ! Mark is staying on an exchange visit with his '**correspondant**' in St Julien. He writes a letter to his French class in Ireland, telling them about the town.

St Julien-sur-Seine, le deux juin

Chers/Chères Ami(e)s,

Ça va ? Je suis ici à Saint Julien-sur-Seine. Je reste chez la famille Bonnet.

Ils habitent près de la  ______________. C'est pratique ! Monsieur Bonnet travaille à la .

Il y a une  ______________ et une 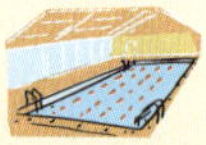 ______________ tout près.

Nous allons à la  ______________ pour acheter du pain tous les jours. Le pain français est délicieux !

Nous allons au  ______________ ce soir et nous espérons aller à la  ______________ demain. Le week-end, il y a un grand  ______________

Je vais au  ______________ samedi.

Qu'est-ce que vous faites en ce moment ? Vous avez des examens ?

Vous allez au  ______________ le week-end ?

Il me tarde de vous voir le 16 

______________.

Dites « bonjour » à tout le monde de ma part.

Amitiés,

Mark

Communication en classe !

- Allez au bureau du directeur tout de suite !
- Restez ici un moment !
- Prenez vos stylos pour écrire une dictée.
- Préparez votre dossier pour lundi !
- Mettez vos cahiers dans le placard, en face du bureau !
- Nous allons à la bibliothèque demain.
- Nous prenons le car pour aller au musée.
- Ouvrez vos livres à la page quatre-vingt-six.

Lexique

achat (m.)	*purchase*
agent de police (m.)	*police officer*
arrondissement (m.)	*district (Paris)*
artisanal(e)	*hand-made/crafted*
assister à	*to attend*
au bout de	*at the end/bottom of*
au centre de	*in the centre of*
au coin de	*on the corner of*
au sommet de	*at the top of (highest point)*
banque (f.)	*bank*
bassin de plongée (m.)	*diving pool*
bibliothèque (f.)	*library*
bijouterie (f.)	*jeweller's*
bureau de tabac	*tobacconist/newsagent*
cathédrale (f.)	*cathedral*
certainement	*of course/certainly*
château (m.)	*castle*
chauffé(e)	*heated*
chez	*at the house of/shop of*
cinéma (m.)	*cinema*
climatisé(e)	*air-conditioned*
coiffeur/euse (m./f.)	*hairdresser*
coin (m.)	*corner*
continuer	*to continue*
(à) droite	*right*
en face de	*facing, opposite*
essence (f.)	*petrol*
éviter	*to avoid*
excusez-moi	*excuse me/I'm sorry*
faire du shopping	*to go shopping*
fermé(e)	*closed*
gare (f.)	*railway station*
gare routière (f.)	*bus station*
(à) gauche	*left*
gratuit	*free of charge*
hôpital (m.)	*hospital*
horaires (m. pl.)	*timetable*
hôtel de ville (f.)	*town hall*
le long de	*along*
libraire (m./f.)	*bookseller*
lilas	*mauve/lilac*
livre de poche (m.)	*paperback*
maire/mairesse (m./f.)	*mayor*
marcher	*to walk*
M.J.C. (f.)	*youth and cultural centre*
moins de	*under/less than*
musée (m.)	*museum*
normand(e)	*from Normandy*
ouvert(e)	*open*
parc (m.)	*park*
pardon	*excuse me/sorry*
papeterie (f.)	*stationery shop*
pâtisserie (f.)	*cake shop*
pharmacie (f.)	*chemist shop*
plaisir (f.)	*pleasure*
poissonnerie (f.)	*fish shop*
policier (m.)	*police officer*
poste (f.)	*post office*
préférer	*to prefer*
prendre	*to take*
près de	*close to*
promenade (f.)	*walk*
renseignements (m. pl.)	*information*
rivière (f.)	*river*
sauf	*except*
souvenir (m.)	*gift, souvenir*
sparadrap (m.)	*sticking plaster*
stade (m.)	*stadium*
station-service (f.)	*petrol station*
syndicat d'initiative (m.)	*tourist office*
tarif (m.)	*cost*
théâtre (m.)	*theatre*
timbre (m.)	*postage stamp*
tour (f.)	*tower*
tourner	*to turn*
tout droit	*straight ahead*
traverser	*to cross*
se trouver	*to be situated*
vélo (m.)	*bicycle*
vente (f.)	*sale*
vue (f.)	*view*

Épreuve

Question 1

Mots cachés ! Trouvez les magasins dans la grille ci-dessous.

p	o	i	s	s	o	n	n	e	r	i	e
b	l	u	l	g	h	s	f	b	â	e	d
o	t	e	b	i	u	o	â	o	k	t	h
g	c	b	u	f	v	t	r	u	w	n	p
u	p	i	v	r	l	o	r	c	i	l	g
i	r	j	h	e	h	c	a	h	u	n	b
q	b	o	u	l	a	n	g	e	r	i	e
t	u	u	n	i	b	k	s	r	d	t	p
i	m	t	q	b	â	v	w	i	r	c	h
f	l	e	u	r	i	s	t	e	n	h	o
s	j	r	d	a	i	j	c	j	i	a	t
o	a	i	m	i	k	m	e	e	s	r	o
r	h	e	d	r	a	i	l	x	h	c	g
l	c	r	d	i	r	m	â	l	m	u	r
t	f	e	e	e	i	n	a	t	u	t	a
r	b	â	r	s	r	o	b	c	a	e	p
c	b	l	q	m	e	i	t	z	n	r	h
l	x	r	p	h	a	r	m	a	c	i	e
z	p	â	t	i	s	s	e	r	i	e	r
s	u	p	e	r	m	a	r	c	h	é	s
t	b	o	u	l	e	x	p	o	m	l	u

boulangerie
librairie
pharmacie
fleuriste
photographe
supermarché
boucherie
charcuterie
poissonnerie
pâtisserie
bijouterie

Question 2

Match the picture to the correct word.

1 la boulangerie	**A** 
2 	**B** le fleuriste
3 la boucherie	**C** 
4 	**D** la gare
5 la pâtisserie	**E** 
6 	**F** l'église
7 la mairie	**G** 
8 	**H** la banque
9 la gare routière	**I** 
10 	**J** la librairie

no.	letter
1	
2	
3	
4	
5	
6	
7	
8	
9	
10	

Question 3

Remplissez les blancs ! Listen to this conversation and fill in the gaps.

Touriste : ______________, Monsieur l'Agent. Il y a un parking ______________ d'ici ?
Policier : Oui, certainement. Il se trouve ______________________ l'église.
Touriste : Et pour aller au ______________ ?
Policier : Continuez tout ______________. Puis prenez la ______________ rue à ______________. C'est au bout de la ______________ de l'église. C'est à ______________ minutes d'ici.
Touriste : ______________, Monsieur l'Agent.
Policier : Je vous en prie.

Question 4

Fill in the blanks with the imperative form of the verbs in brackets, using the singular or the plural ending as required.

1 (*Faire*) ______________ ton lit !
2 Ne (*fumer*) ______________ pas dans le cinéma !
3 Ne (*marcher*) ______________ pas sur le tapis dans le château !
4 (*Finir*) ______________ tes devoirs !
5 (*Acheter*) ______________ vos billets à la gare !
6 Ne (*tourner*) ______________ pas à droite !
7 (*Boire*) ______________ ton lait !
8 (*Fermer*) ______________ la porte de l'église, s'il vous plaît !

For **help** with this exercise, see page 251.

Question 5

Les numéros de téléphone ! Listen to these phone numbers. Complete the gaps.

1 Le syndicat d'initiative 01. ___. 33. ___. 30.
2 La gare routière 01. ___. 24. ___. 25.
3 La bibliothèque 01. ___. ___. ___. 48.
4 La banque 01. ___. ___. 50. ___.
5 L'hôpital 01. ___. ___. ___. ___.
6 La piscine municipale 01. ___. ___. ___. ___.

For **help** with this exercise, see page 261.

Question 6

Write the correct form of the verb '**préférer**' in your copy.

1 Je (*préférer*) habiter en ville.
2 Nous (*préférer*) visiter le château de Versailles.
3 Marc (*préférer*) rester à l'hôtel quand il visite Paris.
4 Tiffaine et Paul (*préférer*) déjeuner au restaurant.
5 Les étudiants (*préférer*) aller au théâtre à Lyon.
6 Je (*préférer*) aller à la librairie pour acheter un livre.

For **help** with this exercise, see page 263.

Question 7

Follow the directions you hear on the CD and write the name of the building you arrive at.

1 ______________________

2 ______________________

3 ______________________

4 ______________________

5 ______________________

Question 8

Read the following information sheet and answer the questions which follow.

Place du Musée

Le musée est ouvert du mardi au dimanche, de 10h00 à 17h00.
La banque est ouverte du lundi au vendredi, de 09h30 à 12h00 et de 14h00 à 17h00.
Le syndicat d'initiative est ouvert tous les jours (juin à septembre), et du lundi au samedi (octobre-mai).
La poste est ouverte du lundi au vendredi, de 09h00 à 17h30 (09h00 à 16h30 le samedi).
Le château est ouvert du mardi au samedi, de 10h00 à 16h00 (12h00 à 16h00 le dimanche).
La pharmacie est ouverte du lundi au samedi, de 08h30 à 18h00 (10h00 à 12h00 le dimanche).

1. Which public building is open every day during the summer?
2. Which public building is open Tuesday-Sunday until 5pm?
3. Which shop opens on Sunday mornings?
4. Which business is closed at lunchtime?
5. Which business closes at 4.30pm on Saturday afternoons?

Question 9

Read the following brochure and answer the questions which follow.

Le Château la Seine

(SITUÉ À 5 KM DE ST JULIEN-SUR-SEINE)

- Promenades dans les jardins – Histoire – Plaisir.
- Au sommet de la tour du château, vous avez une vue de la Seine et de la vieille église de St Luc.
- Déjeuner au petit restaurant en terrasse, au deuxième étage.

Ouvert du 1er juin au 30 septembre

Visites guidées tous les jours à 11h, 15h et 17h.

Renseignements :
Mairie la Seine –
Tél. : 04. 67. 54. 90. 15
Ou
Syndicat d'initiative –
Tél. : 04. 67. 98. 23. 15

1 Where is the castle located?
2 Name **one** thing that you can see from the top of the tower?
3 Where is the restaurant?
4 When is the castle open?
5 Name the **two** places where you can get information about the castle.

Question 10

(a) Ma ville ! Here is a list of the buildings you might find in a typical town. Think about your own town/village. Tick which buildings you would find there.

les magasins	ma ville/mon village
une église	
une école primaire	
un collège	
une bibliothèque	
un château	
une poste	
une gare	
un supermarché	
une banque	
une pharmacie	
une boulangerie	
un cinéma	

(b) Now, write five sentences about your town or village in your copy.

1 J'habite à ________________, une grande/petite ville (un grand/petit village) en Irlande.
2 Dans ma ville, il y a...
3 Nous avons...
4 Au centre, il y a...
5 Il n'y a pas de...

Question 11

You are on holidays in Antibes, in the South of France, with your friend and her family. Write a postcard to your French-speaking cousin, Camille, and say

- Who you are with and where you are staying
- You are having a good time
- Say there is a museum, a swimming-pool and an old (**vieille**) church
- Say you are going to visit Cannes at the weekend

Unité 10

Le sport

Civilisation : Les sports en France

- Sport plays a large part in French life. '**Le foot**', '**le tennis**', '**la natation**', '**le ski**', '**le basket**' and '**le judo**' are among the most popular sports. '**L'Éducation Physique et Sportive** (**EPS**)' is an examination subject in many French schools.
- '**Le cyclisme**' (*cycling*) is one of the most popular sports (www.france-cyclisme.com). '**Le Tour de France**' was first held in 1903. The race, which takes place in July, covers more than 3,000 km and lasts up to three weeks. The route changes from year to year, but always ends on the Champs Élysées in Paris. The leading rider wears '**le maillot jaune**' (*yellow jersey*), but other coloured jerseys are awarded for speed trials and mountain climbing sections.

les Champs Élysées

- The French have their own form of bowling, which is called '**la pétanque**, or '**les boules**' (the rules are slightly different for each game). It is a common sight on summer evenings in parks or villages to see groups playing '**la pétanque**'/'**les boules**' on the flat, sanded area used for this purpose, sometimes called '**le boulodrome**'.

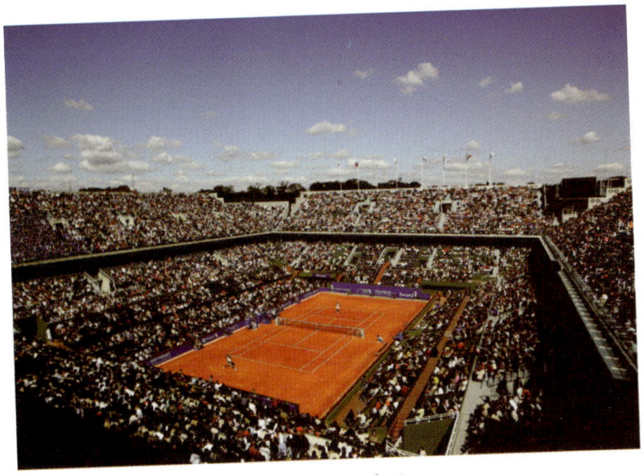

le stade Roland Garros

- '**Le Stade Roland Garros**' in Paris is the venue for major tennis tournaments each year. The French Open is one of the four big Grand Slam events in the tennis calendar. It is thought that the word 'tennis' comes from the verb '**tenir**' (*to hold*) and the scoring system of 'love' (**l'oeuf**), 'deuce' (**jeu à deux**) also has French roots (www.fft.fr).
- Almost every French town has its '**stade municipal**' or '**salle omnisports**'. Popular sports are '**le badminton**', '**le volley-ball**', '**le ping-pong**', '**le basket**', '**le foot en salle**', and '**le judo**'.

Coin grammaire : Team sports ('Les sports d'équipe')

- When you want to say that you play a particular sport, you usually use '**jouer à**' for team sports (**les sports d'équipe**). It is a **regular** '–**er**' verb and, in this case, it is used with the preposition '**à**'.
- Voici le verbe '**jouer**' (*to play*) au présent:

je	jou**e**
tu	jou**es**
il	jou**e**
elle	jou**e**
nous	jou**ons**
vous	jou**ez**
ils/elles	jou**ent**

'Jouer' in the negative

- To make '**jouer**' negative, you use '**ne**' before the verb and '**pas**' after the verb as usual.

Exemples : Je **ne** joue **pas** au foot mercredi.
Nous **ne** jouons **pas** au tennis quand il pleut.

Attention ! '**à**' changes three times:

1. If the noun which follows is **masculine** (most team sports), '**à**' changes to '**au**': Je joue **au** rugby.
2. If the noun which follows is **feminine**, '**à**' changes to '**à la**': Il joue **à la** pétanque.
3. If the noun which follows is **plural**, '**à**' changes to '**aux**': Ils jouent **aux** boules.

le football

le badminton

le rugby

le ping-pong

le basket

le volley

le football gaélique

le hurling

le camogie

le tennis

les boules

le hockey

Exercice 1

Remplissez les blancs avec le verbe '**jouer**' et la préposition appropriée.

1. Je ____________ ____________ ping-pong.
2. Vous ____________ ____________ basket mercredi ?
3. Ma fille ____________ ____________ tennis en juillet.
4. Mes parents ____________ ____________ boules ce soir.
5. Tu ____________ ____________ hockey aujourd'hui ?
6. Ils ____________ ____________ pétanque dans le parc.

Exercice 2

Quels sports ? Write in your copy the names of eight popular sports. You will find them in the grid below by joining two boxes to make each one.

bad-	-ling	ping-	vol-
-ket	foot-	-ley	bas-
hoc-	-pong	-minton	-by
rug-	-key	hur-	-ball

10.1

Écoutons maintenant !

Listen to these six people speaking about a sport. Who plays which sport?

a. 

b. 

c. 

d. 

e. 

f. 

Luc ☐

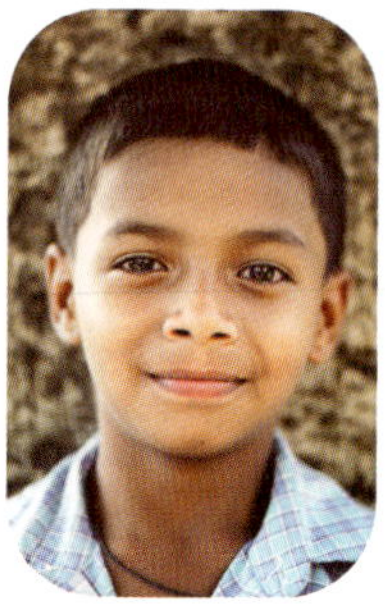

Khalid ☐

Sophie ☐

Léa ☐

Océane ☐

Christophe ☐

Exercice 1

Complétez les phrases suivantes.

1 Luc joue ______ ______________.
2 Sophie joue ______ ______________.
3 Océane joue ______ ______________.
4 Khalid joue ______ ______________.
5 Léa joue ______ ______________.
6 Christophe joue ______ ______________.

Lisons maintenant !

Read these notices from the noticeboard in the '**Club Omnisports**' of St Pierre and answer the questions which follow.

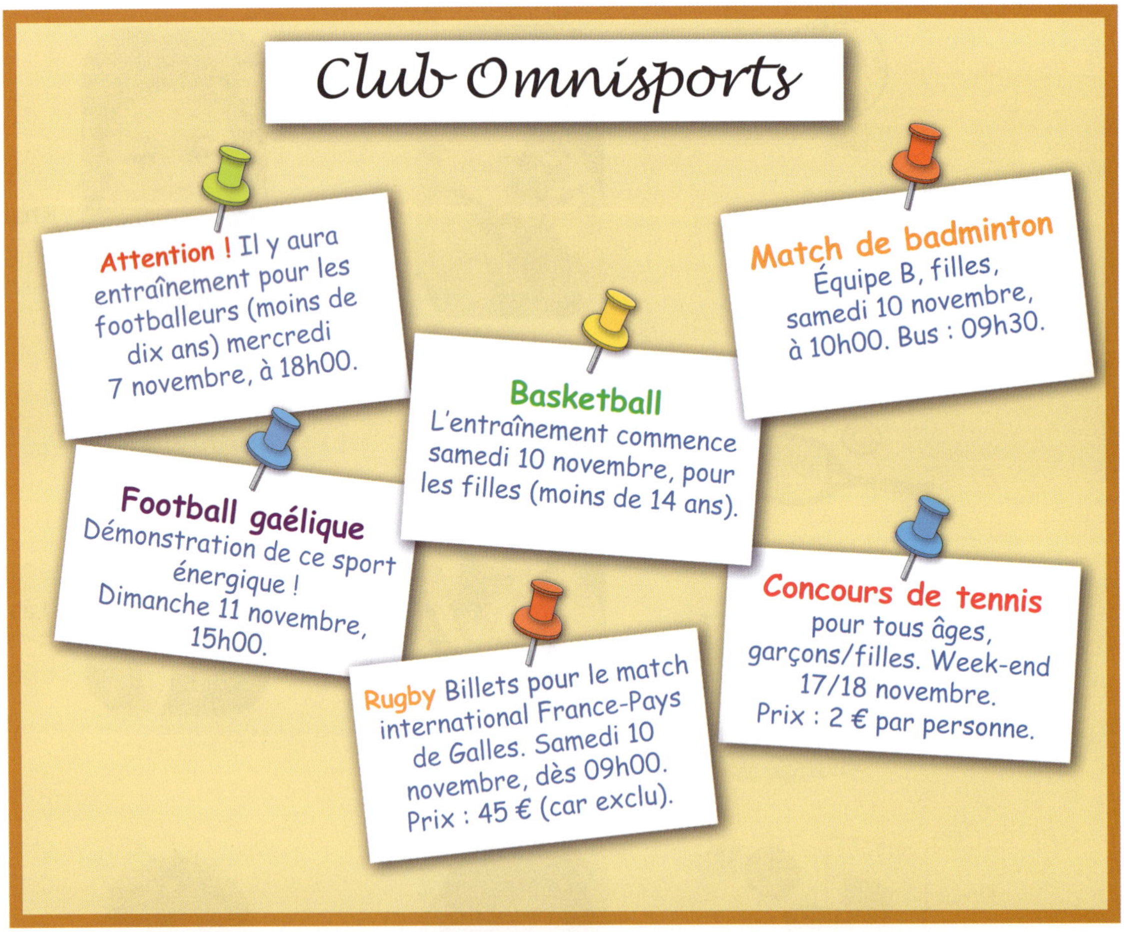

1 Football training is for which age group?
2 When is basketball training starting?
3 Who will have a badminton match on Saturday 10?
4 How is Gaelic football described?
5 Tickets are available for which rugby match?
6 Who can take part in the tennis tournament?

Coin grammaire : Individual sports ('Les sports individuels')

l'équitation

l'athlétisme

la gymnastique

le cyclisme/le vélo

le roller

le skate

le VTT

le golf

- '**Faire**' is used mainly for **individual sports**.
- It is an **irregular** verb and is used with the **preposition** '**de**'.

Tip: Révisez le verbe '**faire**' (page 143).

Attention ! 'de' changes three times:

1. If the noun which follows is masculine (a lot of sports are), '**de** changes to **du**':
   Je fais **du** cyclisme.
2. If the noun which follows is feminine, '**de** changes to '**de la**': Il fait **de la** gymnastique.
3. If the noun which follows begins with a vowel, '**de** changes to '**de l**':
   Ils font **de l**'athlétisme.

'Faire de' in the negative

- To make '**faire de**' negative, put the '**ne**' before the verb and the '**pas**' after it, as usual.

Exemples : Je **ne** fais **pas** de judo.
Vous **ne** faites **pas** de natation.
Ils **ne** font **pas** d'équitation.

Exercice 1

Remplissez les blancs avec le verbe '**faire**' et la préposition qui convient.

1. Je __________ ____ roller.
2. Vous ___________ _____ gymnastique à l'école ?
3. Mon fils __________ ____ golf en vacances.
4. Claude et Patrick __________ _______ skate devant la maison.
5. Tu ______________ _____ athlétisme aujourd'hui ?
6. Ils __________ _______ équitation.

Exercice 2

Écrivez une phrase pour chaque image comme dans l'exemple ci-dessous.

Exemple : le VTT → Ils font du VTT.

le VTT

le tir à l'arc

le roller

la natation

l'athlétisme

le cyclisme

la gymnastique

le golf

le judo

l'équitation

Exercice 3

'**Jouer à**' ou '**faire de**' ? Fill in the following sentences using '**jouer à**' or '**faire de**'.

1 Ils __________ ______ hockey sur le terrain de sport.
2 Anna __________ ______ équitation tous les dimanches.
3 Nous __________ ______ tennis le samedi.
4 Marc __________ ______ rugby avec l'équipe de l'école.
5 Ma tante __________ ______ natation tous les jours.
6 Tu __________ ______ athlétisme ?
7 Je __________ ______ foot avec l'équipe de l'école.
8 Vous __________ ______ badminton ?
9 Je __________ ______ golf en juin.
10 Nous __________ ______ gymnastique dans la salle omnisports.

10.2 Écoutons maintenant !

Listen to these six people talking about sports they like and those they do not like.

	likes	dislikes
1 Caroline		
2 Karim		
3 Sophie		
4 Adeline		
5 Tony		
6 Kévin		

Lisons maintenant !

Read Alexis's email and say if the sentences which follow are true or false (**vrai ou faux**).

Salut Andrew !

Ça va ? Je fais un stage sportif cette semaine dans la salle omnisports. J'y vais tous les jours, sauf le dimanche. Le week-end, je fais du cyclisme avec mes amis. Nous pratiquons un sport différent tous les jours : lundi nous avons rugby, mardi basket, mercredi ping-pong, jeudi judo et samedi karaté.
À part le stage, je joue dans une équipe de foot. L'entraînement est très sérieux. Je m'entraîne le lundi et le mercredi et nous avons un match le samedi après-midi.

Et toi ? Tu joues encore au football gaélique et au hurling ? Merci pour les photos de ces sports. Le hurling est dangereux ?

Réponds-moi vite !
Alexis

		vrai	faux
1	Alexis fait un stage au stade municipal.		
2	Il ne va pas au stage le dimanche.		
3	Il joue au basket le mercredi.		
4	Il s'entraîne pour le foot le lundi et le jeudi.		
5	Il a un match tous les samedis.		
6	Il joue aussi au hurling.		

Giving your opinion

Exercice 1

Faites des paires !

Le rugby…	… c'est un sport passionnant !
La natation…	… c'est un sport compétitif !
L'équitation…	… c'est un sport super !
L'athlétisme…	… c'est un sport fatigant !
Le skate…	… c'est un sport fantastique !
Le hurling…	… c'est un sport rapide !

Parlons maintenant !

Quels sont les sports que tu pratiques ? Travaillez par deux ! Ask your partner the following questions about sports he/she likes.

- Tu joues au… ?
- Tu fais du…?
- Mon sport favori c'est le/la/l'…
- J'adore le/la/l'…
- C'est fantastique !
- C'est fatigant !
- C'est un sport rapide/compétitif !
- Oui, je joue au…/Non, je ne joue pas au…
- Oui, je fais du…/Non, je ne fais pas du…
- Je suis fana du/de la/ de l'…
- J'aime/J'adore/Je préfère/Je déteste…
- C'est super/passionnant !
- C'est trop dangereux !
- C'est trop violent !

Exercice 1

Un sondage ! Travail par groupes de quatre personnes.

Fill out the first column of the table below about yourself and then ask three others in your group, '**en français**', which sports they play. When you finish '**le sondage**', each group must report back saying: **Une**/**deux**/**trois**/**quatre personne(s) joue**/**jouent au**... Or **Une**/**deux**/**trois**/**quatre personne(s) fait**/**font de la**...

When you have finished, you can add all the results together for each sport, to find out which sports are most popular in your class. You might make a poster about it such as the one below and see how your results compare.

✓ = je joue X = je ne joue pas

	1	2	3	4
Tu joues au badminton ?				
Tu joues au hockey ?				
Tu joues au foot ?				
Tu joues au rugby ?				
Tu fais de la natation ?				
Tu joues au basket ?				
Tu joues au ping-pong ?				
Tu joues au tennis ?				
Tu joues au foot gaélique ?				
Tu fais de la gymnastique ?				
Tu joues au camogie ?				
Tu joues au hurling ?				

Voici les résultats d'un sondage dans une classe de 6ème du collège Léonard de Vinci.

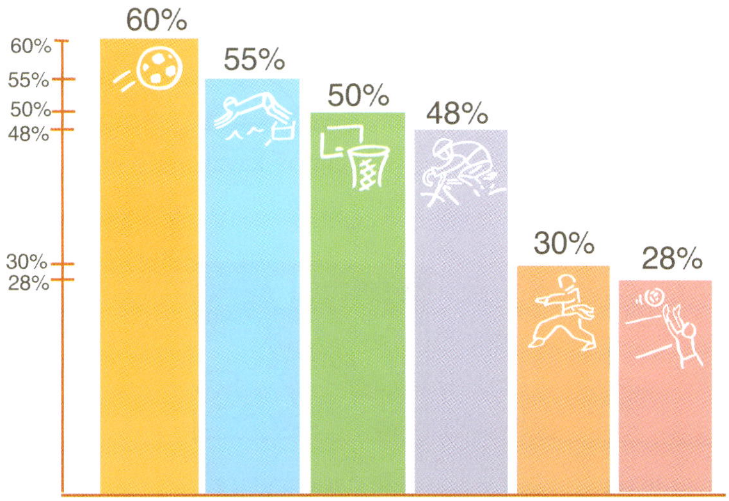

Les saisons

- The four seasons are:

le printemps

l'été

l'automne

l'hiver

Au printemps, je m'entraîne après les vacances de Noël.
En été, je fais de la voile.
En automne, je joue au rugby.
En hiver, je fais du ski.

Rappel !
When saying in spring/summer/autumn/winter you say '**au** printemps', '**en** été', '**en** automne' and '**en** hiver'.

Les sports d'été

Tip: Je fais **du**/**de la**/**de l'**/**des** ...

la planche à voile

la voile

la plongée sous-marine

le surf

le canoë-kayak

le ski nautique

Les sports d'hiver

le ski

le patin à glace

la luge

Exercice 1

Liez le sport avec la bonne saison ! Make a list of the following sports under the headings '**en été**' or '**en hiver**'.

sports
Je fais de la planche à voile.
Je fais du patin à glace.
Je fais du snowboard.
Je fais du ski nautique.
Je fais de la luge.
Je fais du hockey sur glace.
Je fais du volley sur plage.
Je fais du surf.

 en été	 en hiver

Lisons maintenant!

Quel sport ? Say which sports correspond to the drawings.

(a) la planche à voile ____________

(b) le ski ____________

(c) le patin à glace ____________

(d) la voile ____________

(e) la plongée sous-marine ____________

(f) le canoë-kayak ____________

(g) la luge ____________

(h) le surf ____________

Lisons maintenant !

Read the following advertisement and answer the questions which follow.

Sport et nature au bord de la Seine !

Le centre de St Jacques, situé en pleine nature au pied du viaduc de Mauban, propose un grand nombre d'activités sportives pour tout public, à partir de huit ans : VTT, canoë-kayak ou équitation.

Chaque activité se déroule sur une séance de deux heures et est adaptée à l'âge des participants. L'équipement nécessaire est fourni par le centre.

Prix : 18 € pour une séance de deux heures.

Renseignements et inscriptions : 02. 13. 96. 27. 28.

1. What is the minimum age at which you can take part in these activities?
2. Name **two** of the activities suggested.
3. How long is each session?
4. Where do you get the equipment needed?
5. Why would you ring 02.13.96.27.28?

10.3 Écoutons maintenant !

Quels sports ? Quels rendez-vous ? Listen to these conversations and fill in the grid.

	sport	time	meeting place
1			
2			
3			
4			
5			

Civilisation : Les jeux olympiques

- A French man, the Baron de Coubertin, had the idea of organising the modern Olympic Games. He wanted to promote world peace and believed that sport helped to develop a person's character. The games were based on events which were held in Greece, where athletes competed for a crown of olive leaves.
- The first modern Olympic Games took place in Athens in 1896. France hosted the games in 1900 and again in 1924. The Winter Olympics have taken place in Chamonix in the French Alps in 1924, in Grenoble in 1968 and in Albertville in 1992. France has competed at every Olympics.
- The Paralympics were first held in 1960 to cater for those athletes who suffer from a disability. Again, France has had great success at these games.

Lisons maintenant !

Read this article about Assia El Hannouni, who competed for France in the Paralympics in 2004, and answer the questions which follow.

Une athlète courageuse

En gagnant quatre médailles d'or (100m, 200m, 400m et 800m) et en battant le record du monde pour toutes les distances, aux Jeux Paralympiques d'Athènes, Assia El Hannouni est la nouvelle vedette du handisport en France. Assia est née à Dijon le trente mai 1981. À 16 ans, elle découvre qu'elle souffre d'une maladie des yeux et elle perd progressivement la vue. Malgré son handicap, elle a décidé en 1999 de participer à une compétition d'athlétisme handisport à Vittel et son talent était évident. Elle obtient des premiers résultats aux Championnats du monde d'athlétisme en 2003 à Paris lors des compétitions handisports.

Elle est assez grande (1m 78) et elle a un tempérament très compétitif. Sa détermination est impressionnante. Elle court avec un guide et elle se sent en sécurité avec lui. Il la rassure, en lui parlant de la distance et du temps.

1 What did Assia achieve at the Paralympics in 2004?
2 What is her date of birth?
3 When did she first start winning important races?
4 Name **one** of her characteristics?
5 What are the things her guide helps her with during a race?

Les équipements de sport

Exercice 1

Match up the item of sports gear with the sport on the right.

1
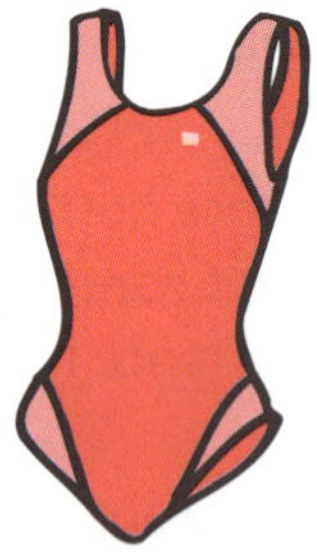
le maillot de bain

2

les chaussures à pointes

3

le ballon ovale

4
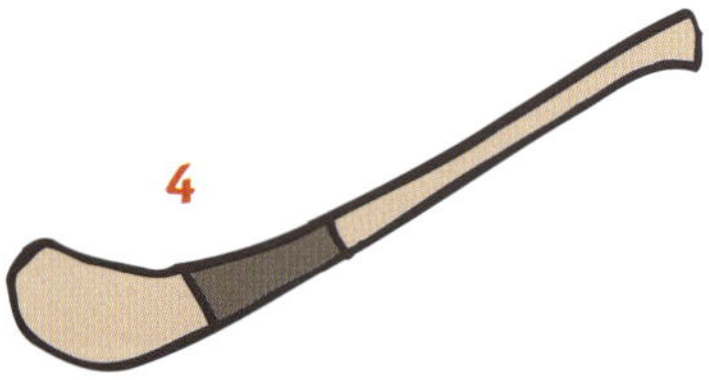
la crosse

5

le ballon rond

6

le maillot jaune

(a) le cyclisme
(b) la natation
(c) le football
(d) le camogie
(e) le rugby
(f) l'athlétisme

10.4

Écoutons maintenant !

These young people are talking about the birthday presents they have received. Say what they received and what sport they play.

	present	sport
1		
2		
3		
4		
5		

Civilisation : Le rugby

- Rugby (**le rugby**) in France is centred in the southwest. France started playing in '**le Tournoi des Cinq Nations**' in 1910, along with '**l'Irlande**', '**l'Angleterre**', '**l'Écosse**' and '**le Pays de Galles**'. In more recent years this tournament has been extended to include '**l'Italie**' and is now '**le Tournoi des Six Nations**'. French club teams also play a leading role in the Heineken European Cup matches (www.ercrugby.com). France hosted the Rugby World Cup in 2007.

Lisons maintenant !

Read this advertisement for sports equipment and answer the questions which follow.

1

15,00 €
Coupe vent, 100% polyester
Du S au XXL, rouge/noir, bleu/noir, vert/bleu-marine

2

12,00 €
Pantalon de sport bicolore,
Homme/Femme 100% polyester
Du S au XXL rouge/noir, bleu/noir.
Version enfant : 10,00 €

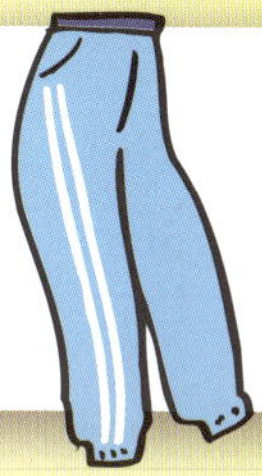

3

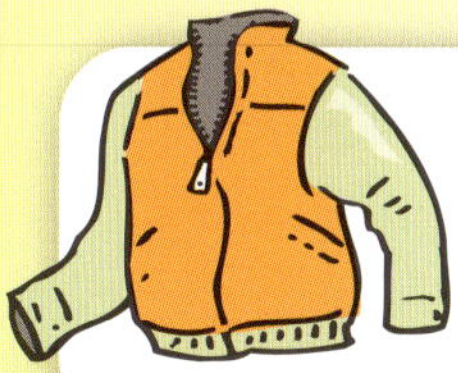

19,00 €
Gilet tricot zippé, 100% coton,
Du S au XXL
Coloris orange

4

6,00 €
Tee-shirts Homme,
100% coton, Du M au XXL
Coloris assortis

5

5,99 € Le lot de 10 !
Paires de Chaussettes de tennis homme ou paires de socquettes femme. Homme : du 39/42 au 43/46, femme : du 35/38 au 39/42. Existe en lot de 10 paires de chaussettes de tennis enfant, du 27 au 40 : 4,99 €

1 Beside red and black, in what other colours can you get this jacket?
2 How much do the track suit bottoms for children cost?
3 What colour is this jacket available in?
4 From what material are the T-shirts made?
5 What can you get for €4.99?

Coin grammaire : The verb 'prendre'

- Here is another irregular verb, '**prendre**' (*to take*). This verb usually means to take, but if a French-speaking person asks you what you will have to eat or to drink he/she will probably say '**Qu'est-ce que tu prends ?**'.
- This is a special use of the verb '**prendre**'. It is also used to give directions.

10.5

Écoutons maintenant !

Écoutez le verbe '**prendre**' au présent.

je	prend**s**
tu	prend**s**
il	prend
elle	prend
nous	pren**ons**
vous	pren**ez**
ils	prenn**ent**
elles	prenn**ent**

Exercice 1

Remplissez la grille avec le verbe '**prendre**'.

je		nous	
tu	prends	vous	prenez
il		ils	
elle	prend	elles	

Civilisation : Le football

- Football (**le foot**) is the nation's most popular sport. Monaco, Paris St Germain, Lyon and Marseille are popular football clubs (www.fff.fr). French footballers have made their name in many European countries. France hosted and won the World Cup in 1998. The '**Stade de France**' in Paris, was built for this tournament. '**Les Bleus**' (*the blues*, the nick-name for the national team) also won the European Cup in 1984 and 2000 (www.fff.fr/bleus/index.shtml) and were finalists in the 2006 World Cup.

Exercice 2

Les ballons ! Match the subject with the correct form of '**prendre**'.

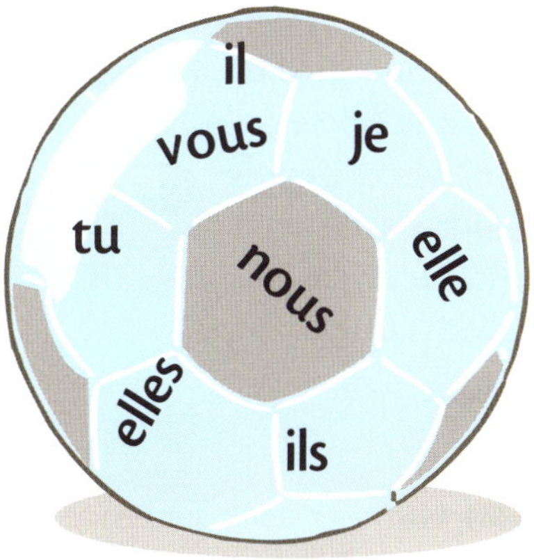

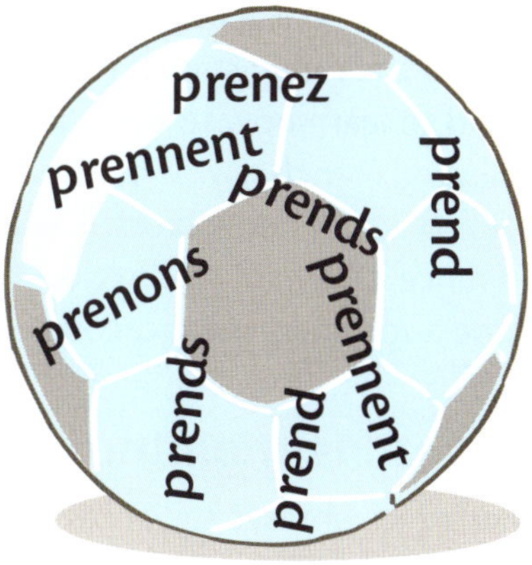

Exercice 3

Complete these sentences using the correct form of the verb '**prendre**' and write them in your copy.

1. Ils pr____nn____nt l'autobus pour aller au match de rugby.
2. Delphine pr____nd le train pour aller au terrain.
3. Luc pr____nd un taxi pour aller au stade.
4. Monsieur Clavel pr____nd un café en ville.
5. Est-ce que tu pr____nds l'autobus pour aller à la piscine ?
6. Nous pr____nons un taxi pour aller au stade.

Exercice 4

Un peu de fun ! Here is a game you can play with your partner to help you to learn the names for sports.

1. Prends la cinquième lettre du mot 'football'.
2. Prends la troisième lettre du mot 'skate'.
3. Prends la première lettre du mot 'ski'.
4. Prends la quatrième lettre du mot 'hockey'.
5. Prends la deuxième lettre du mot 'tennis'.
6. Prends la septième lettre du mot 'badminton'.
7. Qu'est que c'est ?

Using **Exercise 4** as an example, try making a quiz of your own.

Civilisation : L'équitation

- Horse-riding is a popular pastime in France. Young people go to the riding stables (**les manèges**) to learn riding skills and to learn how to take care of their ponies and horses. Several French towns have '**un hippodrome**', where people go to watch horse races. The most famous horse race in France is '**le Prix de l'Arc de Triomphe**' held each year in the autumn at the racecourse near Paris called '**Longchamps**'.

Rappel ! un cheval, des chevaux

Écoutons maintenant !

10.6

Mettez les phrases suivantes dans le bon ordre. Number each sentence in the order in which you hear it. The first one is done for you.

☐	Il adore les carottes et le chocolat.	☐	Je fais de l'équitation le samedi matin au manège.
☐	Je participe aux concours hippiques.	☐	Mon cheval préféré s'appelle Toto.
☐	J'ai quatre médailles.	1	Salut, je m'appelle Martine.
☐	J'ai douze ans et j'adore les animaux, surtout les chevaux.	☐	Mon passe-temps préféré est l'équitation.
☐	Il a trois ans.	☐	Il est grand et blanc.

Lisons maintenant !

Read the document below and answer the questions which follow.

Musée vivant du cheval

Démonstrations tous les jours, sauf le samedi

'Les poneys font leur spectacle'

Animations poneys

Mercredi : 14h00 Samedi : 11h00

Pendant les vacances, le musée est ouvert tous les jours.

Pendant les mois de novembre, décembre, janvier et février, le musée est ouvert le week-end.

Venez voir nos trente chevaux blancs : animations, histoire et démonstrations !

1 On what days do the pony shows take place?
2 During which months is the museum open only at the weekend?
3 Give **one** detail about the horses.

Coin grammaire : Possessive adjectives plural ('Les adjectifs possessifs pluriels')

- In **Unité 4**, you learned how to say '**my**', '**your**', '**his**' and '**her**' in French (see page 89). Now we will look at the **plural** form of these **possessive adjectives**. Remember that the form you use depends on the **noun which follows** the adjective!

	before masc. sing. nouns	before fem. sing. nouns	before all plural nouns
our	notre	notre	nos
your (pl.)	votre	votre	vos
their	leur	leur	leurs

Nous supportons **notre** équipe de badminton. → You use **notre**, because '**équipe**' is fem. sing.
Portez **vos** baskets dans la salle omnisports. → You use **vos**, because '**baskets**' are plural.
Ils vont à **leur** entraînement régulièrement. → You use **leur**, because '**entraînement**' is masc. sing.

Exercice 1

Complétez les phrases suivantes avec l'adjectif possessif qui convient.

1 Nous avons ___________ entraînement le lundi
2 Vous voulez vendre ___________ vélo ?
3 Thomas et Karim habitent Lyon. Mais quelle est ___________ adresse ?
4 ___________ amis viennent au match avec nous.
5 N'oubliez pas ___________ raquettes !
6 Ils jouent au tennis avec ___________ équipe.
7 Vous avez ___________ maillots de bain ?
8 Ils ne peuvent pas trouver ___________ baskets.

Les résultats !

Je suis
un champion :
je marque
des buts !
(*I score goals*)

La France gagne le match !

Munster bat Biarritz !

L'Irlande perd le match !

Les Brésiliens sont les champions !

10.7

Écoutons maintenant !

Les résultats ! Listen to these sports results and fill in the grid.

	le sport	le score
1		
2		
3		
4		
5		

Exercice 1

Un quiz ! Choose the correct answer.

1 La France a gagné la Coupe du Monde de football en
(*a*) 1994 ; (*b*) 1998 ; (*c*) 2000 ; (*d*) 1996.

2 L'athlète Annissa El Hannouni est née à
(*a*) Marseille ; (*b*) Paris ; (*c*) Lyon ; (*d*) Dijon.

3 Dans une équipe de football, il y a
(*a*) 12 joueurs ; (*b*) 15 joueurs ; (*c*) 14 joueurs ; (*d*) 11 joueurs.

4 Pour faire de l'équitation, il faut avoir
(*a*) un cochon ; (*b*) un cheval ; (*c*) un chien ; (*d*) un chat.

5 On joue au ping-pong sur
(*a*) une chaise ; (*b*) une table ; (*c*) une porte ; (*d*) un lit.

6 Quand on fait de la natation, on porte
(*a*) un maillot jaune ; (*b*) des chaussures à pointe ; (*c*) un maillot de bain ; (*d*) un gilet.

7 Quel pays ne joue pas dans le Tournoi des Six Nations ?
(*a*) L'Argentine ; (*b*) L'Irlande ; (*c*) La France ; (*d*) L'Italie.

8 Quel est le sport qui n'est pas un sport nautique ?
(*a*) Le surf ; (*b*) La voile ; (*c*) La planche à voile ; (*d*) Le judo.

Écrivons maintenant !

(a) Complétez la lettre ci-dessous.

Lyon, le 13 mars

Cher Neil,

Tu vas bien ? Comment va ta famille ? J'ai joué au  ________. C'est mon sport favori. J'adore jouer au foot, je suis défenseur. Mon copain Max joue comme gardien de but.

En hiver, quand il neige, je fais du  ________. Nous allons dans les  ________. Ma mère va souvent à la piscine, car elle aime la  ________. Mon père préfère faire du  ________. Ma soeur Sophie joue au  ________. Sa joueuse préférée s'appelle Amélie Mauresmo. Elle s'intéresse aussi aux chevaux, elle fait de l'  ________.

Je suis membre du club des jeunes dans ma ville et j'y vais tous les mercredis pour jouer au  ________.

Je fais du  ________ avec mon père le week-end. Il y a un terrain de golf près de chez moi.

C'est tout pour le moment. Écris-moi vite et dis-moi ce que tu aimes comme sport.

Amitiés,

Guillaume

(b) Now write a letter to your '**correspondant(e)**', Julien/Julie, using the letter above as a model. Based on what you have learned in this unit, say as many things as you can about the sports you and your family play or like.

Communication en classe !

- Faites attention !
- Le match commence à cinq heures.
- Portez des baskets sur le court !
- Ne portez pas vos baskets en classe !
- Mettez votre matériel de sport dans le placard !
- Ne laissez pas votre crosse ici !
- Regardez les détails du match sur le tableau d'affichage !
- Quel est le score ?

Lexique

abonnement (m.)	*subscription*
Angleterre (f.)	*England*
animation (f.)	*entertainment*
à la fin de	*at the end of*
à partir de	*from*
arts martiaux (m. pl.)	*martial arts*
au pied de	*at the foot of*
avoir besoin de	*to need*
balle (f.)	*ball (tennis, etc.)*
ballon (m.)	*ball (football, etc.)*
basket (m.)	*basketball*
battre	*to beat*
billet (m.)	*ticket*
championnat (m.)	*championship*
chaussettes (f. pl.)	*socks*
chaussures à pointe (f. pl.)	*spiked running shoes*
concours (m.)	*competition*
coupe (f.)	*cup/trophy*
coupe-vent (m.)	*windcheater*
courir	*to run*
crosse de hockey (f.)	*hockey stick*
débutant(e)	*beginner*
défenseur (m.)	*defender*
se dérouler	*to take place*
Écosse (f.)	*Scotland*
s'entraîner	*to train*
équipe (f.)	*team*
équipement de sport (m.)	*sports equipment*
équitation (f.)	*horse riding*
entraînement (m.)	*training*
faire (du)	*to make/do/play*
fatigant(e)	*tiring*
en salle (m.)	*indoor*
fourni(e)	*provided*
gagner	*to win*
gardien de but (m.)	*goalkeeper*
gilet (m.)	*sleeveless jacket*
golf (m.)	*golf*
hippodrome (m.)	*racetrack*
jeu (m.)	*game*
luge (f.)	*tobogganing*
maillot de bain (m.)	*swimsuit*
maillot jaune (m.)	*yellow jersey*
maladie (f.)	*illness*
malgré	*despite*
manège (m.)	*riding stables*
médaille (f.)	*medal*
moins de	*under/less of*
natation (f.)	*swimming*
or (m.)	*gold*
pantalon (m.)	*trousers*
participer	*to take part*
passe-temps (m.)	*pastime*
passionnant(e)	*exciting*
patin à glace (m.)	*ice skating*
Pays de Galles (m.)	*Wales*
pendant	*during*
perdre	*to lose*
ping-pong (m.)	*table tennis*
planche à voile (f.)	*windsurfing*
plongée (f.)	*diving*
plongée sous marine (f.)	*deep sea diving*
porter	*to wear*
pratiquer	*to take part/practise*
rapide (m./f.)	*fast*
rassurer	*to reassure*
rendez-vous (m.)	*meeting (place)*
renseignements (m. pl.)	*information*
résultat (m.)	*result*
se retrouver	*to meet*
roi (m.)	*king*
séance (f.)	*session*
ski nautique (m.)	*waterskiing*
stade (m.)	*stadium*
stage (m.)	*course*
sur glace	*on ice*
taille (f.)	*size*
tir à l'arc (m.)	*archery*
tournoi (m.)	*tournament*
trop	*too much/too many*
vedette (f.)	*star*
vélo (m.)	*bicycle*
victoire (f.)	*win/victory*
vite	*fast/quickly*
voile (f.)	*sailing*
VTT (vélo tout terrain) (m.)	*mountain biking*
vue (f.)	*sight/vision*
yeux (m. pl.)	*eyes*

Épreuve

Question 1

Match the following signs and pictures. Put the letters which correspond to the numbers in the boxes.

1		A	le ping-pong
2	l'équitation	B	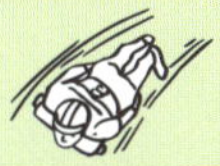
3		C	la voile
4	le vélo	D	
5	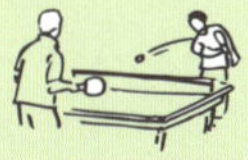	E	le canoë-kayak
6	le patin à glace	F	
7		G	la natation
8	la gymnastique	H	
9		I	le tir à l'arc
10	la luge	J	

Nº	letter
1	
2	
3	
4	
5	
6	
7	
8	
9	
10	

Question 2

Écoutez les conversations et répondez aux questions.

Interview 1

1 What age is Marie-Claire?
2 What is her favourite sport?
3 What subject does she enjoy at school?
4 Name **one** sport in which she represents her school?
5 What does she do each Thursday?

Interview 2

1 Where does Jean-François work?
2 What does he do there?
3 Name **two** sports for which there are competitions.
4 What sports does he do himself to relax?

Question 3

1 What type of lessons are offered?
2 Where will the lessons take place?
3 For how many weeks will the course last?
4 Are the lessons designed for
(*a*) beginners; (*b*) life-guards;
(*c*) improvers; (*d*) experienced swimmers? ☐
5 How can you contact Madame Ménard?

Question 4

Write the correct form of the verb '**prendre**'.

1 Je ____________________ le train pour aller à la patinoire.
2 Nous ____________________ l'autobus chez moi après le match.
3 Marc ____________________ le ballon avec lui.
4 Tiffaine et Paul ____________________ un car pour aller au stade.
5 Les étudiants ____________________ les casques.
6 Est-ce que vous ____________________ la crosse pour le hockey ?

For **help** with this exercise, **see page 290**.

Question 5

Listen and answer the questions.

1. What sport is the subject of the first news item?
2. What sport is holding world championship in Denmark?
3. What has Fabien Barthez just done?
4. Which team has won four medals in the karate championship?
5. In what sport did France win five gold medals?

Question 6

Match the sport to the place with which it is associated.

1	Je joue au foot...	(a)	à la piscine.
2	Je fais du ski...	(b)	dans le manège.
3	Je fais du roller...	(c)	à la mer.
4	Je joue au ping-pong...	(d)	sur un court.
5	Je fais de l'équitation...	(e)	dans les Alpes.
6	Je fais de la voile...	(f)	dans le rollerdrome.
7	Je fais de la natation...	(g)	sur une table.
8	Je joue au tennis...	(h)	sur un terrain de foot.

Question 7

Insert the correct possessive adjective in these sentences.

1. Les Irlandais gagnent _________ match.
2. Suzanne, vous avez _________ baskets ?
3. Nous supportons _________ équipe de ping-pong pour la compétition.
4. Les athlètes battent _________ record pour le championnat du monde.
5. Mettez _________ matériel pour le match dans le car !
6. Nous portons _________ maillots quand nous allons à la piscine.

For **help** with this exercise, **see page 293**.

Question 8

Read this article on the European Rugby Cup and answer the questions which follow.

L'Europe à l'heure du rugby

Premier match de la Coupe d'Europe de rugby ce vendredi 20 octobre. En 12 ans, cette épreuve a conquis le public français.

Plus de 16 000 places ont déjà été vendues pour la finale de la Coupe d'Europe qui se disputera le 20 mai 2007 au stade de Twickenham à Londres (Angleterre). En douze ans d'existence, cette épreuve, aussi appelée H Cup, a ainsi conquis un large public.

La Coupe d'Europe réunit des clubs irlandais, italiens, écossais, gallois, anglais et français. Cette année, sept clubs français participent au tournoi : Toulouse, Biarritz, Paris, Perpignan, Agen, Bourgoin et Castres.

L'Angleterre détient le record (elle a gagné cinq finales), la France compte quatre victoires, dont trois de Toulouse.

1. When will the first match take place?
2. What is the other name for the European Cup?
3. Apart from France, name **two** other countries whose clubs will be represented.
4. How many French clubs will take part this time?
5. How many times has Toulouse won the European Cup?

Question 9

Listen to Philip as he writes an email to Simon and fill in the gaps.

Simon !

Me voici en vacances dans un camping. Il fait ______________ ici dans le sud. Je fais de la ______________ tous les jours. Je fais du ______________ sur la plage avec mes nouveaux amis.

Il y a tant à faire – le ______________, le volley et le tennis. J'apprends à faire du ______________, c'est un art martial. C'est super !

Ma mère adore la ______________ et elle fait de la natation tous les jours. Papa fait du ______________ avec mon oncle le matin. Le soir tout le monde joue aux ______________. Mon frère Kévin fait de la ______________ sur le lac et il est content.

Envoie un courriel demain avec toutes les nouvelles. Tu as un ______________ samedi ? Tu t'entraînes avec l'équipe ce soir ?

Je te quitte, mes amis arrivent !

Phil

Question 10

Read the following advertisement and answer the questions which follow.

pendant les mois de juin, juillet, août

Enfants de dix à seize ans

Matin : 9h–12h
Après-midi : 14h–17h

Tarif

Demi-journée 20,00 € (*3 heures de cours*)
À la semaine 90,00 € (*soit 5 demi-journées*)

Rendez-vous tous les jours : le quai des pêcheurs, rue du Port.

Il est impératif de savoir nager !

Pour tous renseignements et inscriptions, veuillez contacter directement le bureau de l'École de Voile.

1. During which months will the courses take place?
2. For what age group are the courses intended?
3. How many hours tuition will you get for €20?
4. Where is the meeting place each day?
5. How do you get information?

Coin pronunciation: Be careful when pronouncing French words which end in or contain '–tion'! They have a different sound to English. They should sound like 'see-ong': 'nata**tion**', 'équita**tion**', 'na**tion**', 'na**tion**al', 'détermina**tion**', 'réac**tion**'.

Unité 11

Mes passe-temps

Civilisation : Les passe-temps

- French teenagers are no different to those of any other country. They like to listen to music, go to concerts, watch TV, hang out with friends, surf the internet and read. However, because of the length of their school day, combined with a homework schedule, they have less time during the week for these pastimes. It is mainly at the weekend or on Wednesdays that they have time for a hobby (**un passe-temps**).

11.1 Écoutons maintenant !

Listen to these young people talking about what they like to do and link them to the picture which illustrates this hobby.

Océane ____________

Luc ____________

Sophie ____________

Christophe ____________

Léa ____________

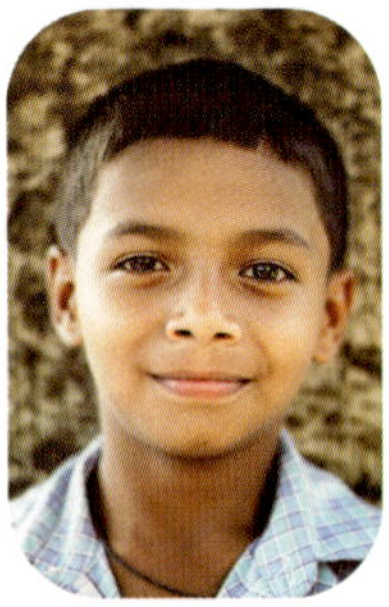
Khalid ____________

a.

la lecture

b.

la philatélie

c.

la danse

d.

la peinture

e.

jouer de la guitare

f.

surfer sur le Net

Lisons maintenant !

Read the following notice board and answer the questions which follow.

Cours de danse
Samedi, 10h00-12h00
Jazz, hip-hop, salsa
Commence le 8 janvier.

CLUB DE PHILATÉLIE
Mercredi, 16h00-17h00
Nous accueillons de nouveaux membres !

Salle d'informatique
Ouverte tous les jours, à partir de 16h00.
Samedi : 10h00-19h00

CINÉCLUB
Samedi 10 janvier
'Les Choristes', film suivi d'une discussion.
Billet : 3,00 €
(boisson chaude pour tout le monde)

Cours de guitare
Mercredi : débutants, 16h00-17h00
Moyens : 17h00-18h00

Ping-pong
Samedi 10 janvier, 11h00
Match contre l'équipe de MJC St Jacques,
Liste des joueurs sur le tableau d'affichage de sport.

Cours de peinture
Samedi matin 11h00–12h00
Commence le 20 janvier, dix semaines
50,00 € par personne (matériel inclus)

Jeux de société
Samedi matin, 10h30
Échecs, jeux de dames, cartes, Monopoly.
Matériel disponible au bureau de l'animateur
(caution : 2,00 € par personne)

Café de l'Amitié
Ouvert tous les jours
(sauf le dimanche)
Boissons, snacks
Tables baby-foot et ping-pong !

1. What types of dance can you take a class in?
2. When does the stamp club meet?
3. When is the computer room available?
4. What does the €3 for the film club include?
5. Where will you find the team names for the table tennis match?
6. How long will the painting course last?
7. What do you pay €2 for if you want to play a board-game?
8. When is the café closed?

Exercice 1

À la MJC ! Complete these sentences with a suitable verb.

fais · envoie · échange · apprends · regarde · bois · joue · amuse

1 Je ________________ au Monopoly.
2 Je ________________ des films.
3 Je ________________ du baby-foot.
4 J' ________________ des timbres.
5 J' ________________ à jouer de la guitare.
6 Je m' ________________ à jouer aux cartes.
7 Je ________________ un coca au café de l'Amitié.
8 J' ________________ des courriels à mes amis.

Parlons et écrivons maintenant !

(a) Travaillons à deux ! Qu'est-ce que tu aimes faire le week-end ? Qu'est-ce que tu n'aimes pas faire ? Ask your partner the following questions and make a list of what he/she likes and does not like doing. Use the grid below to help you.

Posez les questions	Répondez
– Tu aimes danser/écouter… ?	– Oui, j'aime…/Non, je n'aime pas…

	aime ✓	n'aime pas X
danser		
écouter de la musique		
aller au cinéma		
jouer aux cartes		
lire des romans/magazines		
surfer sur le Net		
jouer d'un instrument		
regarder la télévision		
faire de la peinture		

(b) Now write a short report on your findings in your copy.

Exemple : Caoimhe aime danser. Elle aime faire de la peinture et écouter de la musique. Elle n'aime pas jouer aux jeux vidéo et elle déteste jouer aux cartes !

Civilisation : La musique

- Some teenagers play musical instruments and many of them listen to (**écouter**) music on their iPods (**iPods**) and CD players (**les lecteurs CD**). Many download (**télécharger**) music from the internet (**l'Internet**).They attend concerts (**les concerts**) and musicals (**les spectacles de musique**) also. Each year '**la Fête de la Musique**' is held throughout France. Usually held in June, towns and villages organise musical events to celebrate the day: street music, concerts, workshops, etc. The aim is to encourage everyone to enjoy music of all sorts.

Tu aimes la musique ?

le rock
le jazz
le rap
le hip hop
le hard-rock
la musique classique
la techno
la pop
la musique traditionnelle

Les instruments

Écoutons maintenant !

11.2

Écoutez et remplissez le tableau ci-dessous.

1 la guitare

2 la batterie

3 le violon

4 la flûte à bec

5 le piano

6 le clavier

name	instrument	favourite type of music
Luc		
Christophe		
Khalid		
Sophie		
Léa		
Océane		

Coin grammaire : 'Jouer de'

Rappel ! You use '**jouer à**' to play a sport. See page 276.

- '**Jouer**' is used to say you play a musical instrument. It is a regular '**–er**' verb and is used with the preposition '**de**'.
- Voici le verbe '**jouer**' (*to play*) au présent.

je	jou**e**
tu	jou**es**
il	jou**e**
elle	jou**e**
nous	jou**ons**
vous	jou**ez**
ils/elles	jou**ent**

Exercice 1

La forme négative ! Write the negative form of the verb '**jouer**' in your copy.

Exemple : Je **ne** joue **pas**, etc.

Attention ! '**de**' changes three times depending on the noun which follows:

1. If the noun is masculine, '**de**' changes to '**du**'. — Je joue **du** violon.
2. If the noun is feminine, '**de**' changes to '**de la**'. — Il joue **de la** guitare.
3. If the noun begins with a vowel, '**de**' changes to '**de l'**'. — Nous jouons **de l'**accordéon.

Exercice 2

Choose one item from each circle to make a sentence starting from the centre.

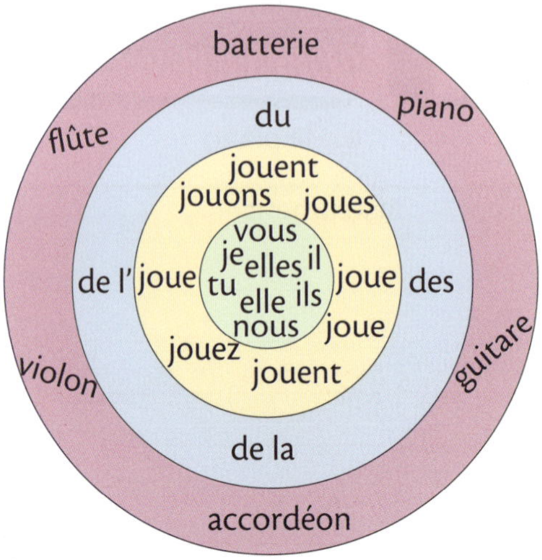

Exercice 3

Remplissez les blancs avec le verbe '**jouer**' et la préposition qui convient.

1

Je ______ ______
______ batterie.

2

Vous ______
beaucoup ______ piano ?

3

Ma fille ______ ______
______ flûte.

4

Louise et Farid ______
______ ______ accordéon.

5

Tu ______ ______
______ guitare ?

6

Ils ______ ______
violon.

- French teenagers follow many famous singers (**chanteurs/euses**) and bands (**les groupes**). They often listen to American or English singers, which helps them when it comes to learning English!

Lisons maintenant !

Read the profile of Avril Lavigne and answer the questions which follow.

AVRIL LAVIGNE

Nom : Lavigne
Prénom : Avril Ramona
Née : le vingt-sept septembre mil neuf cent quatre-vingt quatre
À : Ontario, Canada
Famille : un frère, Matt, une sœur, Michelle
Mari : Deryck Whibley, chanteur de Sum 41. Ils se sont mariés le 15/07/06.
Animal : un chien, qui s'appelle Sam
Artistes préférés : Alanis Morissette, Sum 41, les Beach Boys
Vedettes de cinéma préférées : Toby Maguire, Sandra Bullock
Son parcours : Elle a commencé à chanter à deux ans et à jouer de la guitare à douze, sur la guitare de son père. Elle a passé son enfance à Pananese, une petite ville de cinq mille habitants. À 14 ans, elle a gagné le premier prix d'un concours de chanteurs amateurs à la radio.
Elle écrit ses chansons (parfois en collaboration avec d'autres musiciens). Elle fait partie de la chorale d'une église. Elle a vendu plus de quatre millions de copies de son album *Let Go* (2002). En 2004, *Under my Skin* a été un grand succès. En 2006, elle a chanté pour le film d'animation *Over the Hedge*. Elle vient de signer un contrat pour commencer une carrière de comédienne dans un film *Fast Food Nation* avec Patricia Arquette et Ethan Hawke.

1. When was Avril Lavigne born?
2. Who else is there in her family?
3. What is her husband's career?
4. Who is Sam?
5. What did she start doing when she was two years old?
6. What happened when she was fourteen?
7. How many copies did her album *Let Go* sell?
8. What new career change is she starting?

Civilisation : Le cinéma

- French people are great cinema-goers. Did you know that the first public projection of a film in the world took place in France?
- The brothers Auguste and Louis Lumière pioneered their new invention, the '**cinématographe**' and showed the first ever film in the Grand Café in Paris on December 28, 1895.
- Each year '**la Fête du Cinéma**' takes place in France, towards the end of June. It lasts three days, during which people are encouraged to go along to their local cinemas. Once you buy a ticket for one showing (**une séance**), you get '**un passeport**' which allows you to attend all the other films for €2 each time! French films have had world-wide success in recent years: '**Le Fabuleux Destin d'Amélie Poulain**', '**La Marche de l'Empereur**', '**Les Choristes**' have been seen all round the world and broken box-office records.

- In keeping with the great interest in cinema, '**le Futuroscope**', a theme park dedicated to film technology, was opened in 1987. At that time it had the largest screen in Europe – 600m. Since then, the park has grown adding new technologies. In 1990, '**Cyberavenue**' was opened – 800m of multimedia internet, video and virtual reality games. It is now the second most visited theme park in France. In '**Cinéma 360°**', the viewer is completely surrounded by the film being shown.

11.3

Écoutons maintenant !

Six teenagers talk about going to the cinema. How often do they go to the cinema?

	how often they go to the cinema
Océane	
Léa	
Luc	
Christophe	
Sophie	
Khalid	

Lisons maintenant !

Read the following cinema listing and say who will go to which film.

J'adore les films d'aventure et de suspense.
Laurent
CINÉMA REX
17-24 novembre
Azur et Asmar – dessin animé
Le Dahlia noir – film d'espionnage
Le diable s'habille en Prada – comédie
Indigènes – drame
Ne le dis à personne ! – film à suspense
Scoop – comédie/policier
Mes films favoris sont les films dramatiques.
Clarisse
Les films d'espionnage m'amusent beaucoup.
Michel
Quand je vais au cinéma, je veux rire. J'adore les comédies !
Louise
Je vais emmener ma petite soeur voir un film, un dessin animé.
Claudine
Pour moi, un bon film policier est ce que je préfère.
Mélanie

1 Laurent va voir ______________________.
2 Clarisse va voir ______________________.
3 Louise va voir ______________________.
4 Claudine et sa sœur vont voir ______________________.
5 Mélanie va voir ______________________.
6 Michel va voir ______________________.

Parlons maintenant !

Avec votre partenaire, discutez des films que vous aimez. Utilisez les phrases suivantes :

– Tu aimes aller au cinéma ?	– Oui, c'est mon passe-temps favori. – Je suis fana de cinéma. – Oui, assez. – Non, je n'aime pas aller au cinéma.
– Tu vas souvent au cinéma ?	– Oui, je vais au ciné toutes les semaines/ le week-end/pendant les vacances. – Oui, je vais au ciné une/deux/trois fois par mois.
– Tu aimes quel genre de film ?	– J'aime les comédies/les films policiers/les films de suspense,...
– Tu as une vedette préférée ?	– Oui, j'adore Leonardo di Caprio/Brad Pitt/Scarlett Johansson.

Lisons maintenant !

Read this article about a film festival which is specially for young people.

Mon 1er Festival

Pour sa deuxième édition, le festival du cinéma pour les 3–15 ans est organisé pendant les vacances de la Toussaint, du 25 au 30 octobre 2006.
Ce festival se déroule dans sept salles de cinéma parisiennes.
Il y aura de nombreuses surprises !
Cette année, le thème est 'En route pour l'aventure !' On découvre des pirates, des monstres et des héros.

Trois séances par jour :
10h00, 14h00 et 16h00 en semaine · 11h00, 14h00 et 16h00 le week-end
Prix d'entrée par séance : 4,00 € (5 séances achetées, la 6e gratuite)

1 This festival has been running for (*a*) 2 years; (*b*) 3 years; (*c*) 15 years? ☐
2 In which city is it held?
3 Can you work out the theme of the festival?
4 How do the times of showing vary at the weekend?
5 How do you get one free entrance?

11.4 Écoutons maintenant !

Qui dit quoi ? Lucie et Julie parlent de cinéma. Which of the young people made the following statements? Tick the correct box in the grid.

statements	Lucie	Julie
1 Cinema tickets are quite dear.		
2 She loves to eat popcorn when she goes to the cinema.		
3 She reads film magazines.		
4 Her favourite films are comedies.		
5 She often rents a DVD.		
6 She goes to the cinema with friends.		
7 She prefers French films.		
8 She goes to the cinema festival in June.		

Civilisation : Les nouvelles technologies

Internet: Did you know?

- 61% des jeunes préfèrent Internet comme moyen de communication.
- 80% des jeunes ont un ordinateur dans leur maison.
- 60% des jeunes se connectent chaque jour à Internet.

Sondage réalisé en 2006 par Médiamétrie.

11.5

Écoutons maintenant !

Écoutez les jeunes qui parlent de l'ordinateur et remplissez la grille. Fill in the order in which the comments are made.

1 Uses the internet for homework.	
2 Uses the internet for music.	
3 Surfs the internet.	
4 Uses the computer for sending emails.	
5 Stores photos on the computer.	

Écrivons maintenant !

(a) **Courriel-Symbole !** Lisez ci-dessous le courriel de Fabien et remplacez les symboles par des mots.

Salut Deirdre !

Ce week-end je vais chez Danni regarder un  ____________________ avec des amis. Nous faisons ça tous les week-ends. Dans ma famille, nous adorons la technologie.

Ma mère adore regarder la  ____________________ le soir. Elle adore les jeux télévisés. Mon père travaille beaucoup sur l'  ____________________ à la banque, où il travaille. À la maison, il adore surfer sur le Net. Théo, mon frère, télécharge de la musique sur  ____________________. Ma sœur, Laure, envoie des  ____________________ à sa correspondante espagnole. J'ai reçu un  ____________________ pour mon anniversaire, c'est super ! Et toi ? Comment est ta famille ? Est-ce que beaucoup de familles en Irlande ont Internet ?

Amitiés,

Fabien

(b) Write back to Fabien telling him the ways in which your family uses technology.

Parlons maintenant !

(a) **Sondage en classe !** One student asks the class the question and then counts the answers given. Students take it in turn to ask the questions, count the results and fill in the results on the grid.

– Tu joues aux jeux vidéo ?	– Oui, je joue/Non, je ne joue pas...
– Tu regardes des DVD ?	– Oui, je regarde des DVD/Non, je ne regarde pas de DVD.
– Tu as un ordinateur chez toi ?	– Oui, j'ai/Non, je n'ai pas d'....
– Tu surfes sur le Net ?	– Oui, je surfe/Non, je ne surfe pas...
– Tu as un portable ?	– Oui, j'ai/Non, je n'ai pas de...

	nombre d'élèves		nombre d'élèves
jouent aux jeux vidéo		ne jouent pas aux jeux vidéo	
regardent des DVD		ne regardent pas de DVD	
ont un ordinateur		n'ont pas d'ordinateur	
surfent sur le Net		ne surfent pas sur le Net	
ont un portable		n'ont pas de portable	

(b) Write up the totals in the form of a poster in your classroom.

Exercice 1

Testez-vous ! Answer the following questions and check the results below to see if you are a technology addict.

1. Si tu perds ton portable,
   (*a*) ça ne te dérange pas ;
   (*b*) tu attends de recevoir un nouveau portable en cadeau ;
   (*c*) tu achètes un nouveau portable tout de suite. ☐
2. Tu surfes sur le Net
   (*a*) jamais ; (*b*) le week-end ; (*c*) chaque soir. ☐
3. Tu joues aux jeux vidéo
   (*a*) jamais ; (*b*) quelquefois ; (*c*) tous les jours. ☐
4. Tu as une collection de
   (*a*) timbres ; (*b*) cartes postales ; (*c*) DVD. ☐
5. Pour ton anniversaire, tu préfères recevoir
   (*a*) un livre ; (*b*) un jean ; (*c*) un jeu vidéo. ☐
6. Combien de courriels envoies-tu par semaine ?
   (*a*) zéro ; (*b*) une dizaine ; (*c*) plus de vingt. ☐

Civilisation : La lecture

- Reading is a pastime which is popular among French teenagers, whether it is novels, magazines or comics. Each year, the annual '**Fête Nationale du Livre**' is held in October. The aim is to get everyone to read. There are free talks by authors in cafés, libraries and bookshops. As a lot of people read while they are commuting, the train company, the '**SNCF**', organises readings and lectures by authors and book illustrators in many of the main railway stations.

Lisons maintenant !

Quelle personne ? Read these extracts about reading and answer the questions which follow.

Christophe : J'adore la lecture. Je lis de tout : des romans, des bandes dessinées et des magazines – surtout des magazines de foot comme *Onze*. Je lis tous les jours avant de m'endormir. Mon livre favori est *Le Seigneur des Anneaux*. C'est extra !

Léa : Je suis une vraie fana de lecture. Je lis tous les jours en allant à l'école (j'habite assez loin du collège). J'aime Harry Potter. *Harry Potter et le Prince de Sang-Mêlé* est mon livre préféré. Je crois que J.K. Rowling écrit des romans fantastiques. J'aime aussi les romans d'Eoin Colfer, un auteur irlandais.

Océane : Moi, je n'aime pas beaucoup lire les romans. Mais j'achète des magazines toutes les semaines. Je préfère les magazines comme *StarClub*. Je lis les histoires de toutes les vedettes, les paroles des chansons et les interviews avec les chanteurs et chanteuses.

Luc : Ma journée scolaire est très longue et je lis le soir pour me relaxer. Je lis des bandes dessinées. J'ai une grande collection : Astérix, Tintin, Lucky Luke, Agrippine, etc. Je lis aussi des biographies de vedettes de sports.

Sophie : Moi, j'adore les animaux, surtout les chevaux. Mon auteur préféré s'appelle Lauren Brooke. Elle écrit une série qui s'appelle *Heartland*, l'histoire de Laura et de chevaux. Ses romans sont très appréciés en France.

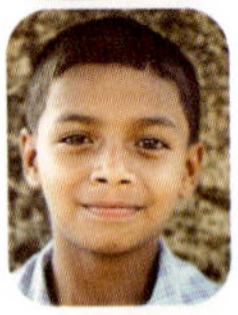

Khalid : Je lis tous les jours. J'aime les auteurs classiques comme Alexandre Dumas ou Jules Verne. Ils écrivent des romans d'aventure qui sont super !

Who is the person who

1. likes an Irish author?
2. prefers classical adventure stories?
3. reads before going to sleep?
4. prefers reading comic books?
5. loves a series about animals?
6. likes to read profiles of the stars?

Coin grammaire : The verbs 'écrire', 'dire' and 'lire'

- When the people in the last exercise were talking about their favourite books, two verbs, '**écrire**' (*to write*) and '**lire**' (*to read*), appear quite often. These verbs are **irregular** and must be learned. However, they are somewhat similar to each other, as is '**dire**' (*to say*). These verbs are often learned together.

11.6 Écoutons maintenant !

Listen to how these verbs sound.

j'	écri**s**	je	di**s**	je	li**s**
tu	écri**s**	tu	di**s**	tu	li**s**
il	écri**t**	il	di**t**	il	li**t**
elle	écri**t**	elle	di**t**	elle	li**t**
nous	écri**vons**	nous	di**sons**	nous	li**sons**
vous	écri**vez**	vous	di**tes** (**attention !**)	vous	li**sez**
ils	écri**vent**	ils	di**sent**	ils	li**sent**
elles	écri**vent**	elles	di**sent**	elles	li**sent**

Exercice 1

Remplissez le tableau ci-dessous.

j'	écris				
		tu	dis		
il	écrit			il	lit
		elle	dit		
nous	écrivons	nous	disons		
				vous	lisez
		ils	disent		
elles	écrivent			elles	lisent

Exercice 2

Remplissez les blancs en utilisant les verbes '**écrire**', '**dire**' or '**lire**'.

1 Laure ____________ un magazine.
2 Paul ____________ une lettre.
3 Théo et Philippe ____________ au revoir.
4 Manon et Tony ____________ sur le tableau.
5 Elles ____________ les affiches.
6 La classe ____________ bonjour au professeur.
7 Tu ____________ une carte postale ?
8 Tu ____________ quel roman ?

Parlons maintenant !

Posez les questions suivantes à votre partenaire.

– Tu lis souvent ?	– Je lis tous les jours/quelquefois/rarement. – Je n'aime pas lire.
– Tu vas souvent à la bibliothèque ?	– Je vais toutes les semaines/quelquefois à la bibliothèque. – Non, je ne vais pas souvent/ne vais jamais à la bibliothèque. – Il n'y a pas de bibliothèque près de chez moi.
– Tu lis des magazines ?	– Oui, je lis des magazines.
– Quels magazines lis-tu ?	– Je lis des magazines de sport/de mode/de films/de musique.
– Qui est ton auteur favori ?	– Mon auteur favori s'appelle…
– Quel est ton livre préféré ?	– Mon livre préféré est…

Civilisation : La télévision

- In France, there is a wide range of TV stations available. Watching television is a very popular pastime. In fact, watching television is the most popular pastime of all French people. They watch TV on average 3 hours 15 minutes per day. Because of satellite and cable channels, French viewers can access more than 180 channels. Some cities have their own TV stations (**La Chaîne Marseille**, **TV7 Bordeaux**, **Télé Lyon Métropole**). Among young people, programmes (**les émissions**) such as '**Star Academy**' and '**Fort Boyard**', and a Spanish series '**Un, Dos, Tres**' are very popular. Other programmes you may know are '**La loi de Los Angeles**', '**Urgences**', '**FBI : portés disparus**', '**Lost : les disparus**', '**Qui veut gagner des millions ?**'.

11.7 Écoutons maintenant !

Remplissez le tableau ci-dessous.

	age	when television is watched	favourite programme(s)
1 Monsieur Royale			
2 Madame Delabre			
3 Sara			
4 Antoine			
5 Kévin			
6 Solène			

Parlons maintenant !

Avec un partenaire, parlez de la télévision !

La danse

11.8

Écoutons maintenant !

Listen to Marine talk about her dance class. Put the sentences in the correct order.

1	Bonjour. Je m'appelle Marine.	1
2	Le thème du spectacle est *L'Eau*.	
3	Je vais à un cours de danse tous les mercredis.	
4	J'aime bien danser et créer une chorégraphie.	
5	Tout le monde a des idées et le prof nous écoute.	
6	La danse moderne est très énergique.	
7	Nous allons présenter notre spectacle le mois prochain au théâtre Royal.	
8	Il y a environ vingt jeunes dans le groupe, des garçons et des filles.	
9	C'est une bonne expérience.	
10	Notre professeur est chorégraphe et nous préparons un spectacle de danse moderne.	

Lisons maintenant !

Océane parle ! Read the text below and answer the questions which follow.

'Je danse le hip-hop!'

Ma passion, c'est la danse. J'aime surtout le hip-hop. C'est un genre de musique qui vient de New York. J'écoute de la musique hip-hop sur mon lecteur CD. Je vais à un cours de danse toutes les semaines. Mon prof de danse s'appelle Miko. Ma danseuse préférée s'appelle Sofia Boutella. Elle danse pour la chanteuse Madonna et pour la nouvelle campagne de Nike à la télévision.

1. What does she say about hip-hop music?
2. How often does she take dance classes?
3. Who is Miko?
4. Name **two** things she says about Sofia Boutella.
5. Find the French for 'especially', 'I listen', 'CD player', 'singer'.

Civilisation : La philatélie

- Nowadays, we use fewer postage stamps (**le timbre**) because we can communicate by email and fax. However, the hobby of stamp-collection (**la philatélie**) is still popular in France. Some collect stamps by theme, such as famous people, animals or flowers. 3.5 billion French stamps are printed each year in Périgueux, in the Dordogne region.

Lisons maintenant

Read what these young people say about their stamp collections.

Je collectionne des timbres depuis quatre ans. Le thème de ma collection est le cheval. J'ai des timbres de tous les pays du monde. Mon timbre favori vient de l'Irlande.

Camille, 14 ans

Le thème de ma collection, c'est les personnages historiques. Je cherche dans les catalogues pour acheter des timbres anciens. J'ai un timbre qui vaut 100 euros ! Mais je ne veux pas vendre ce timbre pour le moment !

Max, 13 ans

Ma collection est assez importante maintenant. J'ai plus de 2000 timbres sur les moyens de transport : des trains, des avions, des voitures, même des vélos ! Je les trouve dans des salons ou à des brocantes. Je suis membre d'un club au collège. Nous sommes environ vingt membres.

Benjamin, 14 ans

Je suis fana de philatélie. J'achète des timbres sur Internet et dans des catalogues. Le thème de ma collection, c'est le football. J'ai une bonne collection, plus de 2500. Je paie entre 5 et 10 euros pour un timbre, pas plus !

Laure, 15 ans

Je collectionne les timbres depuis un mois. Je suis débutant ! Je ne sais pas quel thème je vais choisir, peut-être les requins, car je m'intéresse beaucoup aux animaux marins. Je suis membre d'un club car on peut échanger des timbres.

Louis, 13 ans

Who is the person…

1. who has just started collecting stamps?
2. who has a stamp which is worth a good deal of money?
3. whose collection is about horses?
4. who sets a limit to what they pay for a stamp?
5. who belongs to a club at school?

Écoutons maintenant!

• Les collections! Qui collectionne quoi? Who collects which item?

les pin's

les BD

les timbres-poste

Luc

Océane

les porte-clés

Christophe

Sophie

Khalid

les cartes postales

Coin grammaire: The verb 'sortir'

- Of course, going out with friends is another way of spending time at the weekend. For this, you need to learn the verb 'sortir' (to go out). This is another irregular verb.
- Be careful not to confuse this verb with 'aller' (see page 73) which simply means 'to go', and 'partir', which means 'to leave' in the sense of departing.

Écoutons maintenant! Écoutez le verbe 'sortir' au présent.

- The second sec	
je	sors
tu	sors
il	sort
elle	sort
nous	sortons
vous	sortez
ils	sortent
elles	sortent

Exercice 1

Remplissez le tableau avec le verbe 'sortir'.

je	
tu	sors
il	
elle	sort
nous	
vous	sortez
ils	
elles	

Exercice 2

Écrivez le verbe 'sortir' à la forme négative au présent.

Exemple: Je ne sors pas, etc.

trois cent dix-neuf Mes passe-temps 319

Exercice 3

Fill in the correct form of '**sortir**'.

Communication en classe !

- Vous avez des passe-temps ?
- Qu'est-ce que vous faites le week-end ?
- Vous allez au cinéma/Vous regardez la télé ?
- Qu'est-ce que tu dis ?
- Dites-moi où vous allez le week-end.
- Écrivez vos devoirs dans vos carnets !
- Paul, écris la réponse au tableau !
- Pour ce soir, lisez les deux paragraphes page 5.
- Suzanne, lis la question 3 !
- Qu'est-ce que tu lis en ce moment ?
- Vous sortez le week-end ?
- Où est-ce que vous sortez le samedi ?

Lexique

à destination de	*aimed at/bound for*
accueillir	*to welcome*
affiche (f.)	*poster*
ancien/ienne	*old/ancient*
animateur/trice	*organiser*
apprendre	*to learn*
assister à	*to attend*
auteur (m./f.)	*author*
bandes dessinées (f. pl.)	*comic books*
berger/ère	*shepherd*
caution (f.)	*refundable deposit*
chaîne (f.)	*TV channel*
chanteur/euse	*singer*
chorégraphie (f.)	*choreography*
chorale (f.)	*choir*
collectionner	*to collect*
comédie (f.)	*comedy*
comédien/ienne	*actor/actress*
courriel (m.)	*email*
cours (m.)	*class*
créer	*to create*
danse (f.)	*dancing*
danser	*to dance*
débutant(e)	*beginner*
déranger	*to disturb/annoy*
dessin animé (m.)	*cartoon*
diffuser	*to broadcast/show*
disponible	*available*
dire	*to say*
dos (m.)	*back*
drame (m.)	*drama*
échecs (m. pl.)	*chess*
écrire	*to write*
émission (f.)	*programme*
emmener	*to take (somebody/ something)*
enfance (f.)	*childhood*
envoyer	*to send*
environ	*about*
étranger/ère	*foreign/foreigner*
faire partie de	*to be part of*
fana de (m./f.)	*fan of*
fauteuil (m.)	*cinema seat/armchair*
film à suspense (m.)	*thriller*
film d'animation (m.)	*cartoon film*
film d'espionnage (m.)	*spy film*
film policier (m.)	*detective film*
genre (m.)	*type/kind*
grâce à	*thanks to*
gratuit(e)	*free of charge*
grimper	*to climb*
hardi(e)	*bold/daring*
idée (f.)	*idée*
jamais	*never*
jeu de dames (m.)	*draughts*
jeu video (m.)	*video game*
lecture (f.)	*reading*
lire	*to read*
louer	*to rent/hire*
se marier	*to get married*
mode (f.)	*fashion*
moyen/enne	*intermediate level/average*
musique (f.)	*music*
orgue électronique (m.)	*electric organ*
peinture (f.)	*painting*
philatélie (f.)	*stamp-collecting*
piano (m.)	*piano*
pin's (m.)	*pin-badge*
portable (m.)	*mobile phone*
porte-clés (m.)	*key-ring*
quelquefois	*sometimes*
raconter	*to tell/relate*
rarement	*rarely*
roman (m.)	*novel*
salle d'informatique (f.)	*computer room*
se connecter	*to go on line*
séance (f.)	*showing*
sortir	*to go out*
spectacle (m.)	*show*
suivi(e) de	*followed by*
timbre (m.)	*postage stamp*
vacances de la Toussaint (f. pl.)	*mid-term break in November*
vedette (f.)	*star*
venir de (+ infinitive)	*to have just done*
violon (m.)	*violin*

Épreuve

Question 1

Find the words to do with hobbies in the wordsearch below.

N	U	P	I	U	W	A	J	F	A	Y	V	C	N	W
E	R	B	M	I	T	W	E	U	G	S	T	N	L	L
N	F	C	N	G	Q	O	U	L	C	E	P	K	V	E
F	N	B	Y	Z	R	B	X	C	N	F	E	V	D	I
F	C	O	R	T	J	U	D	R	F	H	H	S	P	R
P	E	I	N	T	U	R	E	P	F	P	X	H	B	R
O	G	O	A	L	B	T	S	T	Y	S	I	F	O	U
J	E	Z	D	X	N	C	O	E	N	L	J	U	O	O
U	C	S	B	I	O	U	C	L	A	A	E	Y	T	C
Q	P	D	N	N	B	R	I	T	E	U	H	E	H	K
M	E	L	C	A	T	C	E	P	S	C	E	C	E	P
S	A	E	H	P	D	L	T	Z	W	E	T	W	A	N
F	R	L	L	Z	I	O	E	O	B	Y	P	U	T	C
T	Y	H	V	E	W	O	B	Z	O	K	B	M	R	R
L	V	A	Y	H	S	L	P	R	S	W	G	H	E	E

CHANTEUR
DANSE
LECTURE
SPECTACLE
CONCERT
INTERNET

PEINTURE
THEATRE
COURRIEL
JEUX DE SOCIETE
PHILATELIE
TIMBRE

Question 2

Remplissez les blancs avec le verbe '**jouer**' et la bonne préposition.

1 Nous __________ __________ piano.
2 Niall et Claire __________ _____ _____ batterie.
3 Christophe __________ _____ _____ guitare.
4 Nathalie __________ _____ _____ flûte.
5 Tu __________ _____ _____ violon ?
6 Je __________ _____ _____ accordéon.

For **help** with this exercise, **see page 306**.

Question 3

Listen and fill in the following details concerning Gwen Stefani.

Date of Birth: ________________ 1969
Where she started her career: ________________
The album *Love, Angel, Music, Baby* was her ________________ album.
Other interests: ________________________________

Nationality of her husband: ________________
What happened during the summer:

____

Question 4

Read this article and answer the questions which follow.

UN CINÉMA PAS ORDINAIRE !

À 3 000 mètres d'altitude, on ne trouve pas un cinéma à tous les coins de montagne ! À dos de cheval, un projectionniste hardi, Zarylbeck, grimpe vers les campements des bergers semi-nomades. Quand la nuit tombe, il diffuse sur un drap blanc des films français, italiens ou américains. Pas de fauteuil de multiplex, pas de paquet de pop-corn à la main. Comme les habitants ne parlent pas les langues étrangères, Zarylbeck raconte l'histoire lui-même au public !

1. How did Zarylbeck reach his destination?
2. What did he use as a screen?
3. Name **one** thing that is missing in this cinema.
4. Apart from American films, what other films did he show?
5. Why did Zarylbeck have to tell the story of each film himself?

Question 5

Listen to what Karima says and fill in the blanks in the text.

Salut ! Karima ici. Chez nous tout le monde lit. Il y a beaucoup de ________________ à la maison, car ma mère travaille dans une ________________. Qu'est-ce que nous lisons ? Mon petit frère, Hichem, adore lire les ________________ et il a une grande collection. Il aime aussi les romans de science-fiction. Ma sœur, Jasmine, qui a ________________ ans, lit des ________________. Elle va souvent au ________________ et elle adore lire les profils des ________________ de cinéma. Papa préfère les ________________ policiers et il lit aussi des biographies. Maman lit de tout ! Et moi, qu'est-ce que je lis ? J'adore les ________________. J'achète *Wapiti* et *Le monde des animaux*. J'aime aussi les magazines ________________, car je suis une vraie fana de foot.

Question 6

Read the following descriptions of TV programmes for younger viewers and answer the questions which follow.

Samedi 16

18h15 *Les Boblins*
Les aventures de sept personnages aux couleurs de l'arc-en-ciel qui vivent en harmonie avec les plantes et les animaux.

19h55 *Hôpital Hilltop*
La série *Urgences* adaptée pour les enfants.

20h50 *La Guerre des Fées*
Les aventures d'Anabel et Murray, un magicien qui n'a pas beaucoup de succès.

Dimanche 17

16h45 *BB3B*
Pour les jumeaux Lucie et Louis, le petit frère qui vient d'arriver à la maison est peut-être un martien ! Comment convaincre les parents ?

17h50 *Dimanche évasion*
Un documentaire qui raconte les aventures de deux petits oursons.

18h30 *Allô la terre, ici les Martin*
La famille Martin s'adapte mal à voyager dans l'espace dans leur navette spatiale SOS.

Which programme

1. is about a pair of twins who think their new baby brother is a Martian?
2. is about two bear cubs?
3. is an adaptation of the adult programme *ER*?
4. is about a family trying to live in a space ship?
5. is about an unsuccessful magician?

Question 7

Write the correct form of the verbs in brackets.

1 Je (*lire*) ______________ un magazine toutes les semaines.
2 Il (*écrire*) ______________ une lettre à sa marraine.
3 Sophie (*dire*) ______________ au revoir à sa grand-mère à la gare.
4 Nous (*lire*) ______________ un roman pour le Junior Certificate.
5 Elles (*écrire*) ______________ leurs devoirs de français.
6 Je (*dire*) « Bonsoir » ______________ à Monsieur Dubois.
7 Vous (*lire*) ______________ beaucoup ?
8 Tu (*écrire*) ______________ une carte postale à Madame Doyle ?
9 Julien et Marcelline (*lire*) ______________ *Le Seigneur des anneaux.*
10 Qu'est-ce que vous (*dire*) ______________ ? Il est malade !

Question 8

Using the verb '**sortir**', write the following sentences in your copy and translate them into English.

1 Est-ce que vous s___rt___z beaucoup ?
2 James et Denise s___rt___nt ce soir.
3 Luke s___rt chaque vendredi au spectacle.
4 Je s___rs au concert de temps en temps.
5 Tombra, Victor et Claire s___rt___nt pour aller au festival de musique à Galway ce week-end.
6 Tu s___rs avec tes amis mardi soir ?

For **help** with this exercise, **see page 319**.

Question 9

Complete the letter using the words in the box below.

Longford, le 2 janvier

Chère Sandra,

Merci de ta carte de Noël et pour le ___________. C'est super ! J'adore ce groupe. Tu sais que je joue de la ___________ dans un groupe avec mes amis. Nous répétons ensemble dans la cave de ma maison tous les ___________.
À part la musique, j'adore aller au ___________. J'aime les films à ___________. Je vais au cinéma ___________ fois par mois. Ma vedette ___________ s'appelle Leonardo di Caprio. Tu as une vedette favorite ?
Le soir, nous regardons la télé. Tout le monde a une émission préférée. Mon père adore les ___________. Mon frère et moi regardons les émissions ___________. Tu aimes lire ? Tu as un auteur favori ? J'aime les ___________ de Tolkien. Ils sont fantastiques !

C'est tout pour l'instant.
Amitiés,
Sinéad

sportives – CD – week-ends – favorite – documentaires – guitare – cinéma – deux – romans – suspense

Verbes irréguliers au présent

aller *to go*	
je	vais
tu	vas
il	va
elle	va
nous	allons
vous	allez
ils	vont
elles	vont

avoir *to have*	
j'	ai
tu	as
il	a
elle	a
nous	avons
vous	avez
ils	ont
elles	ont

boire *to drink*	
je	bois
tu	bois
il	boit
elle	boit
nous	buvons
vous	buvez
ils	boivent
elles	boivent

dire *to say*	
je	dis
tu	dis
il	dit
elle	dit
nous	disons
vous	dites
ils	disent
elles	disent

écrire *to write*	
j'	écris
tu	écris
il	écrit
elle	écrit
nous	écrivons
vous	écrivez
ils	écrivent
elles	écrivent

être *to be*	
je	suis
tu	es
il	est
elle	est
nous	sommes
vous	êtes
ils	sont
elles	sont

faire *to do*	
je	fais
tu	fais
il	fait
elle	fait
nous	faisons
vous	faites
ils	font
elles	font

lire *to read*	
je	lis
tu	lis
il	lit
elle	lit
nous	lisons
vous	lisez
ils	lisent
elles	lisent

mettre *to put*	
je	mets
tu	mets
il	met
elle	met
nous	mettons
vous	mettez
ils	mettent
elles	mettent

prendre *to take*	
je	prends
tu	prends
il	prend
elle	prend
nous	prenons
vous	prenez
ils	prennent
elles	prennent

sortir *to go out*	
je	sors
tu	sors
il	sort
elle	sort
nous	sortons
vous	sortez
ils	sortent
elles	sortent

venir *to come*	
je	viens
tu	viens
il	vient
elle	vient
nous	venons
vous	venez
ils	viennent
elles	viennent

vouloir *to wish/to want*			
je	veux	nous	voulons
tu	veux	vous	voulez
il	veut	ils	veulent
elle	veut	elles	veulent

Exercice 1

Mettez les verbes suivants entre parenthèses au présent.

1. Bernard (*aller*) _______________ en ville samedi.
2. Ils (*aller*) _______________ au spectacle de leur lycée.
3. Ma tante et ma marraine (*avoir*) _______________ trente-cinq ans.
4. Tu (*avoir*) _______________ faim ?
5. Est-ce que vous (*boire*) _______________ beaucoup d'eau ?
6. L'acteur (*dire*) _______________ qu'il est content.
7. J'(*écrire*) _______________ le soir.
8. Nous (*être*) _______________ contents.
9. Ils (*faire*) _______________ le ménage pour leur voisin.
10. Il (*faire*) _______________ soleil pendant l'été.
11. James et Sheila (*lire*) _______________ des romans.
12. L'enfant (*lire*) _______________ des bandes dessinées.
13. Est-ce que vous (*mettre*) _______________ la table pour le petit-déjeuner ?
14. Je (*prendre*) _______________ mon déjeuner à deux heures.
15. Elle (*prendre*) _______________ l'avion à l'aéroport.
16. Nous (*sortir*) _______________ avec nos amis.
17. Ils (*venir*) _______________ tard au concert.
18. Mon oncle (*vouloir*) _______________ du potage.
19. Je (*vouloir*) _______________ l'addition, s'il vous plaît.
20. Est-ce que vous (*vouloir*) _______________ des champignons ?

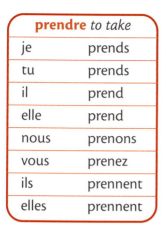